"'Urgently needed' is my first reaction. Ron Susek is not up in some ivory tower. His education as executive interim pastor in the middle of a local church firestorm put him on solid ground, right in the heat of the potentially destructive forces of conflict. Thanks, Ron; you've done a great service to the entire church."

—David Mainse, Crossroads

"Ron Susek has one of the most fertile minds around. In Firestorm his writing is comprehensive and solidly scriptural. This book is not only needed but also essential, and it could not come at a better time. I wish it were required reading for every pastor and staff member in America, as well as for every deacon and elder. It is written with passion and precision, it has practical helps, and it will help your church avoid or recover from destructive division."

—Vander Warner Jr., president, Home Before Dark, Ltd.

"It's a clear-cut issue: evangelicals must either discover the importance of the unity of the Spirit as commanded in Ephesians 4:3 or discover what it means to live without the backing of God. In Firestorm Ron Susek proves that we can even disagree agreeably. His book is a significant and much-needed contribution!"

—Dr. John DeBrine, host of *Songtime USA*

"With literary skill, spiritual insight, godly wisdom, and genuine concern for the body of Christ, my good friend, Ron Susek, has produced in *Firestorm* a unique book. I warmly commend it to pastors, elders, deacons, and all involved in the leadership of a local church. Here is a classic work born out of firsthand observation and experience. It offers practical solutions to perennial problems which surface in any congregation of God's people. To be forewarned is to be forearmed!"

—Rev. Keith Skelton, senior pastor,
The Open Door Church, Chambersburg, Pa.

"Church conflicts seem to be increasing, so we welcome a volume like this that will be helpful to pastors who find themselves in tense, hostile circumstances."

—Luder Whitlock, president, Reformed Theological Seminary

"Ron Susek has written a most informative and helpful manual for pastors and church leaders. Because of its honesty, compassion, and authenticity, it is far above the level of other books dealing with the same issues. Leaders and nonleaders alike will greatly benefit from reading this detailed study of tensions, frictions, and devastations sometimes found in the Christian church, and they will learn how to overcome them."

—Dr. Reinhold Kerstan, professor emeritus of preaching and communications, McMaster University

"Many a church and pastor have been deeply wounded as a result of conflicts which have produced a painful separation. *Firestorm* is a significant tool both for prevention and healing. It should be seriously studied by every congregation, pastor, and seminary student. The fire should be recognized before it becomes a firestorm."

—Dr. Donald R. Hubbard, pastor emeritus, Calvary Baptist Church, New York, NY

"Simple mistakes, well-intentioned blunders, selfish ambition, power plays, dysfunctional ecclesiastical structures—from this volatile mix, firestorms can result. This book shows how firestorms may be prevented and how to recover from them."

—Stuart Briscoe, senior pastor, Elmbrook Church

"For many years I have respected, encouraged, and commended the preaching and counseling ministries of my colleague, Ron Susek. I am delighted that he has now distilled the wisdom and experience of his days in the 'trenches' in his new book, Firestorm. It is a masterpiece of pastoralia. For seminary students—and even for senior pastors—there are lessons, warnings, and insights rarely found in literature of this kind. It is a must-read, and I warmly commend it to my colleagues in the ministry."

—Dr. Stephen F. Olford, founder and senior lecturer, The Stephen Olford Center for Biblical Preaching

FIRESTORM

FireStorm

PREVENTING

AND OVERCOMING

CHURCH CONFLICTS

RON SUSEK

FOREWORD BY D. JAMES KENNEDY

Baker Books

A Division of Baker Book House Co
Grand Rapids, Michigan 49516

Published by Baker Books
a division of Baker Book House Company
P.O. Box 6287, Grand Rapids, MI 49516-6287

Fourth printing, October 2001

Printed in the United States of America

Library of Congress Cataloging-in-Publication Data

Susek, Ron.
    Firestorm : preventing and overcoming church conflicts / Ron Susek ; foreword by D. James Kennedy.
        p.   cm.
    Includes bibliographical references.
    ISBN 0-8010-9091-1 (pbk.)
    1. Church controversies. 2. Conflict management—Religious aspects—Christianity. I. Title.
    BV652.9.S87   1999
    250—dc21   99–16924

For current information about all releases from Baker Book House, visit our web site:
http://www.bakerbooks.com

To Jesus Christ and his church

While conflict within the church does not always indicate that Satan is active, it is clear evidence that the Holy Spirit is absent (1 Cor. 14:33). May this book be used by God to help bring the church out of conflict and into conformity with Christ's prayer that we become one as he and the Father are one (John 17:22). Only then will God be glorified and the world have a basis to believe (John 17:21).

Contents

PART 4: OUT OF THE ASHES

FOREWORD

It has been the conclusion of most literarians that the primary determinant of a book's quality has to be authenticity. Above all else, the author has to know the subject, must be an authority whether by hands-on experience or by acquired knowledge. The more difficult the topic, the greater is the demand for mastery over the subject matter.

In this book, Ron Susck deals with a tragic phenomenon that, for countless thousands of dedicated Christians, has been one of the most traumatic and anguishing experiences through which they have passed. The very title of *Firestorm* suggests the devastating nature of his subject. But because he brings to the challenge a unique combination of unflinching courage, unfailing compassion, and uncommon experience, this author comes up with solutions that are workable in the most delicate situations. He has produced a book that is authentic in every dimension.

In the most detailed analysis of the nature of church "splits" that I have ever seen, there is some encouragement to be drawn from the fact that "firestorms" actually have a life cycle, with identifiable symptoms in six progressive stages. Another section of the book goes into the conceivable causes of church conflict—a most helpful portion because it alerts everyone to the potential sources of trouble, which deserve eternal vigilance if the ultimate danger is to be avoided. Then, following a thorough discussion on real "firefighting techniques" themselves—that is, the preventing and overcoming of major conflagrations—the author provides key insights to the process of rebuilding a church which has been damaged by internal dissension.

The remarkable aspect of this book is how Ron Susek manages to coalesce his knowledge of "how to" minutiae in dealing with the mundane entanglements of human nature, with his evangelist's zeal for the divine welfare of a suffering church. By interlacing Scriptural references throughout the book, his overarching message is that Christ loved his church and gave his life for it. It is that everlasting love that, once received into the hearts of troubled people, has the power to quench any firestorm that may threaten their individual lives or their corporate church life.

—D. James Kennedy

INTRODUCTION

This book is about church conflict—the kind that is so destructive I've selected the title *Firestorm*.

I did not choose to write this book; it demanded to be written after I was privileged to assist a southern Pennsylvania church through recovery from one of the ugliest firestorms a church could endure. The bad news about that conflict was that it sent a wonder-story of church growth to the brink of oblivion. The good news was that a remnant fought back from the brink in a manner pleasing to God, and the church stands today—greatly reduced in numbers but vibrant in spirit.

This is not the story of that church, but the learning curve over the firestorm's two-year period, and its subsequent recovery, was so sharp I asked the church elders if I may write a book about the principles we learned. They said, "Please do, with our blessing."

The *Lancaster* (Pa.) *Sunday News* has correctly stated that "problems can erupt whether congregations are large or small, rural or urban, liberal or fundamental." Can major church conflict be overcome? Yes. But not without stretching those involved beyond measure. If the conflict turns into a full-blown firestorm, it will require God working far beyond human capabilities to bring the church back from destruction.

While working with Myerstown (Pa.) Grace Brethren Church at the invitation of the elders and congregation to help it recover from its horrific firestorm, I learned firsthand the wisdom of the words of

Dr. Roy Roberts, a nearby pastor: "No church is more than twenty-four hours away from a major conflict breaking out. In less than a year, it can destroy years of hard work and growth."

Roy had no way of knowing that one small misjudgment would lead to a destructive firestorm in his own church, resulting in months of humiliation and eventual expulsion. Not long after that, Roy, who was in his early fifties, suffered a major stroke, the cause of which could be traced back to the stress he suffered.

Frankly, by conventional measuring sticks, there was not a chance in the world for Myerstown Grace Brethren Church to survive—*but it did!* And that is the message of this book. If that congregation could overcome in the strength and wisdom of the Lord, any congregation can. This "Gideon's army" turned back formidable forces to again be rightfully called Myerstown *Grace* Brethren Church.

The obvious question in this or any other firestorm is, What went wrong? However, there was no time to discover the answer. The church was on the verge of collapse, and the remnant was in despair, so the first task was to gain freedom from a collective sense of guilt and unworthiness. Developing deeper relationships based upon mutual respect was invaluable. The elders chose to make biblically correct decisions no matter the cost. Quiet and humble in spirit, they never forced decisions upon the church but explained the *what* and *why* of their actions. The church's financial picture was bleak. Survival was a stretch. Every dollar went to make debt-retirement payments and meet the costs of bare-bones operation. When the church became restless in the long search for the right pastor, we instituted a monthly day of fasting and prayer, and it continues to this day. God's hand was evident when, following the first day of prayer, serious negotiations began with Rev. Keith Shearer, who six months later became the new pastor. By the end of my stay, God had delivered MGBC from the destructive force of her firestorm. Two and a half years after the arrival of its new pastor, the church engaged in a major remodeling program, with corresponding signs of increasing spiritual health.

If I were asked what was the greatest factor in this church's recovery, I would say *believing and obeying God!* Sound simplistic? I hope not, because it certainly wasn't. To believe God meant doing everything his way. That often ran against the grain of human logic. It definitely smashed head-on into our comfort zones, which preferred to avoid rather than confront serious problems. But we were determined to see God part a modern-day Red Sea.

The lessons learned from these experiences and extended research are what I want to put into your hands, in hopes that the Myerstown victory will become a common tale for many churches. I am not free to expand on the Myerstown story, because that could improperly reopen some old wounds. But this book is based on many experiences of actual people and events in places ranging from Maine to California. You may even think you recognize your story in it. One pastor who read a draft of the book said, "My wife and I laughed and cried as we read our way through almost every paragraph. We thought Ron must have written this book while sitting in the back pew of our church."

Perhaps, in a way, I am telling your story, because the principles of human behavior are universal. In that sense, you'll see similarities between these composite stories and your church. But from this point forward, though real people are involved, every name will be fictitious unless otherwise stated.

The life cycle of a church firestorm has six observable phases, and as we trace them all, we'll stop at each phase for analysis and suggested actions. Watch for the potpourri of blunders, misjudgments, and misconduct by everyone—from the pastor to the staff, from the elders to the congregation.

My intent is to show the flesh-and-blood realities behind every ministry—for two reasons. First, it is necessary to see that there are very few innocent victims. They exist, but are rare. Friction between two people generally results from abrasiveness on both sides. Second, I hope you will be able to identify the sources of your conflict by observing them in others. You'll learn to discern the signs of conflict and properly respond to them.

If you are a pastor, absorb the sections especially designed for you. Then get copies into the hands of your church leaders and have them carefully read sections designed for them. Go on a retreat together for discussion and planning as an act of spiritual fire prevention. Also, there are sections church members need to read to discover their role and responsibility.

I have only one regret with this book, and it's the regret of every writer: You should see the stuff the publisher made me cut to get this information between two covers! But my friend and guide at Baker Book House, Paul Engle, believes the church will get along just fine without it, and that's probably so. There is a bright side to this. If, after you've finished reading, you would like more information about people to contact (such as consultants) or places to go (i.e., resource centers), I have a file bulging larger every month with material I'd be glad to send your way. So just get in touch. My postal and e-mail addresses are at the back of the book.

As my days of being designated "executive interim leader" of the unconquerable church in Myerstown drew to a close, I found a part of me not wanting to leave. I experienced increasing pain when people expressed regret over my impending departure. Warm smiles, hugs, and handshakes were ways of saying, "We're friends for life." To my pleasant surprise, however, rather than meaning "it's over" with their good-byes, many chose to support my present ministry in prayer. Even now, the pastor and church are reaching out with me through this book, hoping to empower pastors and churches everywhere to overcome firestorms.

PART 1

LIFE CYCLE OF A FIRESTORM

Firestorms have an observable life cycle. Just as a firestorm in nature can be predicted by weather patterns, so can patterns in human relationships reveal where a group is in the life cycle of a firestorm.

Leadership must know the weather patterns and be prepared for quick action to rescue a church from ruin. Indecision is as dangerous as making wrong decisions. A firestorm that runs full cycle can result in spiritual deadness that lasts for generations . . . provided the church survives at all.

1

SPARKS

> Consider what a great forest is set on fire by a small spark.
>
> James 3:5

Fires generally start from a small spark. Sparks of conflict between people are generated all the time and rarely go out. They can smolder, often for years, in a deep emotional memory bank before erupting into a firestorm. To assume they will vanish is a grave mistake. So it was for Steve Gates and Central Baptist Church of Pittsburgh, Pennsylvania.

Steve graduated from seminary at age twenty-five, filled with quixotic fervor. Two weeks later he was a candidate for Central's senior pastor position. His talent and demeanor were about to sweep him past the maturing process of first holding associate positions and land him the top job at the outset. But ambition and ability cannot replace maturation under a mentor. No one on the pastoral search committee could have asked the right questions to unmask the impairments and hidden agendas beneath Steve's sparkling veneer. Only pressure and time could reveal such things—even to Steve himself.

Nor did Steve know all the right questions to ask the committee. Could he really succeed as a young pastor following Dr. Jim Barnes, who had founded, then pastored the congregation of two hundred and forty for thirty-seven years? Was he developed enough to perceive the complexities of existing relationships? He gave no hint that anything was too big to handle.

Over the next three days of Steve's candidacy, he appeared to be a godsend. The church leaders said they wanted Central to grow, and Steve had the goods. His striking appearance enhanced his commanding elocution. He championed Baptist traditions. His snappy suits were a jump-start into the present from Dr. Barnes's tired, unpressed trousers. Yesss! . . . he'll even reach the youth. This thought quieted some older people who had doubts.

What about doctrine and theology? Very important! Steve scored high. Conservative views aligned. But there was another consideration . . . unmentioned, but vital—*culture.* While Steve dressed executive straight, there were unspoken differences in attitudes. Style of music, method of worship, manner of praying, and a thousand other unseen likes and dislikes lay hidden, ready to take on doctrinal ferocity if crossed. The church's culture formed a river of heartfelt familiarity, a sense of safety and identity, even establishing people's sense of well-being. Board members didn't catch Steve placating, rather than honoring, them with his answers. And Steve didn't perceive the importance of an established culture. He didn't realize how deeply personal preferences could be defended as divinely inspired. But everyone liked him. He knew it and assumed this meant they would be thrilled when the *real* Steve emerged—the explosively zealous young man with untested plans. He underestimated the "sacredness" of culture, as well as the strength of invisible power structures.

For instance, there was Ned Friendly, who held no office but had shared a close, mutually-significant friendship with Dr. Barnes. Serious church issues were discussed on the golf course, and Ned's fingerprints could be seen all over the outcome. Board member Bob Barkley was a willful, demanding, impetuous man in his mid-thirties. Being a salesman by day and a sports enthusiast by night, he thought all problems could be overcome with a good quarterback and a motivational slogan. Trustee Mark Mulrooney had taken over a large family business but still lived in the shadow of his eccentric father, whose ways drove Mark to obsession with correctness and conformity. While Mark didn't flaunt his wealth, it was known that his large tithes often delivered the church from shortfalls. And then there was Jim Bender, who was actually his wife's spokesman on the board. Unlike his wife, he lacked strong personal ideas and convictions. Everyone knew that what he said at one board meeting may change by the next, all depending on how his wife reacted at home.

Steve was unable to read these dynamics because he lacked the quiet, unobtrusive love with which a seasoned pastor slowly enters an established culture. He was assessing how the money people could help him fulfill his dreams. He was not aware that many wanted a Dr. Barnes reincarnated in Steve's youthful skin. Acceptance on both sides could only come by adjustments over time. The unanswered question was whether they would respect and reinforce each other until time made them one.

Cultures also have systemic problems, and CBC was no exception. Abusive power, even sin, lay deep in the structure. For instance, Bob Bulrich and Ivan Erikson had an unresolved dispute. Bob's son had romanced Ivan's daughter into engagement, then betrayed her for another. Ivan's daughter had started taking drugs, then had a child out of wedlock, all of which Ivan blamed on Bob's son. Ivan also resented Bob for acting as though his son had done no harm.

Bob, on the other hand, resented Ivan, thinking he should "act like a man" and just get over it. The old wound festered into bitterness, preventing the two families from agreeing on any church decision. Bob found sordid delight in knowing that he could flick the wound, causing it to thump anew, by opposing Ivan's ideas. Friends sided with each family, forming contentious power blocks.

Steve, too young to have been ripened on the vine and crushed in the winepress, was driven by impatient idealism, not weathered wisdom. More like Napoleon than Paul, he didn't understand the timing of grace. Nor did he detect that the board was concealing existing problems with spiritual cosmetics, making the church sound like a preview of heaven. Steve was shown the rope of opportunity but not the hangman's noose at the end.

The weekend of Steve's candidacy drew to a close. It was time for the vote. Steve passed, at least for the present. He became Central Baptist's senior pastor. But already small sparks of disagreement had started a slow burn that eventually would explode into a full-blown firestorm.

The proverbial honeymoon began. Pastor Steve Gates and wife Heather were anxious to get started. They had two children, Michael, age three, and Michelle, eighteen months. Any lingering doubts within the congregation were diminished by Heather's warm, naive personality and the laughter of two innocent children.

But it wasn't long before Steve bumped into resistance. Attitudes differed over church growth. While growth was desirable, the methods to be used and the changes it would bring caused division.

The first five years whisked by as Steve worked with tornadic force, always trying to compress two days' work into one. To him, the mandate was clear: The church said it wanted to grow, and he was the person to lead the charge. He was overflowing with ideas and dreams, all of which were fanned by attending numerous seminars on church growth. He launched efforts to increase membership—a bus ministry, concerts with Christian celebrities, well-known guest speakers, competition with attendance rewards—all well-intended.

The silent resistance Steve encountered resulted from opposition to that one accursed word—*change*. Steve lowered his head like a linebacker and charged the opposition, accusing dissenters of lacking spiritual concern for the lost. In time, some viewed Steve as a threat to the way "God had led them" for thirty-seven years. Some familiar comfort zones were shrinking, pushed in by such occasions as the day Steve invited recording star Wanda Blondell to perform in a concert costing eighty-five hundred dollars. The church had to kick in three thousand dollars to pay her when ticket sales fell below expectations. Some on the board were angry that this never had been approved. Others argued that they must stand behind the pastor, since he was sent by God. Still another group didn't like the kind of people Wanda's upbeat music attracted. Younger people, though, wanted to smash the organ and have someone like Wanda every week. Steve secretly felt the foot-draggers were satanic plants. The church had never faced questions like, "Are we ready for change, or are we demanding conformity?" "Can we make concessions, or are we expecting compliance?" "Will we forfeit comfort, or cling to convenience?" Suddenly those questions were raised with a jolt.

Sparks that wouldn't die out started falling among the pews. Older men on the board wanted to harness and direct Steve's energies. He viewed them as trying to tie him down. Younger members of the board urged him on. Like Solomon's son Rehoboam, Steve deepened his resolve to lead the charge of the young rather than be a spiritual father to all ages.

The end of the first five years marked a pivotal moment. Attendance pushed five hundred. The church had to enlarge its facility or experience loss. Steve sat dreaming. Vision inspired vision. He envisioned not only a new auditorium with an educational wing but also a large campus housing an academy and a retirement facility. He foresaw a compound where missionaries could recuperate. He was intrigued by the idea of starting a seminary. He jotted down a generic name for it: Kingdom Seminary. Subconsciously he saw this as a way to assure his posterity, so he tore up that piece of paper and wrote another name: Gates Theological Seminary. He felt a flush of warmth at the thought of a life-size bronze of himself, raised before an ivy-draped stone archway. Popularity whispered into his ear that people would want this bronze, even though it was foreign to apostolic attitudes.

His second five years became a frenzy of new projects: radio broadcasts, television programs, and buildings. Numerical growth accelerated. When Steve returned from seminars with new ideas, they had to be instituted immediately. Unfortunately, no one was able to see the bad seeds being sown among the good.

Steve, like many young ministers, fastened his eyes on another spiritual leader, who was rising in prominence. He patterned his ministry after this man's success. He didn't sort the good from the bad but adopted everything just because it seemed to work. Steve focused on a model, not a mentor. The model was a heavy-handed leader who led by entrepreneurial dictate, not servant leadership—a serious flaw. But because attendance shot over a thousand, pragmatism ruled: If it worked, it must be right.

Despite the conflicts, the church was still in the early stage of experiencing occasional falling sparks, a happy time when people were relating to each other with goodwill, measured respect, humor, tolerance, and anticipation of more good things to come. As in all congregations, new problems always were emerging, but they never threatened the church as a whole.

There was an ongoing feud between Joan and Barbara, two choir members locked in fierce rivalry over solo opportunities. Then there was Fred the custodian, who threatened to quit if certain elders didn't stop parking on the grass by the entrance. Numerous com-

plaints surfaced about the language Fred used when someone
walked on a floor he had just polished.

Many people grappled with personal and family problems, often
affecting relationships within the church. Sarah, for instance, who
had been emotionally abused by a domineering father, had a distorted view of manhood and womanhood. She saw all men as power
freaks and thought women had to fight for their rights.

Dave and Carol Goodman left the church because the services
were too "professional and showy," conflicting with their simple Ply-
mouth Brethren background. A small charismatic group pressed for
a more experiential faith. Another group thought Steve was too conservative for the University of Pittsburgh intellectuals.

Financial growth brought its own problems. At budget time, cries
for more funds came from every department. This led to serious staff
tensions and committee conflicts. Henrietta Blander insisted that
music was the key ingredient to church growth. Dwayne and Sylvia
Ferndon argued that the music was too traditional and that the youth
were the future of the church, so programs for them were where the
big dollars should go. And so it was that each division thought its
planet was the center of the universe.

Then came conflicts among the seven full-time staff members and
three volunteers. Steve discovered that, while all the staffers he had
hired agreed to their job descriptions, hidden agendas were tucked
into their back pockets. Within three months, each was doing things
the way he or she thought God's work should be done. Steve worked
hard to keep the staff united in spirit and purpose. Then came the
unexpected. He noticed some staffers were carving out chunks of
church members as loyalists around themselves. These became political power blocks to be used as bargaining chips for achieving their
desires. Resentment and distrust grew within the staff.

Still, these were only the normal sparks generated by a group of
any size. Nothing was unmanageable. The church was moving forward. As years passed, Steve and the church won national acclaim.
Denominational leaders pointed their fingers in his direction anytime they wanted to show other pastors "how to do it." But no one
realized the complexity of difficulties that, at times, made Steve want
to leave the ministry.

Slowly, the unthinkable took place. Steve became more absorbed with his goals than in meeting people's needs. He increasingly used his shepherd's staff as a club to drive rather than as a hook to guide. He spurned people for feeling hurt or misunderstood, leaving issues unresolved. To him, talking out problems was a sign of weakness. He raised a wall around himself, not permitting anyone to peer over and see his own flaws. While this appeared as strength to the imperceptive, Steve was violating a cardinal truth: The wall one builds around his heart to keep out future pain locks in present and past problems. The apostle Paul's teaching about finding Christ's strength in weakness made good preaching but didn't get applied to Steve's personal life.

With eyes fastened upon his model, Steve forged ahead. Growth became his benchmark for success. People grew uneasy about the mounting debt. When elders tried to talk to him about cutting back, he sharply chided them for their lack of faith. If anyone persisted with their concerns, he warned them not to "touch God's anointed." He gradually turned from a servant-minister to a demanding master. Still, no one could foresee this ascending rocket exploding in midair. Success gave the illusion of invincibility.

The board should have seen Steve's error, but no one discerned the signs. This was the time when the church should have fulfilled its role, one that even seminaries are not equipped to do—mature pastors. Seminaries can only provide the tools for personal and professional growth. But wisdom and maturity are products of the pressures and practice of pastoring. By not detecting and addressing Steve's improper motivation, the board ultimately failed the church. Herein, the board shared full responsibility for the coming firestorm.

As the church approached the end of the first decade with Steve, some elders believed he no longer was the same person who first came to the church. But he was. People and events were not making Steve what he was; they were unmasking what he was. One day Elder Charles Bradley met with Steve in his office. "Pastor," he said, "some people who are feeling neglected have talked to me. Is there a chance you could do a little more visitation?" Steve sighed with disgust. Charles felt like a fool for mentioning the matter, although he knew he was right.

"Charles," Steve responded, "aren't you satisfied with my sermons?"

"Yes, of course. Everyone thinks you are a great expositor."

"And aren't you pleased with our growth and building programs?"
Steve asked like a trial lawyer.

"Of course, of course, Pastor."

"Well, I can't be out running around to hospitals, nursing homes,
and family picnics, while at the same time building this church."
Steve stood silent, his closing statement made.

Charles walked away, feeling tongue-lashed by a cold, harsh spirit.
He couldn't explain it, just felt it. He felt insignificant and powerless.
As an elder, he should have some access to the pastor's heart. But
the truth was painfully clear. He felt like a worthless pawn, not a co-
servant. His spurned attempt to help Steve started a smoldering frustration in Charles's heart.

In this exchange, Steve was hiding behind his strength, rather than
facing his weakness. He never analyzed himself deeply enough to
realize that his aloofness was rooted in his lack of love for people.
The thought of sitting with a mature saint in a nursing home almost
suffocated him. His mind was churning with ideas on how to preach
to a larger audience by adding more television stations. He was consumed by how to raise money to finance his plans. People? They'd
have to understand and appreciate what they had in a pastor and
stop wanting more.

Charles wasn't the only one to bump into Steve's resolve. Parishioners often left his office from counseling sessions feeling as though
he had not really heard them. Sometimes, when people needed his
help, he was either bent over a new set of blueprints or master-
minding another promotional scheme. They had neither his interest nor his attention.

For instance, while Mary Sadler was unloading her burden to
Steve about her son's disregard for authority, Steve grabbed a pen
and wrote a note. She was pleased to think that he was that inter-
ested in her problem. Steve dismissed himself, claiming to need
some water. He went to the outer office and whispered to his secretary, Paula Harth, to set up an appointment with the contractor for
the retirement village. While he was out, Mary looked at the note,
curious to know what she had said that was so important. She read,

"Get final blueprint draft from Paul Craft." Disappointment surged through her. She was visibly shaken when Steve returned, and abruptly excused herself and left. She felt mugged, violated, cheated. She told no one of her hurt, but unknowingly joined a long list of people who would not stand behind Steve in the hour of fiery trial.

Steve thought that people should simply get over whatever bothered them and move on to the bigger picture. He forgot that in God's heart people *are* the picture. He lost sight of Jesus' priorities. Steve's focus was on crowds, not individuals—a motivation agitated by the lure of celebrity status, a cancer of our media age. He forgot that the only mantle of greatness is to carry a towel of service (John 13:13–17).

Spiritually minded people grew uneasy. They sensed trouble was on the horizon but couldn't define it. Edna Neel and other intercessors felt led to pray, often finding themselves disturbed in the middle of the night. Only God could know how many sparks of unrest flickered in people's hearts.

Let's analyze what is happening in this initial phase. Firestorms ignite from various sparks:

- Someone has an unthreatening complaint about the pastor or board.
- A group is in conflict over a procedural issue.
- Some feel the board is acting unfairly on a problem.
- A group is unhappy about a certain direction the church is taking.
- Someone feels slighted or insulted.
- A pastor may be abusing his position.

The unhappy people generally lack the clout, desire, or fortitude to set a firestorm into motion, so they use small power plays to express their grievance:

- They quit the choir.
- They stop giving.
- They complain to family and friends.

- They formally complain to the board.
- They leave the church.

If enough people suffer injustice (perceived or real), in time a firestorm will erupt.

Most people who raise issues in phase one intend good, not harm, for the church. They simply want to vent and resolve their grievances, after which they will resume normal participation. If they are not satisfied, they may withdraw from involvement. Above all, they are not troublemakers.

The Natural Dynamics of Phase 1

Natural dynamics of human relationships on this level:

1. Real, God-given differences exist in people, such as:

   - *Goals:* What people want to see happen for themselves, their families, and the church.
   - *Needs:* What people require for their children, personal growth, cultural traditions, and religious experience.
   - *Perspectives:* Everyone views issues from a different set of experiences and will naturally approach problems from these various points of view.
   - *Values:* People's codes of right and wrong, worth and worthlessness are determined from a wide range of views, from biblical absolutes to humanistic relativism.
   - *Methods:* How people believe things should be done—how to organize, lead, and have authority roles.
   - *Interests:* Myriad personal preferences, such as style of worship, type of music, architecture.

   We must be very clear at this point that these differences generally are not sinful or evil but God-given. These legitimate differences must be respected and honored, as well as blended (which is basic in spiritual growth), otherwise they will produce a long series of sparks that can ignite a firestorm. On this level, people can still be led to respond to their differences through the following:

- Acceptance (I choose to want you.)
- Adjustment (I choose to change for you.)
- Appreciation (I choose to understand you.)

People are not competing in their differences on this level; rather, they are tolerant and even enjoy their differences. When this normal interaction moves into conflict, harmless differences become emotional focal points. Not all firestorms start with malicious intent, just a lack of maturity in handling these differences. If leadership fails here, people's dispositions will change from collaborative to adversarial.

While leadership ministers, it is God alone who molds. When people's distinctiveness is ignored and an attempt is made to conform everyone to the leadership's image, small fires ignite. Peter wrote of proper leadership, "Not lording it over those entrusted to you, but being examples to the flock" (1 Peter 5:3). True pastoral leadership nurtures the best in people, even if the people's various perspectives cause the pastor's path for the church to meander like a stream in directions that don't fit his straight-line goals. A pastor must be primarily given to the people's good and not his own inflexible goals.

This is not to suggest that the church is run by a disjointed collection of opinions. That would be as ridiculous as a football team on which each man ran in any direction he desired. Randomness is anarchy when applied to human behavior. The Scriptures enjoin people to honor leadership (1 Thess. 5:12–13). Still, leadership is God-given to direct, not dominate.

When leadership dominates, people feel they are doing the leaders' ministry and not being equipped to do *their own* ministry, resulting in either anger or ambivalence. A pastor is not directed to get people to do the pastor's ministry but to equip believers to fulfill *their* ministries (Eph. 4:11–12). When the minister equips people instead of using them to accomplish his own agenda, they generally gain a sense of ownership that makes them highly productive.

2. During this phase, when problems emerge, most people are still focused on issues. They are not attacking each other. There is keen interest in solving a mutual problem.
3. People use respectful, considerate, noncondemning language.
4. In a desire to solve the problem, both sides are not threatened by sharing information and ideas. They are not protecting their positions. Suspicion has not set in.
5. People remain rational in problem-solving. Resolution comes either through informal, personal settlements or in formal ways, such as voting. There is not a sense of mortal loss if one's position doesn't win.
6. People are focused on a resolution that can give everyone a sense of winning because the cause of Christ benefits. Every effort is made to have each person's ideas and contribution be part of the solution. If someone's perspective is bypassed, the greatest care is taken to make the person understand why it would not have worked well at this point. But the person is still made to feel appreciated and needed—not devalued.

Recommendations for Phase 1

- Never allow church growth to shift the emphasis away from the value of the individual. Discipling people does not mean to nurture them until they are mature enough to be ignored. Relationship is central to God's plan. It is generally considered that when a significant percentage of the congregation (10 to 15 percent, according to experts) feels used for the "cause," rather than valued and honored as a worthy part of the cause, then phase two is at the doorstep.
- Hold special meetings twice a year—one with an emphasis for believers, and the other for evangelism. Using the gifts given for equipping the body is crucial (Eph. 4:11–16).
- "Discovering the Real You" is a video series available through SEA that can be helpful in resolving conflict. (See "Recommended Resources.")

- Hold periodic leadership retreats, not for business but for spiritual and relational development.
- Periodically study the biblical purpose and function of the board. Spiritual leadership and business leadership are different functions.
- Promptly respond to complaints and concerns with fairness and justice. Small offenses and misunderstandings rarely go away on their own.
- Conduct an exit interview to find out why people are leaving your church. They may give clues of a coming firestorm.
- At least once a year, take the board and church through the approved master plan. Never assume people are on track without keeping the plan before them. If they lose ownership of the master plan, it has already ceased to be a master plan and is reduced to the pastor's personal plan. Distrust develops if the leader gets too far out in front.
- Keep the staff clear in direction and united in spirit. Personal hidden agendas among staff are among the greatest causes of conflict.

2

PHASE 2

Sparks Igniting a Firestorm

Institutions ultimately rise and fall on the strength of relationships.
When relationships are volatile, sparks can ignite firestorms.

The staff threw an office party to celebrate Steve's fifteenth year as pastor of CBC. His star had steadily risen; the church appeared indestructible. It seemed like only yesterday when Steve arrived, filled with unbounded enthusiasm. Now, Michael and Michelle were in their late teenage years. The hands of the midlife clock had brushed Steve's hair with gray. Hard work had paid off. A new sanctuary, with Sunday school rooms extending from each side, formed the shape of a cross. The driveway leading to the main entrance encircled a fountain spraying water high into the air. While the fountain symbolized the Living Water, the encircling driveway denoted that all were welcome.

But along with success had come fifteen years of unsettled conflicts and irritations. Sparks had kicked up many brush fires. Institutions ultimately rise and fall on the strength of relationships, and relationships were becoming volatile. Steve wanted people to follow him, but he never let people know him. That violated the divine design for heartfelt relationships.

Steve was feeling dry—tired beyond his years. Forces taunted him from every direction in ways unknown to those who have never been

30

in leadership. Like all churches, CBC had various factions, all wanting Steve to champion their cause. One associate, Pastor Bill Kohler, loved to amplify Steve's weaknesses to any who would listen. An aggressive charismatic group pushed hard against noncharismatics. A small group still held the belief that one version of the Bible alone bore divine inspiration. Steve walked a tightrope between these factions.

Further, Steve believed his job hinged upon winning a never-ending popularity contest. He lived with the grinding awareness that Western culture esteems undeveloped youth over seasoned age. Had he passed his prime?

Steve was also plagued by unfair expectations imposed by a few, such as Alex and Cora Preston. They financed a Holy Land tour for Steve's entire family. Sometime later, the Prestons' daughter Cindy had a baby. She dumped her live-in lover because he wanted her to work while he wasted his life on drugs. She turned from her lifestyle and became devoted to Christ. She met a fine young man in the church, and soon they wanted to marry. Alex and Cora met Steve to discuss the use of the sanctuary for the wedding. "I'm sorry," Steve said, "but it is church policy that the sanctuary is not to be used for a wedding of this nature. Everyone knows that she is entering the marriage with another man's child."

"Yes," was the reply, "but she has repented of her sin. She loves the Lord and is marrying a fine young man."

"I understand and feel sympathetic," said Steve, "but this is the policy. It's designed to encourage young people to stay pure and marry properly the first time. I think the world of you both, but there's no way for me to bend this rule without a major problem in the church." Alex and Cora left, seething to think that Steve was such an ingrate after all they had done for him. Though they knew he was right in policy, they couldn't accept the idea that he wouldn't bend the rule for *them*.

The forces didn't stop there. Some were hidden deep within Steve's own psychological profile. His father had never encouraged him as a boy. He was *expected* to succeed. Throughout his childhood and teenage years, he heard things like, You'll never amount to much. . . . You'd better never dishonor the family name. . . . You can't do anything right. Steve's subconscious drive for success was not so much to please God as to gain his dad's approval.

Mimicking the way he was raised, Steve led by negative energy, rarely giving anyone a positive word. His preaching portrayed God as being endlessly disappointed in everyone. He knew his thinking was wrong but avoided analyzing it for fear of the painful results. Bottom line, he hadn't settled who would shape his heart—God or his dad. Laboring to gain acceptance by achievement, he walked a treadmill of despair. Consumed by his own needs, he lacked sensitivity toward others.

This inner conflict reaped some bad consequences in his relationship with Heather. Often she felt like a spiritual slave trying to win his acceptance. Heather was rarely complimented but often criticized by Steve. She at times blurted out, "You should have married someone else . . . someone who would be good enough for you!" She couldn't speak to anyone about her troubled heart without jeopardizing his ministry. Hope waned as disappointment grew. Steve couldn't admit that he was the biggest part of the problem lest he betray his dad. Steve secretly feared that Heather might tire, leave him, and destroy his ministry. His guilt was compounded by the realization that in failing his wife, he was also failing the church.

Beyond this were the invisible powers of darkness faced by every believer. He knew what it was to preach with heavy oppression weighing upon his body and mind. At times he awakened in the middle of the night drenched in cold sweat. His muscles were tightened by the tension in his soul. Fatigued, he would arise early to carry out more duties.

Steve's self-imposed isolation deepened the problem. He refused to seek help for two reasons. First, he believed this would show weakness; second, he trusted no one. Dr. Raymond Noble, a Christian psychologist who attended CBC, saw the symptoms and tried to discuss them with Steve during a private breakfast meeting. Steve immediately pulled down a steel curtain in his mind and turned the conversation to trivia.

Steve's refusal to admit that he wronged people eroded his credibility. Broken relationships accumulated like dead branches on a forest floor—perfect tinder for the sparks to ignite a firestorm. Something deep within warned him that admitting to a mistake wasn't manly. This blocked him from the ultimate source of strength—weakness (1 Cor. 1:27; 2 Cor. 12:8–10). He wasn't convinced of this paradoxical truth. He preached Paul's words about finding strength in weakness but never personalized them. His apologies had a ring of insincerity because they were coupled with explanations that were attempts to make offended parties feel guilty.

The Central Baptist Church scenario points to one vital fact: the entire church, from the pulpit to the pew, was composed of mere humans, each with a personal background of problems and blessings. During the happier years, people had offered mutual encouragement as they sought to grow. They even had found humor in Steve's unwillingness to participate on this level, always carrying himself as though he lacked nothing. But edginess was rapidly growing between people. Differences no longer were tolerated. Friendly humor turned cutting.

Ignoring the warning signs, Steve and the elders plowed ahead with the vision of a virtually closed community in which every phase of life revolved around CBC. They already had the academy and senior citizens' village. Steve also had futuristic dreams of a restaurant, health center, and other income-producing enterprises. Success deafened him to the people's complaints that he was no longer a pastor. Like David, he heard Nathan's words, "Whatever you have in mind, go ahead and do it, for the LORD is with you" (2 Sam. 7:3). Unlike David, he rejected Nathan's follow-up, "No, you are not the man to do these things."

Steve and the elders engaged in a flurry of church growth efforts that looked more like secular marketing techniques than the work of the Holy Spirit. Radio and television became a steroid for growth, allowing little time for discipleship. People would join the church, then be escorted immediately to the choir loft or some other place of service. But the growing crowds were not loyal. Having been attracted by entertainment, they could only be sustained by more of the same. Each week the decibel levels got louder, the music ended on a higher note, and awards for bringing people got more elaborate. The congregation hooted like a studio audience at a game show the Sunday one family won a free trip to the Holy Land. The spiritually minded were saddened, knowing that trouble was soon to erupt.

Late one Friday afternoon, Edna Neel and five other women of prayer met with Steve to discuss the danger of rapid growth without discipleship, as well as the negative impact of Steve's violation of CBC's historical cultural style. Among them was Thelma Worthington, who taught the Women of Faith Sunday school class for older ladies. Steve chided them, as though their concerns suggested a lack of support for him. Tensions deepened when word of Steve's response spread throughout the class, then the church.

The problems at CBC were not too great for a spiritually fit congregation. But because of the weakness resulting from inadequate discipleship, the church couldn't handle the complexities. Steve attended a conference on reaching baby boomers. He saw powerful demonstrations of a "seeker friendly" approach. It was a blend of well-done skits, contemporary music, and a brief message. Success stories abounded.

Steve returned to Pittsburgh insisting upon radical change—*now.* For CBC, this meant crashing the existing culture. However, the church that was successful in the unorthodox "seeker friendly" approach did not overthrow an existing church culture. It started from nothing and built its own distinctive style.

Steve, on the other hand, was violating the promise he had made to honor the culture that had worked so well for his church from its inception. His thirst for change clearly said to the older people, "Get with it, or get out. You're expendable." The response wasn't quiet or soft. Steve found himself surrounded by growing resistance. Elders tried in vain to slow him down. But he was bent on following youthful thought, believing it to be the wave of the future.

Steve ignored the examples of other churches that solved this cultural problem by either slowly blending the two cultures or holding two services, thereby creating two congregations in one building. But Steve expected his people to shed their culture overnight, something that never happens. The intolerant immediately quit the church. The loss was not offset by an increase in young couples who would carry the responsibility of the massive programs of the church, which included serious indebtedness and a hefty missionary budget. As funds dwindled and bills continued, the elders were left with no choice but to slash the missionary budget in half. This forced some missionaries to abandon their ministries on foreign fields and return home. It didn't go unnoticed that Steve forfeited none of his salary and benefits, which approached one hundred thousand dollars.

As weeks rolled into months, anger within the ladies' Sunday school class mounted. Mrs. Worthington tried in vain to get the ladies to let the matter rest. A few of the 230 women became abusive in their comments against Steve and the elders. As reports of the unrest reached Steve's ears, he resolved to take control of the situation by disciplining the whole class. He got the board to order it shut down. His overreaction caused him to lose the power base of these women and their husbands.

Heather, who needed Steve's attention, saw her chance to impress him by taking a bold stand against the disturbed class. She wrote a letter and handed it to one of the ladies to be read to the entire group.

> Dear Thelma,
>
> I am greatly disappointed in the example you are setting for the younger women in our church. It is appalling to see you manifest such wicked deeds of the flesh (2 Cor. 12:20) and the tongue (James 3). Several women have expressed their concern to me, and I feel compelled to admonish you to test yourselves to see if you are truly in the faith (2 Cor. 13:5). I am praying for your repentance and that you will humble yourselves under the mighty hand of God.
>
> Sincerely in Christ, Heather

Even the mature ladies in the group lost patience. Steve and Heather developed a fortress mentality, viewing themselves as victims of an evil plot. Steve's self-concern rendered him incapable of distinguishing between honest questions and sedition. His sermons bore little grace as he hammered on law, casting all dissenters as wicked.

Over the years, Steve and the board had never developed spiritual unity through friendship and prayer. They became hopelessly divided. This threw the congregation into greater confusion. Late night meetings resolved nothing. The pulpit became the soap box for Steve's agenda and not for the feeding of sheep. He unwittingly slipped from holding the high ideals of his youth to nursing a questionable ambition. He failed to learn from Solomon, who had begun his career as the wisest man on earth but ended it as one of the greatest fools.

People couldn't define how Steve had changed, but they knew he had. He had shifted from heeding Christ's teaching about success to holding a secular, pragmatic view. "How can something that seems so right be wrong?" he wondered, forgetting that the end never justifies the means. The board lacked both the spiritual depth and resolve to either restrain or remove him.

Groups formed as people discovered each other's discontent. They did not all have the same concerns but became comrades in unsettled grievances. That unhealthy bond formed the power base for the coming firestorm. The danger escalated when Elder Paul Powers sided with these groups. He hoped to build a consensus for ousting Steve.

The situation turned ugly. The pastor was losing credibility, the board was paralyzed by division and indecision, and an informal coalition championed by Powers was forming between unhappy groups. The board's appeal for the people's loyalty was perceived as an attempt to sidestep the issues. Distrust deepened. People believed they knew the motivation of the other side—those for or against the elders' policies . . . those for or against the pastor . . . those for or against the new style of culture . . . those for or against the cutting of missionary funds . . . ad infinitum.

Now, the spiritual remnant saw why they had been awakened to pray so many nights over the previous year. The firestorm was under way. They intensified their fasting and prayer. There was much talk among the members about the importance of saving their beloved Central Baptist Church, with its rich heritage; after all, they reasoned, it had been raised up by God.

Here are some observable behaviors to be noted as sparks ignite brush fires that combine and progress into a firestorm.

The Natural Dynamics of Phase 2

Natural dynamics of human relationships on this level:

1. People feel uneasy with each other because perceived unfairness or hurt is involved.

   - Humor becomes cutting, disrespectful, and hurtful.
   - Positions and hierarchy start to be used for leverage; i.e.,
     points are made stronger by saying, "The pastor said. . . ."

2. Diversity starts to be despised, not respected. Differences are
   accentuated as bad, not good.

   - The desire for uniformity of viewpoints becomes strong.
   - Diversity is feared as a weakness that will topple the church,
     not strengthen or enhance it.
   - Strong criticism of the way another person or group is doing
     things emerges.

3. People seek out those who agree with their position. Discussions are held to reinforce and promote their concerns.
4. The groups discuss strategies for handling future meetings.
5. People identify with the problem so completely that, if things
   don't go their way, personal loss is felt. Pride is challenged and
   defenses deepen.
6. Language becomes less specific and more general. People will
   say, "They always . . ." or "You can never trust them . . ." or "They
   are not capable of . . . ."
7. Opposition is depersonalized by characterization. In so doing,
   people feel their own pain, but not that of the other group.
8. People stop freely sharing information so the opposing view
   cannot gain an advantage. The spirit between the parties grows
   cold and edgy.
9. Coalitions form, but the well-being of the ministry is still paramount. People meet unofficially in the parking lot, for example,
   to see who is like-minded. The groups have not yet hardened

into formal factions and are still undefined. The conversations are rationalized to be for the well-being of the church.

10. People lose interest in resolve and become concerned about how they will look or fare in the growing conflict. Will they be perceived as push-overs by compromising? Concern for one's personal image deepens.

While phase one can continue for an indefinite number of years, phase two allows only a narrow window of time for stopping the newly arrived firestorm (perhaps three to six months). The conflict rapidly gains momentum.

Recommendations for Phase 2

- Do not take a wait-and-see posture, or you will lose. These dynamics do not die down or go away on their own. Weak leadership says, "We'll wait out the storm and see what happens." That merely fuels the problem.
- Acknowledge that there is a problem and call for fasting and prayer.
- Hold spiritual life meetings with a neutral visiting speaker. Often this will help people return to being under the control of the Holy Spirit.
- Exercise church discipline when it is appropriate. The few people you may lose through discipline at this level cannot compare to the numbers you will lose at the next level.
- Invite a neutral mediator to help settle the disturbance. Some pointers appear in chapter 16, "Firestorm Consultants."

3

FIRESTORM IN FULL FURY

> Once the firestorm erupts, chances of a good recovery virtually disappear. Deep losses are almost inevitable.

Little did Steve realize that, when Elder Jim Ellison handed him a lengthy, handwritten letter of concerns, he was holding the burning fuse—something Jim didn't intend. Steve had been through numerous stare-downs over the years, always winning on the strength of his stubbornness and position. Steve didn't know that this was more than a stare-down. It was an ultimatum.

Jim had outlined two areas of major concern. The first was the continued loss of people due to Steve's culture crash of CBC. The resulting financial strain led to the second area of concern, which was the shifting of designated funds for undesignated purposes. Steve fully intended to repay each account. Still, the practice was unethical without full church and board approval. Jim believed that, in money matters, it was best to avoid all appearance of evil.

Steve shot a letter back to Jim. It was filled with condescending innuendos about Jim's spiritual depth.

Jim was in no mood for another futile debate with Steve. He fired off his resignation from the board of elders. The following Sunday, Steve called him into the office to say Jim could no longer teach Sunday school because of insubordination. In light of the respect Jim had among the people, this proved to be a big mistake.

That Sunday Jim pulled a small circle of elders together to share the sequence of events. Elder Fred Botcher raised his heavy eyebrows, indicating it was time for action. Having inherited his family's lumber business, he responded to church problems by proudly explaining how he handled people at the lumberyard—"I fire 'em!" he'd say. So, true to form, he pointed toward the pastor's study and said, "Let's fire 'im."

The impromptu meeting extended through the morning service. Elder Leonard Rollings happened upon the searing session and was quickly brought up to speed. He was a spiritual man who cautioned that they needed to slow down and pray about the matter. Fred Botcher disdainfully grunted.

This discussion burned away what remained of the board's self-imposed discipline of silence. Steve's refusal to let Jim teach was the line drawn in the sand. Steve had overestimated the strength of his past victories and underestimated the erosion of his credibility.

By the end of the morning service, the entire congregation was discussing Steve's dismissal of Jim from teaching. Mary Matthews burst into tears upon hearing elder Frank Hagg say, "I think the pastor has been here too long. Fred Botcher is right. He has lost his marketability, so let's fire him and get someone with wider appeal." Frank was the CEO of a manufacturing company and saw everything on marketing terms. Mary had come to faith under Steve's ministry. She was a quiet, soft-spoken woman of blind loyalty. To hear such words tore so deeply into her soul that she could barely eat or sleep for days.

Steve drove home thinking this was just another passing flare-up. He remained resolved to change the worship service to a "seeker friendly" style, and he wasn't going to change how he handled the church's money. Instead, he viewed this as an evil plot against him. Heather did not share her misgivings with Steve, lest she jeopardize any hope for their relationship.

Steve was on unfamiliar turf, not knowing God well enough to wisely handle such an hour as this. The instinct for self-preservation drove him to emphasizing legalities. He reminded the elders, for instance, that they had signed an agreement forbidding discussions with church members about controversial issues. His preaching became more legalistic, demanding respect for authority. But law can't fix broken spirits and angry hearts. Some people retaliated by studying the church constitution to see how to get rid of Steve. "An eye for an eye" was in, and tolerance was out. Some became ruthless in their efforts to dump Steve. Others warned, "We must not touch God's anointed."

Some on the church staff also joined the free-for-all. The staff of twenty-eight was divided three ways, as were the board and church members. A few were blind loyalists who believed Steve was being unfairly attacked. Another minority, who had had some bad run-ins with Steve, saw this as the opportune time for revenge. The rest of the staff was confused over the issues and hoped that everything would somehow settle down.

Some staff members were guilty of starting problems. For example, Dwayne and Sylvia Ferndon had been hired to work with the youth and head the drama department. They clearly showed contempt for Steve's position. Shortly after they started, their hidden agenda emerged. They antagonized Steve by refusing to submit reports, account for their time, or show up for staff meetings. When they did attend, they acted bored, as though they were the only ones with real insights for ministry. The tension of the firestorm, combined with their indolence and insubordination, drove Steve one Sunday to "strike the rock." He called them into his office during a moment when untamed rage burned in his heart. Their cavalier attitude further incited Steve, who slammed his fist on his desk and swore, saying, "I'm sick of this behavior!" He did not know the couple had violated ethics and law by packing a hidden tape recorder. Although Steve was not given to swearing, this one slip proved deadly. By the following week, copies of the tape had been circulated throughout the underground network of groups, further consolidating resistance. The couple's conduct was never questioned, but Steve was reduced to virtual criminal status.

Steve, on the other hand, had been guilty of generating anger within some of the staff. He responded to those who disagreed with him by increasing his demands, trying to pressure them to repent or resign. Some rebelled and sought to enlarge their loyalty groups within the congregation. As the firestorm erupted, these staff members rallied their groups to resist Steve, even though these people had no particular argument of their own. One former staff member had stayed in the Pittsburgh area, carrying out a venomous campaign of character assassination against Steve. After the firestorm erupted, he reappeared as an unofficial spokesperson.

The annual congregational business meeting fell on the following Thursday. The timing couldn't have been worse. The atmosphere was charged with unrest. It was a mistake to open the meeting, since nothing could be settled with wrongful spirits. After a gingerly stated prayer, the agenda was presented—but soon set aside. Trevor Hasting stood, ignoring the moderator's call for order, and said, "I understand that the pastor is misusing church funds. I hear that the board knows about it and is allowing it to happen. I demand an explanation." He really wanted revenge because his daughter had been sent home from church camp ten years earlier for misbehavior. Trevor's bold usurpation of order was like a bugle playing reveille, awakening anger in a thousand hearts.

Elder Bob Bulrich rose to say, "Well, we think the pastor did things right."

At that, Ivan Erickson, still bitter over his daughter's fate at the hands of Bob's son, jumped to his feet. "I'm sorry, Bob," he blurted, "but I can't let you say that. You know that this was discussed at board meetings. You also know that Jim Ellison got banned from teaching for trying to correct this." Bob was shocked to be confronted before the whole church. He took a heavy breath and stared straight ahead. Ivan's heart pounded as he hoped Bob felt the sledgehammer effect of his words.

Sam Strazinski, who neither attended church often nor understood the problems, interjected an unrelated issue. "I hear the pastor forced Bill Kohler out of the church." Sam was handicapped by his fear of groups. Yet, he became airborne in the stir of the moment, expecting to speak the final word and be an overnight sensation. His voice was pinched and high as he shouted, "Well, I'm sick of the way you elders just let the pastor run you like a bunch of puppets. What's the matter, aren't you men? Look at poor Bill Kohler. He hasn't been able to find a job anywhere. Maybe Bill should be our pastor." Sam sat down feeling insecure over the lack of thunderous applause. He adjusted his glasses in an effort to recompose himself after his surprising burst of boldness. Some of the elders who were not too spiritual felt their manhood threatened and took Sam's insult personally.

Rev. Dick Sturgill, who was the pastor to the seniors, had damaged Steve in many homes, not by open accusation but by innuendo. When someone asked about situations in the church, he smiled knowingly, then said, "Well, there are some things we just can't speak about. But we must be faithful to the Lord no matter what. I will say this, however . . . ." He thought this ingratiated him with people.

He tried to lay low at this meeting but was unmasked when Jake Shank said, "Pastor Sturgill told me just the other day . . . ah, we were down at the golf course . . . ah, that Pastor Gates didn't care if he lost all the older people so long as he got the younger people by his new-fangled seeker friendly meetings. Well, we're the ones who built this place. This is our church. We gotta do something now." Jake was known for saying things as he saw them. Pastor Sturgill never expected to be quoted in public and felt a hot rush under his collar.

There was a slight lull, a great time to stop the meeting. But feisty Sylvia Ferndon sprang up to deliver a showstopper. Lifting her finger high in the manner of a revival preacher, she said, "I want to say something to all you Women of Faith." She knew that the Women of Faith Sunday school class opposed Steve's culture crash. She brazenly looked around the auditorium as though all should duck or be slain, then added, "I want to say that I don't ever want to be like any one of you." She sat down abruptly, defiance bouncing her hair.

Hot coals fell on heads, but not from kindness. Most were shocked at her impudence. She had snapped at women two and three times her age. They had been through struggles and growth she could not understand. By taking aim at these well-intentioned wives, mothers, and grandmothers, Sylvia thought she had struck a blow for righteousness. Instead . . . well, she just struck a blow!

God's work had fallen squarely into human hands. All parties considered their private anger to be the central issue. The main problems of culture crashing and money management were almost obliterated by the smoke rising from all of the smaller fires. The moderator made futile attempts to regain order. As hours passed and smoke thickened, the scene degenerated. Some shouted. Others tearfully ran from the auditorium. One quiet, saintly widow named Martha Henderson stood to speak. Everyone became respectfully quiet. "We need to go to prayer and ask God to send us a revival. We must stop destroying ourselves in this manner. I'm sure the pastor and elders made mistakes, but we all make mistakes. They are only human and need our prayers." She sat down.

Elder Paul Powers spoke. "Of course, those are nice sounding words. But we have to handle this like men." And so they did. The evening ended with relationships burnt crisp and hollow. Free speech turned into speaking freely to the point of destruction.

Let's look at what's happening in phase three. Once the firestorm erupts, chances of a good recovery virtually disappear. Experience suggests that the window of opportunity for strong, corrective action is open only thirty to ninety days. After that, deep losses are almost inevitable. The reason is that this inflamed level of conflict quickly destroys good people while hardening evil people. Perceptions are radically blurred. Jesus said to settle issues (if at all possible) while hearts are still malleable (Matt. 5:25–26).

Any problem can be solved, provided the right spirit prevails. It is generally possible to inspire a right spirit during the first two phases. In the third phase, however, the chance of recapturing a right spirit fades.

When a firestorm ignites, there is an almost overnight collapse of reason, negotiation, tolerance, love, and forgiveness. Factions take on a "we are right, and they are the enemy" mind-set. The following actions result:

- Emotion rules over reason.
- Fleshly behavior is accepted as the only way to handle the problem.
- Legalism obliterates grace. People sound like lawyers in their arguments.
- Man-made rules take supremacy over biblical instruction and spiritual sensitivity.
- Rigidity reigns. Faults of others are spoken about with intolerance.

The church will be devoured if the leaders either do not or cannot insist upon doing all things in a right spirit—a biblical mandate.

The call for spiritual attitudes and conduct is perceived as a manipulation to help the other side win. As a result, spiritual solutions that would have worked during the first two phases stand little chance after the firestorm strikes. The lowest instincts of human nature rise up in unbridled liberty:

- Tempers flare.
- Discussions deteriorate into destructive trading of accusations.
- Winning takes precedence over fairness.
- Justice is replaced by judgmentalism.
- Mercy is buried by retribution.
- The humble, servant nature of Christ is denigrated as weakness.
- Respect for human dignity is abandoned.
- Condemnation of any position except "mine" is justified.

There is no tolerance for human error, since each side depersonalizes the other side as merely an object—the enemy. Mistakes are like open flesh wounds attracting legalistic piranhas who are not satisfied until they have devoured vital organs.

The white-hot blaze of human rage blots out important questions such as these:

- Are we glorifying God?
- Are we maintaining a biblical spirit and methodology?
- Is this best for Christ's sake?
- Do we want our children to witness this?
- Are we doing the work of evangelism?
- Would we be happy for the lost to witness this behavior?
- Will fasting and prayer help correct the problem?
- How would Jesus handle this?

There are serious casualties, although no one accepts or feels guilt for hurting others. People believe they are engaged in a "holy war," and nothing is more dangerous than an evil spirit cloaked in a religious cause.

The first phase is like sparks landing in a forest and can extend indefinitely. The second phase is like the igniting of small fires that don't go out. Only a three- to six-month window of opportunity exists to stop it. In phase three, the small fires intensify and merge into one. The time frame available for stopping the storm and preserving the church as a whole shrinks to three months.

The Natural Dynamics of Phase 3

Natural dynamics of human relationships on this level:

1. People who were civil and Christ-like in peaceful times now treat each other in godless ways. Slander becomes acceptable in talking about the other person or side.
2. People become identified with strong positions, believing their reputations are on the line. They must hold firm or risk looking bad to their group. Friends and family ties increase commitment to a position, since tolerance may strain personal relationships.
3. Casual disagreements become sharp divisions. Leaders and spokespersons emerge on each side.
4. Issues are presented as an either-or ultimatum. The friendly both-and approach is abandoned.
5. Organizational structure is used as a weapon for defeating the other side. Constitutions, bylaws, and rules are used to "prove" the other side wrong.
6. Perception becomes the new reality. Truth is no longer the main issue. How each group perceives truth hardens into "fact."
7. People take up a "holy cause," with each side believing itself to be absolutely right.

   - Apology is avoided, lest it be seen as weakness or betrayal of the "team."
   - Sometimes an apology will lead to the destruction of the person making it, because grace is no longer the ruling spirit. The desire is to win, not settle the dispute.

8. Powerless antagonists attach themselves to causes led by respected people, giving them undeserved credibility. They carry venom from person to person without fear of reprimand or discipline.
9. Winning becomes so important that serving, loving, or going the extra mile is spurned.
10. Each side is sure it knows the wrongful motives and strategies of the other.
11. The pastor is generally put into a no-win position and cannot lead the church out of the crisis alone. Even if the firestorm is over an issue other than the pastor, by the nature of his position, he is caught in the middle and shot at from both sides. Opposing parties want him to champion their cause. Conflict management consultant Dr. Edward Peirce says that 50 percent of the pastors who are harmed at this point do not return to the ministry.

Recommendations for Phase 3

- Although it is dangerously late, immediately seek a crisis management consultant.
- Prayerfully determine if there is an evil core to the firestorm, and start church discipline.
- Keep a strong balance between grace and justice, both in preaching and dealing with people. Grace without justice is weak, indecisive, and manipulative. Justice without grace produces rebellion.
- Consult with a Christian attorney to avoid an unnecessary lawsuit resulting from the manner in which issues are handled.
- Do not be indecisive about issues. The forces at work will "burn Rome" while the leaders are waiting to see how everything turns out. People tolerate minor mistakes in decision-making, provided they are told the reasoning, but they will not tolerate indecision.

4

PHASE 4

CONSUMING WINDS

> The firestorm phase is brief, intense, and destructive. Further, the column of rising heated air induces strong inward winds which fuel the fire, increasing its damage.

Firestorms create their own updrafts that create within them increasing intensity. And so it was the morning after the congregational meeting. The church office was draped in melancholy silence. All were at a loss for words to ease the heavy tension and erase the sense of doom. No one understood what had happened the night before. Having overlooked the preceding years of unresolved conflict, everyone was disoriented by the suddenness and magnitude of the eruption. No one could realize the many ways in which the church had just been gutted—spiritually, morally, financially, numerically.

The energy from the previous night compounded. Phone lines were ablaze. Fury awakened fury. People wanted their positions heard and *felt*. Reason was imprisoned by passion, and passion ignored the facts. Many made their exclamation point by departing. Little could anyone imagine that last Sunday's crowd of 3,800 would be reduced to 2,547 next Sunday—then continue sliding week after week. To lose a third of the congregation in one week plunged the treasury beneath the level needed to meet operating expense. Within three months, two-thirds of the congregation had left. Only a few more than 1,200 remained. Staff members resigned when the hand-writing on the wall spelled "hopeless." Antagonists said it spelled "Ichabod." Other staff members were dismissed because of dwindling resources. After six months, only four remained.

The firestorm that had come with such suddenness refused to leave the same way. Its swirling winds spread a rumor that the pastor had an immoral affair. Although not true, the rumor caused doubt. Doubt shaped perception. Perception formed a new "reality." Soon, the lie was spread as fact. When the elders asked for the name of the guilty woman, none could be given. Nor could proof be found. A new wave of rumors rocked the remnant almost every week. Thus, the winds advanced the storm.

In the early months, the remaining members received phone calls from those who had left, telling them about the "fantastic" churches they had found and encouraging them to leave CBC. The callers' unabated anger blinded them to the disaster this would cause for missionaries, the church's ability to meet obligations to the bank, and most of all, the work of spreading the gospel.

Anonymous letters filled with outlandish accusations and threats showed up in the church office. Some belittled the board, which by now was reduced to half by resignations. The board was constantly having to face another problem. Ned Friendly and Jeremiah Cutler circulated a petition to have Steve removed. In no time, they had seven groups, all with differing complaints, helping with the petition drive. This continued to fuel the firestorm, which burned away more of the remaining timbers. The destructive force intensified each time opposing camps found common ground.

The damaging effects could be charted. After the decline in attendance and revenue came erosion of morale among the faithful, who hoped to stop the crisis and reverse the collapse. And the church's tarnished reputation reduced its chances of growth for years to come. No matter how hard members prayed and worked, the damage worsened. Soon reality warned that, apart from a miracle, they would have to sell the church.

Prayer meetings grew somber and depressing. No one could discern God's will. Unsettling questions swelled: Was it God's time to end the church? Were remaining members to be faithful to this ministry despite the oversized building and enormous debt?

Would they be disobedient by leaving? Would God send a great revival and reverse the loss? Was there an Achan in their midst hindering recovery?

In time the pastor realized his sermons were consumed by the conflict. The greatest casualty of the firestorm was the gospel of Jesus Christ, as the church focused on survival rather than salvation. Not one person had come to salvation, and the baptistry was drained. Freedom of spirit was gone. No one witnessed for Christ, and certainly no one invited people to the church.

Edna Neel gave Steve two of Dr. Mark Bubeck's books, *The Adversary* and *Overcoming the Adversary.* He discovered realities about Satan that he had never considered. In fact, he was able to identify much of the church's trouble in the descriptions of demonic work. Satan became more than an abstract concept. Steve saw him as a real living enemy.

Steve overreacted, however. He made Satan the scapegoat by putting all the blame on his shoulders. This was a threefold mistake. First, it failed to take into account that, while Satan was clearly involved, he only acted upon the opportunity opened by the people's failures. Second, it exempted Steve from examining his own flaws. Third, it was too easy to regard all who disagreed as satanic. Still, Satan's fingerprints could be seen all over this crisis.

Let's analyze what we are seeing during this phase. The ignition phase was brief, intense, and destructive. On the other hand, the winds are gradually intensifying the storm, increasing its damage by taking the issues far beyond their origins. Hearts turn to granite. Formally organized groups develop plans. Different concerns cement into alliances that are resolved to bring down the perceived enemy. Destructive methods are justified. The fact that they are damaging the body of Christ is disregarded.

Also, the winds of the firestorm draw in new fuel. Each new rumor is given headline attention. As additional issues erupt, fatigue sets in on the faithful.

Because powers of darkness continue to escalate human tragedy, it is almost impossible to keep losses minimal. During this stage a church may be reduced to a handful of people fighting for survival, or it may not survive at all. If church discipline has not been employed in the initial wave of the storm, the small evil core has strengthened by this point.

The Natural Dynamics of Phase 4

Natural dynamics of human relationships on this level:

1. Once the conflict has spread to 10 percent of the leadership and 20 percent of the congregation, the storm is full-blown, with swirling winds intensifying it.
2. Facts are hard to find, because arguments have become intensely emotional. There is fear that facts may diminish one's position.
3. Objectivity and moderation are viewed with suspicion.

   - Paranoia sets in.
   - Soft-spoken people are perceived as weak.
   - Spirituality seems impotent.

4. Each side is sure the other side will not change, so fighting is seen as the only option.
5. Permanent damage is done.

   - People who cannot stomach the fight begin to leave.
   - Some leave as a statement of protest.
   - Others feel pressured to leave by family and friends.

6. A subgroup's power and advantage become more important than the parent organization.
7. Irreparable harm comes to the main organization as the damage becomes external. The church loses its good reputation within the community.
8. Even more so than in the previous phase, people have little perception of others' pain because of detachment from the opposition and lack of communication. The opposition is an object no longer given "people" status.

9. Specific issues melt into vague principles and ideologies, as personal perspective, bias, and opinion are elevated to doctrinal status. Some church consultants estimate that only 2 percent of church conflict is over doctrine; the rest is personal. When preferences are elevated to doctrinal status, attacks on personal positions are equated with violating God. Everything becomes a weapon:

   - *Prayer:* The opposing side is corrected by statements made in prayer.
   - *Scripture:* Quotes are used out of context to prove points.
   - *Outside people:* Calls are made to respected leaders to gain support.

10. Distinguishing the difference between satanic activity and human behavior isn't easy, making the spiritual struggle hard to define.
11. Talk about needing revival generally is based upon the simplistic view of God bringing about a quick and easy solution that will get others to see the error of their ways.
12. Board members, overreacting, often improperly use church discipline as a weapon.
13. The departed people will be viewed as weak or sinful by the remnant, which reasons that God is cleansing the church of bad people. While it is generally true that a small core of troublemakers may need to exit, it is more often the failure of leadership to act in time that accounts for the larger loss. It can be a convenient cover-up for failure in leadership to say the mass exodus resulted from God cleansing the church.

Recommendations for Phase 4

- Work closely with a consultant. The greater the authority granted to him at this point, the better are his chances of helping to deliver the ministry.
- Teach solid, biblical truths about our spiritual battle with darkness. These truths are most clear when seen in a real situation and not in theory.

- Do not let people blame the whole situation on Satan, who probably only acted upon the opportunity afforded to him by people's wrongful attitudes and conduct.
- Set up a conference on spiritual warfare, and invite one of the growing list of biblically responsible teachers to speak.
- Do not permit Scripture to be used as a weapon between factions, unless biblical absolutes are being violated.
- The faithful who are not involved in the controversy need ongoing ministry. Be careful that they do not become restless through neglect.
- Do not let the conflict become the pulpit theme.
- Call the congregation to days of fasting and prayer. Without divulging sensitive information, the church must collectively seek God's help.
- Each leader, including the pastor, must determine whether it's best to stay or leave. Sometimes departing is best for both parties.

5

PHASE 5

THE FINAL BURN

> Conflict may lead to litigation. It's disgraceful when the world must do the church's work.

It is said that desperate people do desperate things. Maybe so, but desperation never justifies disobedience. It's probably more accurate to say that desperation reveals a person's true character. It was desperation exacerbated by anger that gave a growing number of people at Central Baptist Church boldness to violate Scripture in an attempt to "make things right."

Eight months after the firestorm struck, the church was slapped with its first lawsuit by Liz, one of the secretaries dismissed due to a lack of funds. Liz's husband Scott was a truck driver. They could only afford to enroll their three children in the academy because of her job at the church. Tuition was halved for church employees. Liz was not too skilled in her profession but made up for it by singing Steve's praises. She had often said within earshot of Steve, "Praise God for this great leader," and, "We have the greatest pastor anyone could ever want." But when her lack of talent made it difficult to find a new job and tuition was raised to full fare, her true character emerged. She went to various parents and teachers to discuss a class action lawsuit against the church in the event that the school should close. The argument was that the church would fail to provide the ongoing education promised in its brochure. Everyone was amazed at her creative energy, something not seen when she had a job.

The threat of the lawsuit reduced vitality among the elders and academy board. The thought of a spiritual institution embroiled in a legal matter shattered innocence. But closing the school seemed imminent. Funds were running out. Teacher salaries were woefully behind. Insecurity bred anger. Some teachers wanted guarantees that they would be paid. Threats of additional suits surfaced.

The retirement village had its own financial problems. Tensions grew between the village and church boards. Harsh words were exchanged. Residents panicked, thinking they might lose their life-long investments. Some argued for the two organizations to sepa-rate, lest the church's problems sink the village, but the village's debt made an independent financial plan impossible. As a result, law-suits were filed by those who demanded immediate repayment of all of their money. People who said their treasures were in heaven fought like pirates on earth. They didn't care who got destroyed, as long as their treasures were secure. For some, Steve was reduced to a scoundrel. Many no longer attended the church, driving past it in search of other churches. Eventually the village became indepen-dent and was promptly turned into a for-profit organization in hopes that investors would save the enterprise.

With the collapse of the academy and loss of the retirement cen-ter, the original dream of a cradle-to-grave ministry focused on CBC was dead. Plans to build an enclosed walkway between the church and the village were dropped. Although people were satisfied that their money was safe again, many harbored bitterness toward the church. A few of the gracious ones still attended services, more out of convenience than loyalty.

The church no longer could afford to be on television and radio, thereby losing its lifeline to new growth. Overdue bills accumulated. High-pressure collection agents further demoralized the staff.

Blame flew in every direction as the institution unraveled—all part of the final burn. Loyalists to Steve blamed the board of elders for being too divided and weak to stop the troublemakers. Critics felt that God's wrath had fallen on the church. Cynics sneered to see the church crumble. Elders were divided in their fault-finding—some blaming Steve, others blaming one another. The cross-networking of finger-pointing further blocked resolution.

Lengthy board meetings were held to discuss how to keep from defaulting on the monthly mortgage payments of $38,000. The bank threatened to call for the loan. The church required $24,000 to meet monthly operation costs and $11,000 to fulfill missionary commitments. An estimated $238,000 was needed for repairs on the building, which if ignored would lead to further deterioration and greater cost. The reduced congregation was only giving a monthly average of $52,000, which nosed the church toward bankruptcy. One small group attended a religious conference on financial stewardship and added to the agony by spreading word that God's wrath was upon the church for going into debt in the first place. That conclusion was not the intent of the conference, but it fit the group's purpose and justified not giving anymore.

The final burn was consuming Steve's private world, too. His son and daughter were now far away at college, but their grades suffered from loss of concentration. They felt insecure as well-intentioned friends wrote and called with differing viewpoints on the turmoil at home. Heather lost her voice under the pressure. She took nerve medicine and used sleeping pills. She could hardly contain her rage toward those who perceived Steve as the culprit. While she well knew his personal struggles and failures, she also knew him as a good man with admirable intentions. Attempts to destroy Steve ravaged her body and mind.

Finally the board's worst nightmare became reality when the bank called in the loan and the church was forced into bankruptcy. The court set up an independent arbitrator. The fountain that had sprayed its symbol of hope and life into the air was shut off. The floodlights that had lit the steeple nightly went black. The marquee that had announced coming events was covered by two gigantic, ghastly red words—*For Sale!*

For Steve, the thought of staying in Pittsburgh with the remnant and starting anew in a smaller building was unbearable. He pulled out the file of a church that had shown interest in calling him as its pastor a few months earlier. He hoped that it was willing to reopen negotiations. The church was halfway across the continent. Steve asked the pulpit search committee not to contact CBC for any reason, stating that it would cause a great disruption if his people thought he was considering another opportunity. He gave glowing reports of the growth and building programs, stopping at the highest figures. He didn't mention the firestorm or decline. In honoring Steve's request, the committee failed its duty to fully investigate all potential pastors.

Steve had no clear sense from God whether to stay at CBC or leave. The ghostly shadow of his father seemed to mock him in his subconscious mind. The firestorm seemed to prove his dad's negative predictions—disqualifying Steve from manhood. But, on the conscious level, Steve's instinct for self-preservation caused him to shift the blame to others. In his honest moments, he believed he should have left CBC two years earlier, an act that would have either saved the church or revealed a systemic problem. But he was still here as the final burn lay smoldering at his feet.

Steve went up on South Hills to sit alone on a bench overlooking the three rivers as they converged at the Point. There was Three Rivers Stadium, where he had occasionally ministered to the Pittsburgh Steelers during pre-game chapels. Dazzling lights danced on the rippling water below. Late evening traffic rushed across the Fort Pitt Bridge. The eastern sky was absorbing the day into blackness. He thought back to the early years when Pittsburgh's energy had inspired him. Now the city seemed friendless, reduced to mere noise. He couldn't sort out who was responsible for the collapse—himself? . . . the elders? . . . the complainers? . . . the congregation? The questions were unbearable and unanswerable. He was powerless to change anything. So, overlooking the city that would go on with or without him, Steve wrote his resignation.

It had taken a decade and a half of unresolved tensions to set the stage for the conflict to erupt. The initial firestorm lasted only a few months, then the winds carried it forward for another year. The final burn went on for several additional months. When Steve stood before the beleaguered remnant and read his resignation, some felt relief, knowing that there was no other recourse. Others wept openly, having so intensely sought God for a miraculous deliverance.

Soon Steve was gone. The broken congregation had to work through the crushing loss of bankruptcy alone. After the liquidation of all assets, it was able to pay debtors only thirty cents on the dollar. The membership, now reduced to six hundred, looked for a place to rent. But CBC's stigma looked like an indelible stain on the cross.

The Natural Dynamics of Phase 5

Natural dynamics of human relationships on this level:

1. Conflict may lead to litigation. It's disgraceful when the world must do the church's work. Avoid litigation if possible, because attorneys are not trained to be sensitive to emotions or spirituality. They will side only with the group paying the bill because their professional ethic demands this. They will affirm the "you-are-right-and-they-are-wrong" mind-set. This intensifies the conflict. Attorneys are trained to be adversarial, not redemptive. Further, it is not biblical for brothers and sisters in Christ to settle things through courts outside of the church. Litigation involving the church is almost always a lose-lose situation.

2. The object now between the groups is to discredit and destroy the opposition. Winning is no longer enough for the groups; destroying the enemy is the passion.

   - Serious violence can break out.
   - Dangerous threats (lawsuits and bodily harm) may be made.

3. The deeper the conflict, the more formal becomes the effort for resolution. The church has gone from mediation to arbitration (someone else makes the decisions for the groups). Notice, for example, the process in Matthew 18:15–17. It begins with two people resolving an issue and progresses to more people assisting the effort. If that fails, it becomes more formal and less relational as the church makes the decision for the people. When that fails, it moves to the formality of the church expelling the unrepentant offender.

4. An outside party officiates the dismantling of the organization. It may be a court, denominational representative, or consultant.

5. At this point in the conflict, the issues are crystal clear to each side, with each side feeling confirmed in its position.

Recommendations for Phase 5

- Make it difficult for the flames to spread by eliminating oxygen. Pull people back from the simple "we-are-right, they-are-wrong" mind-set by getting them to see the complexity of the situation. How? Set up a task force to discover each group's complaint. This will reveal that a spider web of issues is really behind what appears to be a single issue. That complexity must be identified and addressed or there can be no solution.

- Hire a neutral consultant to start a fact-finding procedure and assure fairness to all parties. Hear out each person fully. No progress will come until people have been thoroughly and respectfully heard. Sometimes the emotional energy of a crisis will dissipate once people feel they have been heard and understood. This breeds tolerance.

- Set biblical guidelines to which all who believe the Bible will submit, and set forth Scripture and prayer for each side to consider.

- Help people take ownership of their own fallibility.

- Properly placed humor can often help break down tensions. But it must not favor either side. It will take time for walls to be dismantled.

- The efforts here are designed to turn people's attention away from destroying the perceived enemy and get them to refocus on problem solving, *not* conquering.

- Do not hesitate to terminate nonfunctioning ministries or sell excess property. It is essential to preserve potential resources for future ministry. Failure to do so may result in the eventual loss of everything.

PHASE 6

REBUILDING ON BURNT TIMBERS

The question to be asked is not, "Did our side win?" but, "How can we best glorify God in all that we do now?"

For the first Sunday service after the sale of the church, the members met amid the pungent wood-oil smell of an old gymnasium. All the familiar props were gone. Their beautiful church building was sold to a group of investors who planned to turn the classrooms into a trendy, indoor shopping mall featuring unique shops with everything from coffee beans to handmade crafts. New Age paraphernalia would be sold in a cubicle called "Mother Earth and You." The sanctuary would become a theater for movies and live performances. Retaining the religious flavor in the architecture, the planners named it "Inspiration Mall."

Some of the elders fought back hard feelings toward the hundreds of people who had voted to build the elaborate building, then abandoned it through the firestorm, even delighting over the bankruptcy. But that's the risk of any volunteer organization. People can walk away from their commitments, leaving others with burdens they helped create. The sin was not in the debt but in the abandonment of the cause. Many people had found the Lord through the ministry.

The unexpected collapse was the result of the instability of the human heart—a consideration the leaders had ignored during the years of promise.

The storm had gone through the full cycle. Like Noah, the congregation was emerging into an altered world. But unlike Noah, it was not entering a new, sunny day. The leaders realized their chances of finding a competent pastor were not good. They could not compete with equally valid ministries that offered better salaries. Beyond that, they were still grappling with some unsettled lawsuits, as well as bad-mouthing from departed members. Business people throughout Pittsburgh also had been hurt by the bankruptcy, such as the owner of the local business machine store who lost forty-seven thousand dollars. He warned other stores to sell to the church only on a cash basis.

The remaining faithful felt strongly, however, that they were to endure this humiliation in order to restore the Lord's reputation. The board and congregation followed Elder Jim Ellison's proposal and voted to pay off their debts, even though the bankruptcy released them from such obligation. Thus they burdened themselves with repayment of $973,048, which included everything from media invoices to telephone bills. They knew that to honor this debt would slow any hope of recovery, yet they approached each vendor with their ten-year plan to repay. The creditors were so impressed that they all refused to accept any interest, only principle.

Rev. Harold Ford agreed to come as an interim to help them through the recovery. He was retired but had pastored two churches over forty-two years. Fortunately, what he lacked in physical stamina was more than made up in wisdom, knowledge, and people skills. He proved that age and physical limitation can work to the advantage of a person who has learned to live in the power of the Holy Spirit. Harold's genius for rebuilding the church was found in the thing he had done best—ministering Christ. No skill can match a person who ministers truth and love in the power of the Holy Spirit. He poured himself into the church, discipling and encouraging the people at every opportunity. In addition to all the normal duties, he went to their homes, met one-on-one for lunch, and held special retreats with the elders. He was laying the only foundation that could work—*a healthy spirit leading to good relationships.*

But it wasn't easy. Harold's first Sunday in the pulpit felt more like a funeral than a worship service. He realized that he was dealing with a confused swirl of collective anger, grief, blame, and insecurity. It is hard enough to lead an individual out of a traumatic experience, let alone a group. The more sensitive people wanted to mourn the past, while the more aggressive wanted to move ahead as though nothing had ever happened. Harold set forth an agenda that addressed both the practical and spiritual needs of the church.

Harold knew that the people would never be able to unite over their views of Steve or the issues that had divided the church. Once opinions are hardened, they rarely bend. He didn't fight against the adage, "To change a man against his will is to be of the same opinion still." Instead, Harold resolved to bring the congregation to a higher level of commitment. In one carefully crafted sermon he said, "I know there are intense emotions about the past events. But, as in death, we must surrender the past into the hands of the Lord for his judgment. We must honor what God did in the past and the people through whom he did it. Our focus from now on must be on exalting Christ. The question to be asked is not, 'Did our side win?' but 'How can we best glorify God in all that we do now?' Our worship to God is only as valid as the love, forgiveness, and respect extended to one another."

First, Harold pressed in his sermons the need for cleansing before God. The time was past for seeking to sort out every detail of the conflict. The time had come to cover the matter with the cloak of charity and to cleanse members' hearts with confession, forgiveness, and grace. He encouraged the people to realize that there comes a time when words are not helpful and matters must rest.

Harold affirmed CBC's history, spoke well of Steve, and commended members for their decision to pay the debt. He purposely lumped these three things together. Throughout the church's history, it had produced much fruit for the kingdom. While the firestorm tended to accentuate everyone's failures, including Steve's, all were to be respected as God's children. Moreover, the remnant that had emerged from the ashes possessed enough integrity to pay the church's debt, even though it would demand sacrifice. Slowly the bitterness dissipated as the congregation remembered the good in its past. As elder Charles Bradley said, "We don't feel like a bunch of worthless, no-good people anymore."

Rev. Ford made repentance, restitution, and reconciliation major themes. He knew that there would not be a satisfactory resolution to every situation, but that God at least demanded an effort. He encouraged people to resolve personal differences, even extend forgiveness to those who had angered them by abandonment. He led the board into private church discipline directed toward the people most central to causing the crisis. Getting at truth was the goal. Justice tempered by mercy was the manner in which they preserved the dignity of those they confronted. Some came to proper settlement. Others fought, even slandered the board as a bunch of thugs. It was a difficult and tiring process. When asked why they didn't just ignore these people and move on, Harold would answer, "Because justice is as much the work of the church as love. They are inseparable. God will not bless our future if we do not do his work well in the present."

Another building block was to teach the church about the reality of spiritual conflict and what believers are commanded to do about it. Most in the church responded favorably, discovering truths they had not previously seen about powers of darkness. A few felt threatened and uncomfortable standing on unfamiliar ground. The biblically literate saw the truths in God's Word and even held advanced training in adult Sunday school classes. As people learned how to resist the spiritual enemy in repentance, prayer, and authority, major oppression lifted.

Next, the pastor refocused them on the Great Commission. He made it clear that they had to move away from a survival mind-set and return to the work of seeking the lost. Harold knew the powerful encouragement that would come when they saw people coming to salvation. Slowly this happened. And, indeed, each new believer brought a healing fragrance to the congregation. The members realized they were still usable to God.

Harold strongly pressed the congregation to stop trying to understand the past, but to let the Lord judge it. He told members that in order to see God's blessing, they must commit themselves to acting like the church, which meant ministering to one another. And so he committed himself to showing them how to do that (Eph. 4:11–12). He told them, "I am not here to decipher God's will for you, but to help you determine and do it. You are not here to support me in my ministry—rather, the reverse is true. I want to draw out of you what God is placing within your hearts to do. I will then support and encourage you in every way possible."

However, getting people to be involved in ministry wasn't easy, because every church breaks down to the universal eighty–twenty principle. He was able to inspire a large part of the congregation to do certain things, such as setting up chairs on Saturday nights, but the majority only volunteered once or twice. Then it fell to the faithful few who complained that they had little help. Harold also found that the elders struggled to work hospital and home visitations into their personal schedules. It wasn't long before Harold detected a power play between two elders, both of whom were filling the balloon of good intentions with the helium of strong personalities and determined wills. They were vying for whose ideas would best rebuild the church. It was not a dangerous standoff, and both men conceded to Harold's leadership as he blended their concepts into a unified force.

He handed out a form on which members could indicate how they wanted to serve the Lord. Many were reluctant, still feeling unworthy after the firestorm. Harold encouraged them, however, to realize that God allows hard times and leads his people through them as a vital part of spiritual growth. With rising confidence, most completed the forms. While not all fulfilled their commitments, the ministry took a sharp upturn.

Harold preached sermons on the purpose of suffering and grief in the believer's life, including the church as a whole. The spirit of the congregation sprouted like a spring flower emerging from a winter's frozen crust. Harold made it clear that trouble may be God's chastening hand to cleanse us, and that it also could be unexplainable—allowed for purposes known only to God. He assured them that if they honored and pleased God they would see his compassionate hand of deliverance. His foundational text was Lamentations 3:32, "Though he brings grief, he will show compassion, so great is his unfailing love."

Within three months the congregation had started laughing again, no longer plagued by depressing discussions about the past. One could almost see the dark oppression lifting. It took a year for the people to fully trust Harold's leadership, since they felt deeply confused and betrayed by the behavior of many who had been in leadership. Attendance stabilized at 524, with minimal gains off-setting minimal losses. Monthly debt payments rounded off at $8,109, and while repayment was a tiresome burden, it also acted as a big eraser removing the blemish from the minds of those in the community. People who once cursed and mocked CBC members sang their praises as trustworthy people who honored their word. The congregation was able to bear that debt, plus an additional $16,500 for salaries, operating costs, and missions. But monthly expenses left nothing for outreach development. Members were filled with the anticipation, however, of what they might be able to do in the next ten years with a clean reputation and no debt.

Harold stayed for three and a half years, handing a spiritually renewed congregation to Jeremy Smith, a thirty-seven-year old IBM executive turned minister. With the heart of a pastor, he showed great concern for the spiritual growth and well-being of the congregation.

Many of the departed people remained scattered throughout the Pittsburgh churches—except for the one small group that failed in its attempt to start a new church. Some ceased attending church altogether. About thirty returned to CBC.

As hard as some tried to understand the calamity that had brought down one of Pittsburgh's most promising congregations, no one could quite piece it all together. All agreed, however, that every problem could have been conquered had a spiritual mind-set reigned. People at times discussed how wonderful it would have been to see a miracle restore the church to its former glory. But, in more thoughtful moments, they conceded that they preferred the spiritual growth that accompanied their gradual ascent from the ashes.

The Natural Dynamics of Phase 6

Natural dynamics of human relationships on this level:

1. One group may start a new church, while others scatter to other churches.
2. Some people (often the youth of the families involved) are lost to the faith due to bitterness.
3. There is a period of struggle as different personalities emerge and attempt to remedy the problem or save the ministry.
4. A faithful remnant will stay with the property and ministry as it either dies or struggles on with minimal effectiveness for many years. Members will talk of the good old days. They will not overcome their damaged reputation for a generation. They will hardly be able to financially support the struggling effort.
5. Resentments will linger between the ones who stayed and the ones who departed.
6. With proper leadership and time, the church can reemerge.

Recommendations for Phase 6

- If the pastor resigns, it is vital to hire an interim pastor, or the cycle can start all over again. An interim serves best at this point to prepare the way so the new pastor can have a clean start. Otherwise, the new pastor may have a short-lived, lame-duck ministry resulting from leftover embers and smoke casting the odor of the conflict upon him. A growing number of pastors specialize in this kind of interim ministry.
- Invite a special speaker to assist you in a series of meetings geared to the healing of the remnant. Themes such as unconditional love, forgiveness, and unity are necessary.

PART 2

CAUSES OF A FIRESTORM

The causes and dynamics of human conflict are multitudinous. It is essential to understand some of the major ones in the hope of foreseeing and stopping firestorms.

7

TRIM

The Pastor's
Four Pillars of Strength

> When a pastor becomes the focus of legitimate complaints, almost
> inevitably the problem will be found in one of four areas: truth, rela-
> tionship, integrity, or mission.

The story of Steve Gates and Central Baptist Church was designed
to show the phases of a firestorm to help you determine at which
level your church is functioning. This section will widen the understanding of a firestorm's causes. We'll look at causes within pastors,
boards, congregations, and the surrounding culture. A firestorm,
possibly yours, could come from one or more of the areas to be considered. Let's begin by seeing how pastors can avoid creating their
own firestorms.

Every pastor with whom I have worked has wanted a strong ministry, not a weak one. Yet few have had an objective way to evaluate
their strengths and weaknesses, which directly affect their ministries.
This has led to some unwittingly igniting their own firestorm, then
being totally bewildered by how it happened.

What about you? Like most, you enter the ministry assuming
God's call guarantees your success. You start to lead but do not find

a paved highway from Egypt to the Holy Land, with air-conditioned rest stops. You wonder if you grabbed the wrong road map in seminary. The wind has swept away the footprints of those who have gone before. Soon what began with your "burning bush call" becomes life on hot, barren sands.

Confusion sets in. Your throbbing motivation is hallowed by good intentions, so why doesn't everyone trust you? Your personality isn't sustaining the congregation in quiet adoration. Your preaching isn't sweeping them into unruffled happiness. Your prayers feel pitifully weak, especially when Pharaoh tells you to get out of town—*alone . . . now!* You can't nail down the problem. Self-confidence sags. Because you were called by God, you assume the problem must lie squarely with the people—which often is true. But a fatal mistake is made by not following the disciples' lead in asking, "Lord, is it I?" Sometimes it is.

Evaluating Your Four Pillars of Strength

If you're ready to ask that daring question, then let's look at the four pillars of strength that must stand relatively equal in height to balance the structure of your ministry. Here's an acrostic to aid in retention: TRIM.

> *Truth:* Presenting Christ in *concept* and *communion* (teaching what and whom we believe).
>
> *Relationship:* Presenting Christ in *companionship* (building bonds of trust).
>
> *Integrity:* Presenting Christ in *character* and *conduct* (practical holiness).
>
> *Mission:* Presenting Christ in *conquest* (vision—purpose with a plan).

Do these four pillars come close to the same height in your ministry, or are you already spotting one or two that are much taller than the rest? These pillars can't guarantee success—at least not as we define it—so don't be discouraged if you have them and still face a firestorm. Conflict happened to men like Isaiah, Jeremiah, and Paul—men who certainly cannot be faulted for their trouble. Hindsight tells us that they had phenomenal ministries, so trouble may mean that you are fulfilling God's will. While the four pillars cannot assure prevention of a firestorm, they can enable you to evaluate your performance to see whether you are igniting your own storms.

It matters not whether you pastor seventy-five people in a bucolic postcard setting or seventy-five hundred in a pulsating megalopolis; you're engaged in a struggle on three battlefronts. First, you face people problems. Like Moses, you are leading a *rebellious* nation out of a *resisting* one. That's gargantuan. Second, you deal with satanic pressures. Well-aimed, hot arrows fly at you from the invisible realm (Eph. 6:10–18). Don't rest yet, the worst part comes next. Third, you wrestle with personal inconsistencies (Romans 7).

In light of these three battlefronts, two things are essential: the first is knowing what to do, and the second is evaluating how well you're doing it. By using TRIM, you can teach your board how to assist and evaluate you. Most board members have no clue how to help you evaluate yourself. As a result, they often make up their own criteria, which generally compounds the problem. This can lead to firestorms. Let's look at TRIM in depth.

Truth: Presenting Christ in Concept and Communion

Your preaching imparts *concepts* of truth, causing people to say, "I know the Bible." Your prayers impart *communion* with Christ, causing people to say, "I know the Lord." Both are vital for ministry to be complete. Without an adequate theology, people's relationship with Christ is flawed. Without a relationship, knowledge is meaningless. So your work is to build the precepts of truth in the mind and the Person of truth in the heart.

Paul had this in balance. He taught enormous theology in the book of Ephesians but did not stop on the cerebral level. Dropping from the mind down into the heart he added, "I keep asking that the God of our Lord Jesus Christ . . . may give you the Spirit of wisdom and revelation, so that you may *know him better*" (Eph. 1:17, emphasis added). Paul taught them *about* the Lord but also prayed that they would *know* him.

Your work as a pastor is the same. You prepare for the presenta-
tion of truth and pray for the impartation of the Truth. Hereby you
are a divinely empowered master craftsman, forging the truth of
Christ into the mind and the image of Christ into the heart.

But it doesn't stop there. Your people must learn how the Bible
lies at the foundation of all knowledge. So you study widely to build
bridges from the Bible to the truths revealed in creation. Your people are encouraged to see Christ as the melody line in the grand sym-
phony of creation, not merely as an abstract, unnecessary chord
(Hebrews 1).

This pillar of truth is essential, then, to the well-being of the mind
and the heart. You cannot be weak in this area without potentially
giving rise to a firestorm.

Relationship: Presenting Christ in Companionship

Relationship is woven throughout the fabric of creation. It's the
quintessence of existence. It's not a want; it's a need. It is seen in the
Godhead and in the longing of the human heart. If the Bible bore
another name, it arguably could be called "The Book of Relationship." It is not a book of religion but of the relationship between God,
others, and ourselves.

Christ established his church in oneness: first, by his prayer in
John 17 and, secondly, by his death and resurrection. He made it
possible for us to be one with God when the temple veil rent and he
entered the Holy of Holies to present his blood in our behalf (Matt.
27:51; Hebrews 9). He made us one by tearing down the dividing wall
between Jews and Gentiles (Eph. 2:14–18).

The two greatest commandments are foundational to relationship. Jesus said, "'Love the Lord your God with all your heart and
with all your soul and with all your mind.' This is the first and greatest commandment. And the second is like it: 'Love your neighbor as
yourself.' All the Law and the Prophets hang on these two commandments" (Matt. 22:37–40). So relationship is at the heart of God's
intention for all people.

While the Old Testament stories exhibit what happens when these
two laws are either honored or neglected, the New Testament teaches
how to live them out. Proper relationship between believers is not

optional; rather, it's commanded (John 13:34; Eph. 4:1–3). It is the distinguishing mark of disciples (John 13:35) and an attraction to faith for the world (John 17:21). Drawing people into oneness in Christ, despite their varied backgrounds, temperaments, cultures, preferences, and talents is tedious beyond measure. Still, it's a divine requirement of your work.

This pillar of relationship with God and others is indispensable to the well-being of your church. People are highly tolerant where relationships are strong. Where they are weak, however, intolerance can set off a firestorm.

Integrity: Presenting Christ in Character and Conduct

As Christ is the image of the invisible God, so you are the image of the risen Christ. This is by far the most personal and difficult pillar. People will study under a vulgar craftsman in secular fields, since they only want the craftsman's skill, not his likeness. In ministry, however, like Paul, you must say, "Be ye followers of me, even as I also am of Christ" (1 Cor. 11:1 KJV).

Your life, then, is like a diamond, with countless reflections of the character and conduct of the true Light. Everything about you is as much the message as what you say from the pulpit: how you write a letter, keep appointments, fulfill commitments and responsibilities, handle enemies, treat your family, honor human dignity, hold confidences, confess mistakes, confront failures, shun praise—die to self. Integrity is not established by rigidly keeping rules but by instinctive obedience. It is Christ's life flowing through you that produces integrity.

Mission: Presenting Christ in Conquest

Your primary mission is not planning a new building project, scheming another promotion, or developing a needed program. That's the work of Spirit-filled people appointed to serve. Your mission is the gospel: nothing more, nothing less, nothing else. Your work is to call the lost and disciple the saved. All else must be left to others. Otherwise, your ministry is merely a Styrofoam facade.

Only when your mission is fulfilled are your people adequately equipped for their mission: building a new church, evangelizing a city, discipling new believers, or sending missionaries abroad. While the mission of your church members is multifaceted and global, your mission is more narrow—primarily to deepen the gospel in *them*. This mission statement for pastors was set forth by Jesus Christ: "Feed my sheep. . . . Lead my sheep." Anything less and a firestorm could strike.

How Pastors Choose Their Pillars

A major key to your success as a pastor will be found in how well you balance these four pillars. You may have excused your weak area by thinking that these four pillars merely represent personality traits in a manner something like this:

Truth: Good preaching belongs to the naturally brainy person, the quiet intellectual.

Relationship: This is for the flamboyant personality, the good car salesman.

Integrity: Some people are more straitlaced than others.

Mission: This is for the strong leader type with visions for organizations and buildings.

These pillars are not personality traits; they are responsibilities that must be fulfilled in relatively equal balance.

Do you pick and choose between them, stating that one fits your personality while another doesn't? It's easy to insist that you just don't have the gift for the one(s) you don't like, but that's a lame excuse. God not only calls you to exercise areas in which you feel gifted (which often boils down to the things you *like* to do), but also to develop the craft of ministering to all the needs of his people. When you focus only on the areas you like or that seem to come naturally, at the expense of the other areas, you are playing to your strength. That may prove to be the very thing that will destroy you in the long run.

How Strength Becomes Weakness

Most ministers who start their own firestorms do so by *hiding behind their strengths*. This was illustrated in the life of the famed aviator Charles Lindbergh. His widow was once asked why her husband had not used his fame to enter politics. She said that he was too altruistic, that he was unwilling to debate or compromise his views. Then she made this insightful comment: "His strength became his weakness."

And so it is when you avoid your weakness by hiding behind your strength. Here's how it works. It's Monday morning. You feel like pulp. You rethink yesterday's sermon, rating it somewhere between Charles Stanley and Chuck Swindoll, with a little Billy Graham tossed in for flavor. It wasn't your best, but neither was it your worst. You spent your days in Bible college or seminary slogging through Greek, establishing your epistemology, studying the principles of exegesis, and learning how to spell words like hermeneutics and eschatology. Now, you just want to return to civilization, be a normal person, and enjoy some peace.

Your secretary calls. "Pastor, Ned is on the phone. He wants to meet with you. Shall I set it up?"

"Yes, of course. Make it seven o'clock." The final drop of enthusiasm left over from Sunday falls to the floor.

Your midsection tightens throughout the day. You know Ned is going to start the "we're-not-getting-fed" bit again. He's influencing some in the church to believe that your ministry should end. What really annoys you is the way in which Ned has become so adept at your job. He learned it through the miracle of osmosis from his granddad, a retired circuit riding preacher.

Your anger grows throughout the day. You want to tell Ned to keep his day job and stay off your back. The shadow of dislike for Ned lengthens across your mind until you imagine him as a wife-beating, dog-hating maniac. But, when he walks in, you flash your instant ministerial smile.

He has his followers with him. One sits so erect that you muse, "A rigid spine is a rigid mind," as she speaks with irritating clarity. A second one is a new Christian who's amazed to be called upon to correct you. Ned starts, "Pastor, ah . . . ah . . . well, a lot of people have expressed to us that they don't feel like they're being fed from the pulpit." Wham! . . . You duck behind your pillar of strength and hurl grace-gilded mortars back in defense.

"Well, Ned, I know I'm not the best. And I know that yesterday's sermon was no grand slam. But, when I got back from vacation, I had to spend a lot of time with a family whose grandfather was dying." Ned and his supporters stare unsympathetic holes into your chest. You realize it's futile. This is their fourth visit in six months. Actually they're right. You've been lax in study because you derive an inner strength from socializing. You try hiding behind the pillar of relationship, but they're focusing on the pillar of truth.

Hiding behind your strong pillar will not protect you if a growing number of people are frustrated over your weak one. In fact, by not confronting a weak area, your problem is exacerbated.

TRIM: People's Four Spiritual Needs

Your four pillars of strength (TRIM) correspond with four basic needs in your people—all four of which God sent you to meet. Most often, people cannot define their needs but feel them all the same. And unmet needs in any one of the four areas can produce nasty responses—even firestorms.

Before we look at how your pillars and people's needs correspond, we must establish why those needs exist. We will be able to see more clearly, then, why these four areas are critical to people's fulfillment.

Your people's needs began when Adam sinned. His descendants were plunged into the bondage of satanic lies. The first lie undermines the absolutism of God's Word: "Did God really say . . . ?" (Gen. 3:1). This question implies that human opinion is supreme, relegating God's Word to a mere advisory position. Herein, oneself becomes the new authority. The second lie promises invincibility: "You will not surely die" (Gen. 3:4). From Adam's fall onward, people have lived as though the lie is true—you can live as you desire with no negative consequences. The third lie assures deification: "You will be like God, knowing good and evil" (Gen. 3:5). Indeed knowledge expanded, but it was downward, not upward. Before the fall, Adam and Eve had a heart knowledge of good and a head knowledge of evil. The fall reversed that. Now people have a heart knowledge of evil and a head knowledge of good. The highest of all creation became estranged enemies of the Creator (Rom. 5:10; Phil. 3:18; Col. 1:21).

Attempting to live out those lies creates a hotbed for conflict. Herein lies one of your greatest tasks as a minister. As Moses led God's people from Egypt to the Promised Land, so you are leading them from the kingdom of darkness (lies) to the kingdom of the Son of God (truth) (Col. 1:13–14).

But God must first remove the lies from you before you can remove them from your people. And that takes a long process. Think of it this way: It took God forty years on the back side of the desert to get Egypt out of Moses—to enable Moses to get his people out of Egypt. So it is with you. Getting God's people released from Egypt is only step one in a long, difficult journey. Then begins the process of helping your people to replace the lies of Egypt with the truth of the Promised Land. That's your specific task. One advantage you have, however, is that the Spirit of Truth dwells in your people, giving them yearnings that must be met.

These are the four needs in your people that correspond with the four strengths in you.

Truth: Needing Christ in Concept and Communion

Adam's fall threw your people into a crocodilian pit of satanic lies, crushing their bones in the jaws of deception. Jesus once bluntly told doubters and detractors, "You belong to your father, the devil, and you want to carry out your father's desire" (John 8:44). Conversion released your people from satanic rule. They have new natures (John 3:1–16) to enable them to walk in the freedom of truth (John 8:32). This must be experienced on two levels: in the mind (concepts) and in the heart (communion). The pursuit of truth is not merely the exercise of intellectual curiosity but a paramount *need*.

It matters not how correctly you expound the Word of God to your people. If they sense you have no deep, personal communion with God, a dissonant chord strikes within them. Likewise, if they sense you commune with the Lord but cannot teach them conceptual truth, the music of the heart turns bad. They are not being critical. They have a God-given need for truth that must be met in both their minds and hearts.

Relationship: Needing Companionship with God and People

Satan's deceitful promise of invincibility in the Garden of Eden backfired. Death came. While most people don't acknowledge that they are "the living dead," they experience death's effects all the same. Death means separation, not cessation. People experience its haunting reality in five areas: death toward God, themselves, others, the environment, and their bodies. Let's look at each one.

First, death strangled theology, resulting in confusion about God. Second, death robbed us of proper self-understanding, opening a Pandora's box of psychological disturbances. Third, death invaded people's cherished relationships—trashing marriages, disturbing society, setting nations at war. Fourth, death closed the gates to the Garden of Eden, leaving people to labor in a sweat-producing, hostile environment. Finally, death eventually will swallow their bodies in hungry graves.

The gospel reverses all five deaths by bringing life through oneness with God, a proper view of one's self, restored relationships with others, the promise of a new heaven and earth, and the resurrection of the body. As death means separation, life means union, oneness, belonging. All of that spells *relationship*—one of the greatest needs of the human heart. When neglected, this insistent need results in fears and isolation—the recurrence of death. The result? Firestorms!

Integrity: Needing Proper Character and Conduct

Succumbing to Satan's Garden lies sent a wrecking ball into the soul, shattering the stained-glass window of God's image into a billion fragments. Integrity was destroyed. This left your people with a crying need for both the redemption and restructuring of integrity.

Webster's dictionary captures the rich nuances of the word integrity: "1. the quality or state of being complete; unbroken condition; wholeness; entirety. 2. the quality or state of being unimpaired; perfect condition; soundness. 3. the quality or state of being of sound moral principle; uprightness, honesty, and sincerity."[1] This is the inner wholeness that Paul said only comes from Christ: "For in him dwelleth all the fulness of the Godhead bodily. And *ye are complete in him . . .*" (Col. 2:9–10 KJV, emphasis added).

Self-deification is flawed at the core, since it results in the consequence of the lies—death! Life screams at every turn, "You're not God. You can't be your own person." Yet your people have persisted in the attempt, cutting themselves badly on the splintered glass. They hurt. They need healing. So who is called to center stage? You! First, to be the exhibit of the wholeness brought by Christ, then to assist people at each step in their development toward wholeness. It is the redemption and reconstruction of character that results in transforming conduct.

This is not a self-help program; this is teaching people to believe their position in Christ and trust for the power to practice it. Paul identified the struggle when he wrote, "For what I do is not the good I want to do; no, the evil I do not want to do—this I keep on doing" (Rom. 7:19). He doesn't end with a hopeless struggle, however, but presents Christ as the daily means of victory. "What a wretched man I am! Who will rescue me from this body of death? Thanks be to God—through Jesus Christ our Lord!" (Rom. 7:24–25).

Mission: Needing Identity and Purpose in Life

While your people need to have a direction—and something to do—their effectiveness depends upon your ability to fulfill your mission to them, studiedly applying the gospel to their lives.

When Adam and Eve were thrown out of the Garden, they left with gaping questions in their hearts: "Who am I? Where did I come from? Where am I going? Why am I here? What should I do while I'm here?" The gospel alone answers these questions.

Solomon, too, perceived such questions when he wrote in Ecclesiastes 3:11, "He has also set eternity in the hearts of men. . . ." There is a longing for eternal significance in every heart.

Your people, then, innately sense they're eternal beings. They know they are part of a higher nobility, far above all other creation. Yet, they were born without a clue as to what that means or what to do about it. They have dissipated much of life trying to live out their greatness for themselves, a distortion caused by self-deification. Your mission is to shape Christ in them. This enables them to shape him in others. That's discipleship—the fundamental mission of the church.

Balancing Actions

Can you see how your four pillars of strength correspond with the four major needs in your people? And can you see why you cannot allow one pillar to be shorter than the rest without the imbalance jeopardizing your ministry? If so, then consider the following four steps to balancing your strengths.

One, be honest if a pillar is short, throwing your ministry off balance and provoking a need in your people. Two, balance the four pillars by further developing your weaker pillars. Three, explain TRIM to your board members to equip them with valid criteria for evaluating your effectiveness. Four, inform your leaders that, just as Jesus focused primarily on his twelve disciples, so you are going to focus your strengths on them. Your purpose is to enable them, along with you, to impact your church, then the world.

What if you fulfill TRIM and still face a firestorm? We'll consider this more in depth in chapter 11, "Fire from On High." The importance of TRIM is twofold: to equip you to prevent firestorms and to ensure that you will not be responsible for one that comes.

So, where do you go from here? You have looked at TRIM and perhaps concluded that your ministerial performance is in good shape. You have submitted these four criteria to your board, and they have affirmed you are right on target. Still, trouble is brewing, either on the board or in the congregation. Where do you look next?

It's time now to examine the motivations built into everyone: yourself, the board, the congregation. What drives people to act as they do? We will look at some of the forces that the field of psychology has fingered as largely responsible for determining our actions.

8 SOCIAL PYROMANIAC MADNESS

UNDERSTANDING FAMILY AND PSYCHO-SOCIAL NEEDS

We are all wounded by things harmful to healthy development. Some have been damaged severely and have not found adequate healing before entering the ministry. They enter, hoping to find healing in the ministry or serving on boards.

Dr. Roy Johnston, psychologist

Pyromaniacs are individuals impassioned to set fires, with a tragic psychological need to witness the drama. Likewise, some people are infected with a "social pyromaniac madness." They destroy relationships instead of buildings and are found in most churches. At times it is the pastor who, as a social pyromaniac, sets fires, then gets caught in the back-draft. At other times fires are set by strong personalities within the congregation—almost always those in a leadership role. Social pyromaniacs who excel in people skills are the most destructive, since they build confidences, win positions, then undo it all. You can spot them when they:

- fight doctrinal issues that are not essential to the faith,
- relate improperly to men or women,
- are intensely controlling, demanding that everything be done their way,
- make others feel obligated for their success or failure, even their emotional state,
- despise weakness, failure, or inability in others,
- drive others to achieve their self-aggrandizing goals, and
- stir controversy, since they function best in conflict.

Such people develop defenses, making it difficult to help them. They hide their insecurities and fears behind forceful personalities or the positions they hold. They become highly skilled at making themselves appear as victims and not perpetrators of trouble. But it eventually backfires. Either the controller self-destructs, or the subjects rebel.

What drives some people to be socially destructive? The answer invariably lies in our backgrounds. We all drag two elements of our past into the church, which may control some of us far more so than Christ. These elements are past family conflicts and psycho-social needs. Everyone has been shaped by them, and because most people come to Christ primarily for salvation, not transformation, problems in these areas can remain unresolved. Thus, the potential for social pyromania.

Social pyromaniacs are people who use destructive means to support some dysfunction within themselves, resulting from inadequate development in one of these two areas. Pyromaniacs will not perceive their behavior as sin, since their conduct will feel right to them.

All people experience the impact of family conflicts and psycho-social needs, which can be good or bad. We will look only at the bad side for the purpose of understanding why people cause firestorms. Some who haven't resolved these issues feel worthless without a crisis. Calm waters are a sign of failure rather than success, so they stir trouble. They feel threatened by unfamiliar feelings such as love, kindness, and acceptance, so they create chaos. They are emotionally conditioned for pain, not peace.

Destructive Family Backgrounds

You may be in church leadership, subconsciously wanting to help others gain what you lacked as a result of either a broken or dysfunctional home. Your intentions are honorable, but your past keeps injecting venom into your present. You can't shake old thought patterns, inferior and inadequate feelings, turbulent emotions, fears, and resentments. You want to be controlled by God's Spirit, but situations arise that agitate old wounds. You overreact. You wreck relationships. You are either duplicating or despising your negative experiences. Both are destructive responses.

Let's identify some of the common ways in which your family past can prove destructive to present relationships. Dr. Roy Johnston is a psychologist who assists many Christian leaders and missionaries both in the United States and on foreign fields. He provided the list we are about to see. It was examined and approved by psychologist Dr. William Secor, former professor of pastoral counseling and psychology at Trinity Evangelical Divinity School Seminary in Deerfield, Illinois.

Overbearing father. If your father was overpowering and authoritative, he gave no room for the development of your own sense of value as a person. This left you with a throbbing need to prove yourself worthy—a *real* adult—a valid individual. Being an adult and feeling like one are different things.

Your tendency, when you feel ignored or bypassed is to blow up, sulk, get depressed, or cower like a child. You'll become either aggressive or ambivalent during conflict. Whichever the response, it is prideful anger saying, "I will not be ignored anymore." If you're the pastor, you'll tend to be either dictatorial or have short tenures. If you're a board member, you'll tend to create problems where none exist.

You'll experience a lot of anger coupled with fear: anger when you feel your worth is in jeopardy and fear when you feel your maturity is disregarded. This inner conflict is exhausting. Your overreactions destroy relationships.

Controlling mother. Having a controlling mother can produce either an unnatural need for a woman's approval, or an intense resentment toward women. You respond to forceful women by angrily "putting them in their place" or fearfully avoiding them.

A controlling mother tries to govern in two ways. One is to build fear with raging temper tantrums. The other is to manipulate with a doting, smothering love. Both produce a sense of bondage or entrapment in you as a child. In adulthood, you try to break free of the control, but this early sense of imprisonment still will negatively affect your thinking toward women and will impair your judgment in counseling and board interaction.

Broken home. A home can be broken by death, divorce, or separation. Any of these is a serious disturbance. You felt great loss and developed deep insecurity. Life fell apart, security was gone, and God didn't seem to do anything about it. Further, you were helpless to salvage the most sacred thing in your childhood—home. To this day, a panic surges through your heart when you feel out of control, lacking support. You desperately search for reaffirmation that you will not be abandoned.

Alcoholic parent. As a child, you slept most nights with deep insecurities. You still find it hard to trust people. Having been betrayed by an authority figure, you fear further betrayal; after all, if your first guardian was delirious and irresponsible, who can guarantee that another guardian is any better?

Abuse. Verbal, emotional, physical, or sexual abuse in childhood inevitably will leave you feeling inadequate. Self-perception is disfigured as you believe you deserved the cruel things said and done to you. Feelings of rage demand justice for what happened. It's hard to believe passages of Scripture that say you are loved. You're crippled by a need for approval. Criticism is devastating. Exhaustion results from the endless effort to overcome a sense of having been stigmatized. You are sure everyone views you as inferior, inadequate, undesirable.

Rejection. You have developed inner skills to cope with the pain caused by rejection. Feelings of acceptance are foreign—even frightening. Thus, you tend to destroy the very approval you crave. You may even tend to provoke rejection through inappropriate behavior. When you do feel accepted, you suffer guilt over the sense of betraying the family from which acceptance was not received.

Enmeshment. There is a proper place for closeness within a family, but every good thing can be carried to a destructive extreme. That's the difference between enmeshment and closeness. Enmeshment is likened to a pile of spaghetti; individuals become so intertwined that they lose their own identity. Family ties become their identity. To this day you cannot function without Mom or Dad's approval.

Almost inevitably, your parents either needed control or found their fulfillment by living their lives through you. You came under the bondage of having to fulfill their desires. You are not free to serve your mate, or God, outside the enmeshment of your parents.

Individualized family. In contrast to the family smothered by enmeshment, you may have grown up in an individualized family, in which everyone ran his or her own life. There was little or no communication between certain people because they harbored long-term anger. Affirmation or reinforcement were lacking. Today, you have a wall around you, making it difficult for peers to feel secure with you.

Legalistic home. You got the clear message that principles were more important than your value as a person. You were raised on an approval system. If you were good, you were promised love. If you were not, love was withdrawn. Acceptance was based upon appropriate behavior. You tried but never felt accepted. Your parents may have held the view that, by always pointing out your faults, they could motivate you to strive harder to improve. They may have used punishment or put-downs. You responded in one of two ways: you became either excessively lenient or brutally demanding. You now have difficulty balancing love and law.

Libertarian home. A deadly overreaction to the legalistic approach is the lawless home. You were not taught the absolutes of right and wrong. Such choices were based upon how you *felt* about things. The result is that you are inept at giving sound direction today. You also tend to vacillate in your commitments.

If you are a leader who identifies with any of these dysfunctional backgrounds, then you're a candidate for setting a firestorm.

It must be emphasized that these situations are potentially true of every person within the church. It is easy to see how a church can become dysfunctional when these areas have not been properly resolved in troubled lives. You cannot handle church conflict any better than you handle personal conflict. The way you learned to relate to your natural family becomes the way you relate to your spiritual family. You may start problems without realizing you're responsible. You're simply responding to people in the same manner you learned to cope with the pain and confusion of the past.

Overcoming this pain is an exhausting preoccupation, robbing you of the freedom to build relationships. You'll do anything to rise above it. You may try education, marriage, work, materialism—even ministry. There's no solution deeper than the one found in Christ's call to discipleship: "If anyone comes to me and does not hate his father and mother, his wife and children, his brothers and sisters—yes, even his own life—he cannot be my disciple" (Luke 14:26).

This ultimatum forces you to decide who will govern your heart—God or family. To be controlled by the desires, opinions, or needs of family members renders you unable to take orders from Christ. This is idolatry—you are making your family to be a god! You're disqualified from discipleship. Your heart is bound and controlled by earthly relationships (i.e. "Let me go and bury my father." Luke 9:59), not a heavenly one. You cannot bear the cross of sacrifice while enslaved to your past—a controlling parent, advising brothers and sisters, a demanding spouse, or especially, *yourself.*

The depth to which you follow Christ's invitation to be controlled only by him determines the depth to which you can have resolution. Discipleship doesn't deny or ignore the past; rather, it dies to being controlled by the past. When you die to the past's control by making a daily positive commitment to Christ, you are freed to more fully love the people of the past.

Unresolved Psycho-Social Needs

Let's move now to the second area—the five psycho-social needs. These are God-given needs, not merely wants, and they won't go away. The only choice you have is how you'll try to meet them—properly or improperly. You can have no inner sense of well-being without these needs being properly met.

To deny them or improperly fulfill them results in your becoming dysfunctional in relationships. To fulfill them God's way is the only true escape from potential social pyromania, resulting in a healthy life and ministry. You may seek to meet these needs in different ways at different times in your life, but you are constantly searching to satisfy them.

Let's look at these powerful needs, then see how to properly meet them.

1. *Acceptance.* To be a valued and accepted part of a group is essential to a sense of completeness—inner wholeness. George Whitefield, the famed eighteenth-century evangelist, visited a godly recluse. When Whitefield asked about his perspective on being alone, the man told him that trees in a forest do not suffer the storms as much as a tree that stands alone. Likewise it's a God-given need to feel accepted by a group.

   If this need remains unfulfilled, you're likely to stir trouble to gain attention and acceptance, or as a payback for nonacceptance. You can appear socially adjusted while suffering crippling feelings of rejection.

2. *A sense of personal achievement.* No normal person wants to exist just to eat, sleep, and stare into space. There is an inner drive to do something of worth.

   You'll willingly work in obscure, even bad conditions, if you can have a sense of personal achievement. You will have no problem pastoring a small church as long as you feel worthy in accomplishment. If you lack a sense of achievement, however, you'll likely strike a match to your labor, causing a firestorm.

3. *A sense of value to a group.* There is a need to have people affirm that your existence and your efforts are valuable to them. You may reach for this in giving time or money to a cause or ministry.

4. *A sense of safety.* You will not function well if you feel you must always prove yourself to avoid being discarded. You only function freely in a safe, protective atmosphere.

5. *A sense of destiny.* There must be a sense of progress in your life: "I am heading someplace. . . . I am going to achieve this goal. . . . I am moving toward a solution."

These are the areas of psycho-social need. Danger lurks when you are frustrated in one or more of these areas. The worst thing you can do is look to people or positions to fulfill them. When people fail and your position is not fulfilling, your destructive behavior may surprise even yourself.

You can be destroyed easily if you harbor a subconscious hope that people in the church will meet these needs. If they fail, you will become negative, unproductive, isolated, upset, or discouraged.

While I was interviewing Roy Johnston, he commented, "Every man who came out of the ministry whom I have counseled (between 150 and 200) was basically frustrated because he couldn't get the people to do what he wanted them to do. Herein, their five psycho-social needs were not met."

If, as the pastor, you lack inward fulfillment, you'll tend to become dark and heavy in preaching (scolding the people), negative in outlook, hostile and angry in relationships. If you are a board member, you'll tend to be disgruntled about all that the pastor and board want to do, thus destroying your leadership. You will blame others, because taking responsibility for your own behavior is too frightening.

The Spiritual Leader's Resolution

You can't rely upon people to fulfill your psycho-social needs. You must have them satisfied by Christ. That's what the apostle Paul did; otherwise, he could not have handled the neglect of his needs during imprisonments, betrayals, and abandonments.

Paul wrote to the church at Philippi, "I am not saying this because I am in need, for *I have learned* to be content whatever the circumstances. I know what it is to be in need, and I know what it is to have plenty. *I have learned* the secret of being content in any and every situation, whether well fed or hungry, whether living in plenty or in want. *I can do everything through him* who gives me strength" (Phil. 4:11–13, emphasis added). Notice that Paul had to *learn* this. Obviously, at one time Paul was controlled by his psycho-social needs. The transition could not have been easy for one who imprisoned Christians, then voted to execute them. Eventually, however, he found completion in Christ alone.

Does this mean that Paul did not need people or that people did not affect him? Certainly not. Often he departed places, expressing affection with many hugs and tears. He wrote about longing to see people again. Still, these people did not determine his well-being. Christ did.

Likewise, you must learn to find fulfillment in Christ alone, not in family or ministry. Family and ministry are wonderful blessings, but you do not *need* them. Life goes on without them, as many have been forced to learn. If this were not so, then people like Paul would be nonfunctional. While you must properly relate to people, you must not use them to gain a sense of well-being. That role belongs to the Lord alone.

In this chapter, you evaluated the possibility of conflictive family backgrounds or frustrated psycho-social needs as potential tinder for setting off a firestorm. Next, let's discuss how to identify some of the other more common causes of firestorms.

Identifying Common Causes

If you are to avoid a firestorm, it will be essential for your board to determine biblical boundaries for each issue coming your way, then for you to teach them to the congregation.

Culturally Learned Resistance to Authority

You entered church leadership to help people, only to discover some resent you. But why? Because you represent authority, the anathema word of this age. The attitude within many parishioners is governed by the zeitgeist—spirit of the age—and not the Holy Spirit. Authority is distrusted and despised.

People rarely understand their resentment toward authority; they just feel it. They hold an unchallenged assumption that all authority is manipulative, abusive, and oppressive—in short, self-serving. So individualism is the new "authority." The spirit of the age teaches that one's opinion is the only authority that matters.

A pastor whom I know steps into the pulpit one Sunday night to preach. He feels like a cannonball has been shot through his stomach as he watches some disgruntled elders turn their chairs to face the back wall. The whole church sees it, including the youth. What's the message being conveyed? If you dislike or disagree with authority, you can disrespect it. Whether or not there are legitimate problems between this pastor and these men isn't the issue. The elders' reprehensible behavior clearly displays the mood of this age.

What is the origin of such boldness? It springs from the prevailing notion that everyone is an authority unto himself, and a person hardly feels value unless he has reduced and demythologized authority.

A popular slogan from the sixties can still be seen on bumper stickers today: "Question Authority." A more recent one reads, "Question Authority: Fill the Pit." The prophet Habakkuk put his finger directly on the problem when he referred to "guilty men, whose own strength is their god" (Hab. 1:11). And the prophet Isaiah wrote, "Woe to those who call evil good and good evil, who put darkness for light and light for darkness" (Isa. 5:20). So, while this spirit is not unique to our age, there has been a serious resurgence of it since the decade of the sixties.

When Dr. Billy Graham received the Congressional Gold Medal of Honor in 1996, he referred to America as being poised on the brink of self-destruction. He said that we have mistaken license for liberty.

Our culture has developed a climate in which firestorms thrive. Not only does the spirit of the age foster a climate for wrongful attitudes but when a firestorm strikes a church, there is no cultural support. The assumption is that it's good to see another authority brought down. The world is an enormous, dry forest ripe for firestorms, and the church sits like a log cabin surrounded by underbrush.

Rapid Church Growth

The anti-authority spirit of this age can surface in the church when growth occurs too rapidly. While rapid growth is virtually everyone's dream, it often proves to be one's worst nightmare. During times of church growth, you may become so enamored by the growing choir, crowded pews, and larger offerings that you rarely ask tough, sobering questions.

- Is this healthy growth, or are seeds of destruction entering the body?
- Is our discipling process keeping pace with the growth?
- Is this growth man-made or God-sent?

You trust the false assumption that growth means divine blessing. This faulty view is fostered as pastors of fast-growing churches
are invited to speak at conferences, exalted as though they have an
inside track with God. But *quantity* instead of *quality* has never
impressed God—ask Gideon's army. Fast growth without in-depth
discipleship can provide Satan with a Trojan horse. You're in trouble when there is a rapid intake of people inflamed with an anti-
authority spirit.

The early church saw rapid growth, but the Bible reveals the
source of growth: "And the Lord added to their number daily those
who were being saved" (Acts 2:47). The early church was absorbed
with fasting, prayer, the ministry of the Word, and discipling con-
verts to conform to Christ. While rapid growth in itself is not the
problem, our methodology, which is quite unlike that of the early
church, sets the stage for the church to be overrun by the attitudes
and thinking of the world.

Rapid church growth was common during the 1970s and '80s.
Numerous churches mushroomed from a handful of people into
hundreds, then thousands, in record time. Much of their growth
came from learning how to build a fleet of buses, advertise, and
conduct successful programs. I cross no swords with the method-
ologies. If they can be used by the world to sell cars and ham-
burgers, so can they be used for the kingdom. The evil lies not in
the technique but in our shift of faith. Fast-growing churches were
not known for fasting, prayer, or discipleship. In fact, anything too
spiritual was avoided on the grounds that, "Our people aren't ready
for that," or, "People just won't come out for things like that." Con-
tests, celebrities, and higher decibels from the latest musicians
became the attractions. We unwittingly were developing a market
demand, which, if unfulfilled, would backfire. And it has . . . with
firestorms!

Some pastors experienced their firestorms when they decided to
stop the show and turn people to the throne of God. They found
themselves surrounded by immature people who had never developed a taste for spiritual thinking. The backlash for turning spiritual could be likened to a person interrupting a crowd in the middle of a Super Bowl to say, "We're going to spend the next hour in
Bible study, prayer, and meditation." He'd be shouted down and cast

out of the stadium. That can happen to any pastor who may interrupt fleshly church programs.

Marketing Jesus

Many pastors have experienced the brutal result of marketing Jesus. As pastors marketed Jesus, so their people marketed them. For example, during a breakfast meeting a corporate head was asked what he thought could have spared his church from the firestorm that gutted its membership. He boasted, "I can tell you exactly how the problem could have been solved." Surely you would expect the man to speak of fasting and prayer, repentance and restoration. No, his "solution" was typical of this era. He said, "The pastor was no longer marketable, so we needed to fire him and get someone who was more marketable." Before we fully fault this man for his spiritual ignorance, we must remember that he had watched his pastor commercially market Jesus.

The marketing mind asks, Does our pastor market well to the demographic group we want to reach? Is he sellable to younger couples? Do older people like him?

The business brain asks, Can this man excite people enough to raise the money it takes to run this place? Can he lead us in a building program?

The sports mind asks, Is he a winning coach? Can he inspire enough enthusiasm to help us grow (win)?

But God doesn't choose slick business minds or pep-rally coaches. He chooses men who are nothing in the eyes of the world to bring to nothing the thing that is (1 Cor. 1:27–29). Until the church understands this and seeks the power of God, not the popularity of the pastor, you'll never be safe in the church.

Freedom and Form Clash

During the 1960s the secular world made a radical shift from reason to experience in its search for truth. Drugs were purported as the means to a "religious" experience that would expand perception and answer life's hardest questions.

Christianity made a corresponding shift. Prior to the sixties, most doctrinal discussions were about concepts. Today they are about experiences. This has led to severe tensions between structure and freedom, absolute truth and relative experiences, and authority and self-expression.

It is not my purpose to share my convictions in these areas but to encourage discussion between church leaders so that you may determine your parameters before trouble begins. Otherwise, your church is vulnerable to split in an instant. Following is one such event that actually occurred in a Pentecostal church.

The pastor was greeting the congregation when a woman approached him. "Pastor," she said, "I have been given the gift of dancing in the Spirit." She wanted to "spread the blessing" to his church. She had been to meetings where people were free to express themselves in any way they believed the Spirit led. She wanted assurance that there would be no restriction on the "spirit" in this church.

"Well," said the pastor, with measured wisdom about people claiming to be Spirit-led, "I am not in agreement with your perceived gift. I would prefer you not to exercise it in this church."

They discussed his position of authority to govern conduct and the exercise of gifts in the church. She agreed to honor his authority . . . until the following Sunday, that is.

There she sat, near the front. The congregation was worshipping in music when the "spirit" prompted her to make her move. Of course, to her the "spirit" should be obeyed over the pastor—no matter how godly or wise he may be, no matter how God-given his authority, no matter how correct his biblical position.

The congregation was instantly polarized as she pirouetted across the front of the church. All attention was transferred from God to her as she gracefully spun, glided, and leaped before the bemused spiritual spectators. Worship turned to wonderment. Her talent was good, not sinful, but she had chosen the wrong time and place to exercise it. Worship of God and performing with a talent are different things. The congregation watched to see if the shepherd would care for the flock or let the dancing troubadour take charge. Some silently cheered her "freedom in the spirit," while others were appalled at her defiance of authority.

The pastor rose to his feet and stepped to the microphone. The dancer was midflight in a gazelle-like leap as his voice boomed out, "Please, sit down." The expression on her face turned to the horror of the damned. She was angered that he would hinder the "spirit." She sat down . . . embarrassed . . . but still immature about true freedom in the Holy Spirit.

Her action instantly split the church. A small but significant group in the church quit, accusing the pastor of being too controlling. To them, freedom in the Holy Spirit meant anyone doing anything at any time. The imposition of any discipline was equated with trying to control the Holy Spirit. They reflected the religious counterpart of the "do-your-own-thing" culture, a tragic leftover from the sixties.

Most of the congregation, on the other hand, praised the pastor for doing his job well. They understood that the Holy Spirit of God always conducts himself within the structures of law, order, and decency—a conduct God ordained and that reflects behavior in heaven. The question had nothing to do with the art form of dance finding a place in the church. The issue here was a lack of submission to authority—a demonstration of the lost attitude of godliness in our age.

This pastor got off lightly, losing only about forty people. The dancer has pranced off to other churches, but not without leaving a disturbance in the trail of her act. Unfortunately, her "liberty" to dance where and when she desires, or as she would say, "When the spirit leads," is an exhibit of one of the internal forces lighting fires of conflict in churches; that is, equating one's urges with the Holy Spirit's voice.

The importance of being prepared before the dancer or her equivalent shows up in your church cannot be overly stressed. She *is* on her way. Not only her, but a Pandora's box of other doctrinal and behavioral viruses. It is essential, if you are to avoid a firestorm, for your board to determine biblical boundaries for each issue coming your way, then for you to teach them to the congregation. If people are well trained, then "the dancer" will only be a passing amusement. If they are not, then "she" can split the church.

Systemic Problems

When an undercurrent hinders the church's progress, it's called systemic, meaning that the underlying problem affects the entire church system. Often such a church can be detected by a quick turnover of pastors. Sometimes firestorms that flare up from systemic conflict cannot be avoided or stopped, since they smolder until suddenly bursting into flames. Often you must permit them to ignite, then burn themselves out. This will be hard for you as a sensitive pastor, but the most well-intentioned and capable person cannot stop the inevitable.

Perhaps you are at such a church. You fantasized about being able to handle the problems where others have failed. You are forgetting one major principle: Every generation has great prophets who are sent by God but are destroyed by the people. It is the people's response, more than the prophet's message and skill, that determines success or failure. Don't assume you are uniquely equipped to overcome spiritual hardness of heart. Neither Isaiah nor Jeremiah could do it.

Here's what you come up against. You arrive with great expectations, only to find the church immovable. Everything you suggest is shot down; everything you try gets trampled. You look under the rug and discover a whole different congregation. You see anger, tension, even rage rooted in the past, resulting in power plays and disputes. Communication is gridlocked, cooperation deadlocked. You expect them to respond to you as the great deliverer sent from the Savior, only to find that they try to make you the scapegoat for their problems. A few people may try to explain things to you, even sympathize with you, but to no avail. These few become your pallbearers when you finally leave—beaten, angry, confused. You're experiencing a systemic problem—a problem deep in the system that has nothing to do with you but can paralyze your ministry all the same.

The congregation attempted to make you responsible for its problem, but gave you no authority to resolve it. And if you exercised bold leadership to root out the systemic problem, they turned their energy on rooting you out. People who despise each other will create a common enemy to despise together. This doesn't resolve their problem but gives them a sordid sense of camaraderie as they focus their energy on the object of their joint dissatisfaction. The choices you have for handling this problem are found in chapter 13, "Bold Spiritual Leadership."

Culture Crashing

Culture crashing occurs when a pastor (or any other staff member) accepts a position in a church with an established culture, then tries to radically change the culture. This is primarily seen in efforts to make old churches young, traditional churches contemporary, or worship services "seeker friendly." The intent to draw sinners, not saints, to God is good but should not be at the expense of an existing culture, unless, of course, the church is dying and in desperate need of some kind of change to become effective again.

You have every right to develop any cultural church style you want, provided you start your own church. But, when you crash an established church, you seriously violate Christ, ripping the garments of his bride. That's sin. Here's why. First, it is a moral violation to crash a culture. Missionaries have learned the hard way that their job is to take the gospel *into* a culture, not change the culture. If ethics demand that foreign cultures remain intact, then the same ethics demand that an established culture in any church be honored. Second, it's egotistical immaturity to tear down a culture just because you didn't help to build it. Third, it's downright stealing to take a salary under the guise of pastoring a certain culture, then violate and trash it.

Your work is to root out sin, not destroy culture. It is ruthless ignorance to pound people with guilt for clinging to a thirty- to fifty-year pattern of life instead of supporting your desire to dress, sing, and worship differently. You must honor the culture in which they learned to follow the Lord Jesus Christ.

Wounded People Sometimes Wound

You entered the ministry to help people on the deepest levels of need—resolving inner problems through the power of the gospel.

But ministering to wounded people is much like walking through a minefield. It's impossible to know when something you say or do may accidentally trigger a concealed explosive. Firestorms are often started by people who misunderstand a statement or intention, have a memory revived that causes fear and distrust of you, or feel the need to hurt because they have been hurt.

Deeply wounded people can have altered perceptions resulting from childhood violations, dissociative disorders, or demonic harassment. Such was the situation with Martha (not her real name), who was the sweetest Christian woman you could meet, quiet in spirit, a servant in the church. Her artistic skills kept the church communication centers creative and attractive.

One Sunday evening the pastor saw her near one of her creations and stopped to introduce her to some guests. The pastor touched her cheek as a gesture of appreciation and said, "This is the lady who does this excellent work." Everyone admired and complimented her creations.

The following week this shy, talented lady asked to meet with the pastor. After a great deal of struggle to overcome embarrassment, she said, "Pastor, when you touched me, it erupted some terrible fantasies that I used to have."

"Really," he replied. "Would you tell me about them?"

"Well . . . ah," she stammered, "I have this fantasy of being beaten by bad people. They leave me bruised and bloodied on the steps of a church. The pastor picks me up, holds and comforts me."

Over the next few weeks of counseling it was discovered that this woman had been badly abused as a child, resulting in a mild dissociative identity disorder (DID). She had intense reactions to authority figures, since one had abused her. She was searching for a pure authority who would not violate her. A simple touch on the cheek evoked longings that she could not fully understand. The potential danger would be for her to misconstrue the pastor's motive and interpret his kindness as being sensual.

By God's grace, this story has a happy ending, as many do. The pastor was able to assist her to some degree, then recommend her to people better trained in dealing with DID. She is doing very well today. But not every story ends this way. Innocent ministers have had their reputations ruined by wounded people making false accusations. What would be a normal word or gesture to someone from a healthy background is viewed in a totally different manner by a victim of abuse. For instance, one woman, who was severely abused and suffers today from multiple sclerosis, entered a candy store in her motorized wheelchair. A kind elderly gentleman, feeling sympathy for her, offered to buy her candy. Overcome by panic, she rushed out of the store in search of her husband. While her rational mind told her the man was just being kind, her emotional memory bank filled her with a sense of being threatened.

Another danger faced when working with wounded people is that they may try to make you feel responsible for their survival. Their desperate need for acceptance and assurance makes them cling like a vine, trying to entwine around every part of your life. You'll hear such a person say, "You don't care about me," or "I can tell you don't want to hear from me again," or "Can't you give me more time? You help me so much."

Before long the person is calling your home or office anytime the urge strikes. For you to end a conversation triggers a sense of rejection. On the other hand, showing kindness results in a greater takeover of your life.

Most abused people have distorted views of authority, either intensely hating it or placing unreasonable expectations upon it. For example, in another actual case, an attractive woman would cuddle near older authority figures. One pastor, much her senior, perceived the wrong signal from this and made advances. She nearly committed suicide. She was subconsciously in search of the safety and sense of belonging found in a pure grandfather, because hers had violated her.

While she had no recollection of her childhood crisis, the emotional repercussions were like fingerprints left at a crime scene. Emotions that are separated from cognitive recall can lead to bizarre behavior. Her emotional need to regain what was robbed in childhood demanded fulfillment. Until this was uncovered and resolved, she sent signals that appeared sensual—the opposite of her need.

Women are not the only ones carrying enormous baggage into local churches. War wounds, along with other violations, scar men's souls dating back to World War II. The impact of sin upon any civilization leaves shattered souls.

When a troubled person lashes out with false allegations against you, a question mark forms in people's minds that isn't easy to erase. Even proof of innocence never gets the chalkboard perfectly clean. Rarely does the victim intend to ruin you. It's just that wounded people often wound. It's a knee-jerk response, a fearful reaction from the past. While you must respond to hurting people, you can't be too guarded against a potential explosion.

Multiple Staff and Hidden Agendas

Your big dream is to have a large, multiple staff church. You fantasize that your staff will work happily together to build a great church. Finally you have it, and—Blam!—your fantasy explodes. Discontent rolls in like a London fog, such as in the following true story.

A consultant is invited to meet with church staff members to determine why they lack coordination and direction. The pastor is asked to be quiet and listen. Each of the seven other staff members is asked to explain his or her vision for the church. Seven agendas unfold.

Then the consultant asks the pastor, "Do any one of these sound like your vision?"

The pastor looks in need of a long overdue vacation as he responds, "Only one comes close." Here are some of the conflicting attitudes and visions:

The visitation pastor has a good view of his function but not of the overview. He maturely understands that serving God means doing his part on the team to fulfill the singular vision of the pastor and board, but he is powerless to build this conviction in the others.

The youth pastor is totally absorbed in his department, with no appreciation of how the other players fit. He sees them as threats to his budget desires, indicating that the whole church should exist for the youth.

The music director's response is awkward, hesitant, and tense. This pastor had salvaged him from a fiasco in his previous church job. But pride doesn't allow appreciation to endure. His agenda is to have a major musical production each Sunday, with the pastor bringing a short devotional at the end. Since the pastor won't comply, the music director is secretly plotting to get rid of him.

The Christian education director is a team player but has no idea what the rest of the team does. She expresses frustration over the youth pastor's attitude about funding, reminding him that every department is valid.

The office manager, who is in charge of coordinating the staff, expresses disturbance over the way these warring factions pressure her for loyalty, each one pulling on her for favors.

At first glance this pastor may appear to be failing to articulate his vision. Not so. Everyone understands the vision, but some have their own. The breakdown comes in the hidden agendas. Your church hires people with either signed or informal agreements and expectations. Everyone smiles as though entering heaven's gates. You tell your spouse that the dream team has arrived. Within three months, however, the team members aren't doing precisely what they agreed to do. In some cases they find better ways to do it. That's good. Generally, however, you find them shifting from what they were hired to do to what they *want* to do.

During staff meetings, you start to moralize about how each is a vital part of the whole picture. You tell them what great things will happen if everyone does their job in cooperation with one another. Their eyes are glazed and their ears are plugged. What's happening? Their minds are conjuring up how to work around you to continue with their own agendas.

Did they lie when they took their jobs? Some, perhaps, but not most. A hidden agenda can be so deep and subtle that even the employee isn't aware of it. These agendas seem natural and right as they surface in response to the pressures and problems of the jobs. If a person is with you long enough, new hidden agendas will surface as needs, desires, and perceptions change with age.

Your headaches become migraine over people in Christian ministry. The secular world understands that self-interest lies at the heart of motivation. That can be true in Christian ministry, too, but Christians can cover their motives with spiritual phraseology, forming protective walls around their agendas. They can sound like the apostle Paul himself, who gloried in Christ Jesus (Phil. 3:3), made Christ his all sufficiency (Phil. 4:13), was ready to suffer the loss of all things for Christ (Phil. 3:7-8), and longed for the well-being of the church (2 Cor. 13:9). While using these phrases, they continue to use the church as a vehicle to achieve *their* desires.

Before you fire everyone tomorrow, remember the regular battles you must fight to keep your own motives pure. Hidden agendas lie within everyone—you and me included—and are driven by various forces:

- Pride that says, "I deserve more."
- Bitterness that says, "They owe me for what they did to me."
- Ambition that says, "I must establish my importance."
- Fear that says, "I might be rejected, so I'd better get a strong foothold."
- Lust that says, "I want gratification."
- Bias that says, "I don't like certain people."
- Selfishness that says, "I should have a bigger ministry, with more money."

People with hidden agendas can get nasty when their agendas are threatened. For instance, you decide to make a staff member accountable—indeed, that's your duty. You're defied. You must either reprimand or remove the person. It's firestorm time. First, the person puts a spin on his or her activity, making it sound vital and spiritual. You are made to appear nonvisionary and unspiritual. Second, you discover that the person has carved a political power block out of the congregation and made it a bargaining chip for negotiation. The situation escalates from dealing with a problem employee to resolving a major church disruption. The very person who smilingly told you at the beginning how honored he or she felt to work with a great leader like you attempts to hold you hostage. And, indeed, you may lose people because of this defiant staff member.

Dale (not his real name) is a prime example of how destructive hidden agendas can be. He departed from a large church after several years of conflict with the senior pastor. He had some valid complaints, but also had used divide-and-conquer methods, attempting to fulfill his hidden agenda to be the senior pastor. Dale badly tore the wedding gown of Christ's bride during his exit.

In time Dale was hired by another church. The senior pastor of the new church never inquired about his track record. Soon Dale's desire to be a senior pastor resurfaced. The original pastor wanted to plant a new church, while Dale wanted to enlarge the existing one. There is nothing wrong with conflicting visions, but it was Dale's role to submit to the senior pastor's directive. He circumvented this with one small technicality: When Dale had taken the job, he'd asked to be called an associate pastor, not an assistant. The young senior pastor, trusting Dale's integrity, had been blind to the entrapment, until Dale claimed this gave him equal authority. Dale's divide-and-conquer mind-set kicked into gear, and he split the church, going down the road to form his own.

Empire Building, Not Kingdom Building

Having aimed scrutiny at staff members, now get brutally honest with your own hidden agendas. You, like all ministers, fight incredible forces lurking deep within your heart. It can happen slowly, subtly, as pure intentions degenerate into using the church to satisfy personal desires. The moment you go from "feeding" the sheep to "using" them, you are in violation of Christ.

Indicators that you may be building a personal empire rather than Christ's kingdom include driving your staff and congregation with production pressure, pushing them to do things that are important to your self-made image, demanding from your staff improper loyalty to you as a person, "ruling" by fear, not love. One church secretary who served under such a pastor called this "negative adrenaline flow."

You become intolerant of a staff member who is struggling to develop in a certain area, perceiving it as a weakness that hinders the rapid achievement of your goals. That's the opposite of the patience shown by Christ, who was surrounded by a fumbling team of disciples but built them into men who changed the course of world history in God's power.

Let's take some pages from King Saul's life to see the patterns of an empire builder. Such a person will:

- *Not wait on the Lord.* Samuel wasn't on time for the sacrifice, so Saul did it himself. Likewise, there are struggling churches everywhere echoing the failed efforts of those who would not wait on the Lord to unfold and fulfill his plans.

- *Not obey God.* Saul spared the king of the Amalekites, along with the best of the sheep and cattle. Likewise, men today use the church to take the best for themselves.

- *Lie.* Saul deceitfully claimed to have obeyed the Lord. Likewise, self-driven leaders lie because forthrightness reveals the hidden agenda that could lead to repentance or removal. And to walk in truth is to give up the control of one's life. Truth demands our subjection; lying attempts to conceal self-government.

- *Shift the blame for failure to others.* Saul blamed the soldiers for his disobedience. Likewise, self-driven leaders are hard on subordinates. The staff is expected to bear the blame for the pastor's failures, while the pastor maintains a well-polished public image.

- *Not repent.* Saul confessed that he had sinned, then tried to kill young David. That's not repentance. Likewise, the self-driven leader will try to destroy anyone perceived as a rival. Saul eventually fell on his own sword, as do all self-driven leaders.

Underlying Saul's behavior is the age-old problem of ownership. When God gives a responsibility, don't possess it. The kingdom belongs to God. You're a caretaker, not an owner. If you impose yourself upon people, rather than develop Christ in them, a firestorm is guaranteed. The Lord will see to that.

The Fact of the Human Heart

After two years of sifting through the firestorm that had struck the Myerstown Grace Brethren Church, I had discovered many causes of the conflict but still lacked understanding of *why* it had happened. Who had done what to whom was evident, but why they had done it was illusive. I tried to learn facts, hoping to formulate reasons leading to an understanding that would bring closure and safeguard the future. Both proved impossible, because everyone had a different perception of the same set of facts.

One thing clearly emerged that is common to human conflict: People deify their opinions, which results in throwing off moral and spiritual restraints, because their opinions *feel* right. And when the freedom of opinion leads people to believe they have the right of judgment, they take wrongful liberty of expression. This leads to massive destruction.

What is at the heart of this attitude? The Bible spells out the nature of sin: "There is no one righteous, not even one; there is no one who understands, no one who seeks God. All have turned away, they have together become worthless; there is no one who does good, not even one. . . . Their mouths are full of cursing and bitterness. Their feet are swift to shed blood; ruin and misery mark their ways, and the way of peace they do not know. There is no fear of God before their eyes" (Romans 3:10–12, 14–18).

Doesn't that well describe the disposition you have witnessed during conflict? Yet people view their worst behavior as a *mistake*, not depravity. And that is only if they will admit to being wrong at all.

Here's the point: The greatest threat to your church is human nature. It underlies all the previous causes we just considered. It generates an endless supply of evil schemes. The well-being of your church will largely depend upon teaching people to wage a daily war on their own flesh (Romans 6; Eph. 4:23), separate from the ways of the world (Isa. 52:11), and give no ground of opportunity to Satan (Eph. 4:27).

These are only some of the common causes of firestorms, but there are many more. It is critical for church elders to periodically examine this list anew, even expand it according to their own experiences, and prayerfully discuss how to diffuse any firestorms that are beginning to smolder within the congregation. Remember that it's easy to put out the sparks, but nearly impossible to suffocate a full-blown firestorm.

Having looked at some of the human factors contributing to conflicts, let's turn now to Satan's role. After all, we are in a spiritual war, and to deny Satan's involvement is to be ill-equipped to face a firestorm.

10 FIRE FROM THE ABYSS

> There can be no sound theology without a sound demonology.
>
> Dr. Berkouwer, Free University of Amsterdam

Yes, there is a Satan who gladly adds fuel to the firestorm in your church that was set in motion by human behavior. While the consideration of Satan doesn't negate human responsibility, his role as a master arsonist must be understood.

Unbelief Doesn't Change Reality

Who wants you to know there is a real devil? God. Who wants you to learn about this devil? God. Knowledge about Satan comes not from wide-eyed storytellers passing down legend or myth but from divine revelation. This information doesn't exempt you from fierce battles with the devil, but it can equip you to beat him.

I hope you're not stuck in the blind alley of believing Satan is a mythological explanation of the darker side of human nature. While much of this book deals with the dark reality of human nature, Satan's role must be acknowledged, or you'll be powerless against an otherwise beatable foe.

The Bible gives clear instructions: Don't be outwitted by Satan (2 Cor. 2:11), and don't be taken captive to do his will (2 Tim. 2:26). Those warnings are made to Christians and clearly indicate things you need for victory. In fact, the Scriptures declare that hell's gates cannot overcome the church (Matt. 16:18).

Here are some actions we are commanded to take in our spiritual struggle with Satan: stand firm (Eph. 6:14), put on the full armor (Eph. 6:11), run (1 Cor. 9:24; Heb. 12:1), fight (2 Cor. 10:4; 1 Tim. 1:18), endure (2 Tim. 2:3), press on (Phil. 3:12), resist (1 Peter 5:9), overcome (Rom. 12:21; 1 John 2:13–14; 4:4).

A quick scan of Scripture reveals Satan's activity throughout history. He:

- attacked God's throne in eternity past (Isa. 14:12–17; Rev. 12:1-6),
- deceived our original parents in the Garden of Eden (Genesis 3),
- inspired David to number his troops (1 Chronicles 21),
- tempted Jesus in the wilderness (Matt. 4:1–11),
- entered Judas for the betrayal of Christ (Luke 22:3),
- fought the church at Rome (Rom. 8:31–39; 16:20),
- resisted Paul's travels (1 Thess. 2:18),
- tormented Paul (2 Cor. 12:7),
- will rally the world against Christ at Armageddon (Rev. 16:16), and
- is doomed for total destruction (Rev. 20:7–10).

Dr. Erwin Lutzer, pastor of the Moody Memorial Church in Chicago, wrote regarding this spiritual struggle:

> We're in a war.
> We can't plead pacifism.
> We can't run from the bullets.
> We can't hide from the bombs.
> We can't plead medical deferment.
> If you have never felt the war within, I can't identify.[2]

It's incongruous to sing "A Mighty Fortress Is Our God," then either ignore or deny the reality of this closely fought battle with Satan. Satan *is* involved in your church's conflict. That's a reality that doubting cannot change.

My Experience at Myerstown

I experienced firsthand Satan's resolve to destroy a church when he's given the chance. By my second year at the MGBC, I found myself unbearably exhausted, not from responsibilities but from resistance—Satan's. Although the firestorm had already passed through the church before my arrival, there were still occasional outbreaks of strange behavior: intense anger, irrational conduct, destructive discussions, unreasonableness, senseless power plays, and even threats. Not all of this behavior could be attributed solely to human nature.

One Sunday night, while returning home from the evening service, I tried to capture in words what I was experiencing. I scribbled the following thoughts on an envelope, then transferred them to my journal.

> Often I drive home from Myerstown feeling as though a plug is pulled out of my inner being, and all the energy of my spirit and soul is drained. The emptiness combined with the weighty oppression make it hard to breathe—literally.
>
> I feel like personal restoration and deliverance for the church will be impossible.
>
> This terrible agony of heart must be something of sharing in the sufferings of Christ. The struggle is great, and the battle lines aren't clearly defined. Who are the evil people? What is Satan's role? What is the battle plan developing in the invisible realm? . . . I am truly wrestling with darkness.
>
> It feels as though I am in a life/death intercession with only momentary victories, such as a good worship service, or a successful counseling session, or a good board meeting. But a deep, dark overcast hangs like night over a flickering campfire. The night cannot put out the flame, but neither can the flame dispel the night.
>
> It will take the Son himself to do that at his own appointed time. The work of the church is to never abandon the flame while awaiting the "Son" rise. He will come!
>
> Too often, however, his morning light reveals only scattered, burnt ashes, rather than the glory of flame meeting flame. My

prayer is that my friends at the church will endure to the morning of a new day.

This will call for patient endurance, fasting, and prayer to keep the congregation intact until the Most High causes the long, dark night to surrender to the Son (Dan. 7:21–22).

Does this describe something of your experience? Well, be assured that your sanity isn't slipping. You're experiencing the disturbance of heart and oppression of mind that Satan can impose. Is this satanic pressure beatable? Yes. We'll look at how to do that later in chapter 15, "Stopping the Hot Wind from Hell." For now, let's go back to the beginning of your firestorm and learn something of how Satan got involved.

Unmasking Satan's Clever Strategy

A clear illustration of how Satan incites trouble is seen in his clever deception of David, as recorded in 1 Chronicles 21. The story begins with Satan inciting David to do something that does not appear evil—numbering his troops. We do not know the historical setting for this incitement. Perhaps David was threatened by the Philistines. As the curtain rises, Satan, who is the master of making evil appear good, carefully studies David: listening . . . watching . . . noting . . . preparing to pounce on a weakness of faith, an area where he can make sin appear proper.

Satan isn't stupid enough to try the beautiful bathing Bathsheba routine again. David has already paid the bitter price of adultery. The spears that took Absalom's life also pierced David's soul, shattering his fatherly dreams. "O my son Absalom!" he openly wept. "If only I had died instead of you—O Absalom, my son, my son!" (2 Sam. 18:33). That pain drove him to build a high fortress of moral protection. Heavily armed guards stood at the gate once vulnerable to lust. No, David would not be responsive to obvious sin. This time Satan would have to look deeper in search of a weakness. Suddenly he finds it. He makes a suggestion that throws common sense into conflict with faith. He incites David to do what every king should do—know his military strength by numbering his troops.

But for David this is a violation of faith—a sin. Why? The Lord alone was to be David's strength, not the size of his army. Paul wrote to the Romans in 14:23, "Everything that does not come from faith is sin." David shifts his faith from God to common sense—so subtle, yet so deadly.

Think back to your firestorm. How did it begin? Someone may have set forth a good sounding plan that was a slight shift from faith to common sense, from divine to man-made plans, thereby lacking God's protection. It was so subtle that few perceived it as a violation against God.

Notice that Satan could incite but not force David. The word incite is strong. It means to arouse, goad, urge—move into action by persuasion. While incitement deeply stirs the heart, it cannot force an action. David could have said no. Likewise, Satan can incite, but not force your church into conflict.

Agreement with Satan Is the Key

Satan can only incite where he finds agreement in the heart. For instance, the power of music is not found in the structure of the chord so much as the response of the heart, which each person has the power to determine. What response did Satan find in David that made him vulnerable to persuasion? We can only surmise. Perhaps it resulted from his rapid rise to power, or from someone mocking David's shepherd background. David may have been trying to prove a point to someone who belittled his achievements. Pride, anger, or revenge may have contributed. We'll never know, but we do know that the key lay not in Satan's incitement but in an unsettled area of David's heart.

So it was in the early stages of your firestorm. Satan found agreement in someone's heart—some unsettled area. He may have whispered it directly or suggested it through another person. All the same, it strengthened what the person wanted to hear. The individual interpreted the incitement as confirmation of what was already felt. The burning incitement was misinterpreted as a spiritual conviction or seen as a strength. The person was unaware of being no longer Spirit-led but rather inflamed from the abyss. Passion overruled reason, and compulsion crushed compassion.

The law to watch for, then, is this: Satan can only incite sinful behavior where he finds agreement in the heart.

When satanic provocation finds heartfelt agreement, there is no limit to the destructive potential, since the offender feels justified. What the bodiless antagonist from hell cannot do alone, Satan achieves through those who welcome his voice. And the higher up in leadership he finds agreement with his prompting, the greater the damage he can incite.

David became delirious in his spiritual blindness, even ignoring his commander Joab's rebuke: "Why does my lord want to do this? Why should he bring guilt on Israel?" (1 Chron. 21:3). Can you think back to the agitation that ignited your firestorm? Someone wanted something so badly that destroying Christ's body was unimportant. For instance, pastor Dr. Jack Sailor (not his real name) proved to be a hard-driving leader, abusively pushing his congregation toward his dreams. This led to an uprising by some to destroy him. Jack's pride caused him to neglect the congregation's needs. His opponents' anger blinded them to the sacredness of the congregation. In the conflict that ensued, the congregation was trashed. Satan incited pride in Jack and anger in his opponents, both resulting in the decimation of the congregation. But keep in mind that Satan could have caused nothing had there not been areas in hearts ready to respond to his incitements.

Look back at your firestorm and you'll see the warnings that went unheeded. For instance, David's command so repulsed Joab that he refused to number the tribes of Levi and Benjamin. Probably you can think of the godly people who warned about the violations of faith. They were ignored, because pride is deaf to God's voice.

Many Pay for the Guilt of One

Satan attacked David, but the fallout landed upon Israel. David was given three choices: three years of famine, three months of defeat by enemies, or three days of plague inflicted by the angel of the Lord. David chose the third one, so as to be in the hands of a gracious God, not merciless men. But God's mercy severely disciplines, too. Seventy thousand soldiers died in the plague.

Through the plague God removed the very thing that captured David's faith—strength by numbering his troops. Reflect on what God allowed to be destroyed in your firestorm. It was the very thing that agreed with Satan's incitement: Someone who needed a new building found it a millstone around his neck, or one craving a position found it the emptiest experience of his life, or one who felt he must have a large congregation found it filled with vipers.

David pled that he be allowed to pay the price himself for committing the sin. I suspect that if the seventy thousand who died had known of David's prayer, there would have been a thunderous amen. But God has so fitly framed the fabric of his people that one cannot sin without a price being paid by many.

What did Satan achieve by inciting David? He brought David into conflict with his God. Likewise, Satan lacks the power to destroy God's people, so he incites them to violate faith, which brings them into conflict with God. God chastens in love and holiness (Heb. 12:1–13). While God is chastening his children (or church), they are certainly in no position to be a mighty force against their foe. To my knowledge, there has never been a church that was effective in evangelism or discipleship during a time of conflict. So while God's people are being chastened, Satan has reduced their effectiveness in plundering his kingdom.

How to Determine Satan's Role

How, then, can you determine Satan's role in instigating, then perpetuating a firestorm? Look for the place where there is agreement with him. Following are some possible areas.

- Is there unconfessed and unresolved sin in the church's past? Many rural churches, for instance, found their well water by the demonic practice of divining. Other churches have destroyed pastors without regret or reparation. Still others have unsettled rifts in their past, which give Satan plenty of opportunities to incite present problems.

- Is there a lack of submission to the board by the pastor? Some insist they are under God's authority alone, refusing the God-ordained authority of the board.
- Is the board violating the pastor through improper control? It is Satan who loves oppressive control. God loves cooperative self-control. Satan overpowers, while God *empowers.*
- Are there people, or families, who hold an improper attitude of ownership of the church?

Satan Tries to Finish What He Starts

Once Satan's incitement sets a firestorm in motion, he doesn't retreat. Quite the contrary, he'll send a hoard of demons to fan the flames. At first he may have incited only one person. As violations multiply, however, Satan will prompt many to spread the destruction.

If you're still bewildered as to how this can happen among God's people, let's look more carefully at the Scriptures. In James 3:14–15, the apostle captures the collaboration that can form between Satan and God's people. He states, "But if you harbor bitter envy and selfish ambition in your hearts, do not boast about it or deny the truth. Such 'wisdom' does not come down from heaven but is earthly, unspiritual, of the devil."

That's blunt. It doesn't get more clearly stated than that. James said that you, a believer, can follow "wisdom" that is of the devil. The revelation clearly states how it happens—harboring sinful thoughts and attitudes.

Human Responsibility

I'm sure some readers at this point would furiously argue that people are still responsible. I agree. This explanation of how Satan operates in a firestorm in no way removes each one's responsibility to resist and overcome him. All I am explaining is how he works when given the opportunity. While Satan may try to inspire evil behavior, we, as the superior creation, must refuse it. But when he finds agreement somewhere in us, lethal damage can be done.

Let's go one level deeper by seeing how Paul explained this interplay between Satan and mankind. In Ephesians 2:1–3 he writes, "As for you, you were dead in your transgressions and sins, in which you used to live when you followed the *ways of this world* and of the *ruler of the kingdom of the air*, the spirit who is now at work in those who are disobedient. All of us also lived among them at one time, gratifying the *cravings of our sinful nature* and following its desires and thoughts" (emphasis added).

Notice from this text how the world, the flesh, and the devil are almost indistinguishable from each other. What makes sense to the one makes sense to the other. When Satan finds agreement in a believer, he only lands upon an area of the heart not cleansed from the former life. That's where his incitement finds the desired response.

But, you may say, that's describing the relationship between nonbelievers and the devil. True. Still, that's the former relationship that believers often slip back into when they allow sin in their hearts. Keep in mind that every warning in the New Testament of what Satan can do to a person is made to believers. Furthermore, it is God who gave us an abundance of revelation about how to overcome our foe.

Now that we have examined Satan's role, we must turn to the One who ultimately determines all things related to a firestorm—God. Let's look next at his sovereign dealings with you and your people.

11

FIRE FROM ON HIGH

I form the light and create darkness, I bring prosperity and create disaster; I, the LORD, do all these things.

Isaiah 45:7

God is a consuming fire.

Deuteronomy 4:24

By now, you may be wondering what to do next. You've taken corrective action in many of the areas already discussed, but still the conflict boils on.

Welcome to the tough reality: *neatly packaged formulas rarely work.* When prayer, fasting, and corrective action don't douse the fire, then God may be working on levels beyond your control without explaining his actions to you. Don't despair. Solution? Remember that he is a holy, consuming fire, so cooperate with him *by faith!*

God's Primary Goal

Although God rarely explains all of his purposes, he has revealed his primary purpose for every situation in your life—whether you're facing a baby's death, a job loss, a prolonged illness or, yes, even a firestorm. In fact, this purpose is declared to be predestined. That should give you a big enough reason to endure. So, you can be sure that God's predetermination for your life is exactly what is unfolding.

This purpose is found in Romans 8:29. Unfortunately, however, it can be overlooked because of the popularity of the verse preceding it. It's at the worst time of your life that well-meaning people quote Romans 8:28: "And we know that in all things God works for the good of those who love him, who have been called according to his purpose." That can be irritating. Your life is burning down around your feet, and they slap you with this verse that implies an easy, happy ending. Frankly, it's more than irritating; it violates God's Word to quote this verse without quoting the following verse. That's where we find "the good" God is bringing out of every situation.

What is the good? Read verse twenty-nine slowly: "For those God foreknew *he also predestined to be conformed to the likeness of his Son*" (emphasis added). There you have it. Absorb it. That's the good God is working in every situation, including firestorms. His highest priority is to conform you to Christ and the great Consuming Fire will stop at nothing less. If you don't share that desire, then you may be pleading with God to end the firestorm while God is prolonging it to fulfill his purposes.

Getting in Sync with God

Bewildered by God's seeming neglect to intervene, you plead for consideration of the beautiful edifice—*built for his glory.* You explain the important programs of the church—*instituted for his purpose.* And you ask him to protect the church's reputation—*established for his name.* These are excellent prayers, so why doesn't God seem to answer? Their focus is secondary to God's predetermined will to shape the image of his Son in your heart. In light of this, it may be wiser to pray that God would turn up the heat. As the eminent Herbert Lockyer Sr., wrote, "In our spiritual experience, the Holy Spirit, reigning within our hearts, is the Fire consuming our lusts and melting our wills into loving obedience."[3]

God's Claims about Himself

Frankly, we must throw off the insipid theology that strips God of sovereignty. The same God who opened the Red Sea sent his people into the Babylonian captivity. Once we accept God as he has revealed

himself, full of both grace and judgment, we can conclude that ultimately all firestorms are either *allowed* or *caused* by God, otherwise
he would not be sovereign. He declared in Isaiah 45:7, "I form the
light and create darkness, I bring prosperity and create disaster; I,
the LORD, do all these things."

Fear not, this does not cast him as a deranged "desert god" with
hair blowing wildly in the wind, swinging an indiscriminate sword
of vengeance. While God does not delight in inflicting pain, our
proud hearts require much heat and pain for God to fulfill his predetermined purpose—to forge us into the image of his Son. In
Lamentations 3:32–33, Jeremiah, the brokenhearted prophet, captured God's compassion when he wrote, "Though he brings grief, he
will show compassion, so great is his unfailing love. For he does not
willingly bring affliction or grief to the children of men."

God is not deranged, but he is determined to accomplish his perfect will. Once convinced that God lovingly and wisely inflicts pain
upon his people, it will be clear why he may be in no rush to end
your firestorm. How many Sundays have you opened your hymnal
to sing "Great Is Thy Faithfulness"? That hymn was lifted out of
Lamentations 3:22–24: "Because of the LORD's great love we are not
consumed, for his compassions never fail. They are new every morning; great is your faithfulness. I say to myself, 'The LORD is my portion; therefore I will wait for him.'"

Jeremiah penned those words while Israel was entering her black
hole of existence—the Babylonian captivity. This was the only time
in the history of the world that God permitted the Jews to be conquered. God's protection upon tiny Israel, despite overwhelming
odds, has been a witness to all people. Why, then, did God allow such
disgrace on this occasion?

The answer is found in his predetermined will. The condition of
Israel's heart has always been uppermost in God's concern. Because
they had turned their hearts away from God while he protected them
in freedom, he disciplined them while preserving them in slavery.
It was their dereliction of heart, not the degradation of slavery, that
concerned God.

And so it is with you and your church. One former associate pastor, who was an innocent victim of a ruthless pastor and weak board,
said that he could find no value in what happened. However, when

asked if he had gained greater wisdom and sensitivity from the fire, he responded positively. That's the deeper purpose of God. This person is by far a more effective minister today than he ever could have been without that firestorm.

Let me illustrate this transforming process by taking you to a ranch near Dubois, Wyoming, the residence of Bud Boller, one of America's premier artists. Lifeless clay sculptures stare from shelves in his log studio—silent reminders of bronzes he created for people like Charlton Heston, Robert Redford, and Paul Harvey. Bud's naturally warm smile and gentle spirit flood the studio with sunny vitality.

For most of us, creativity is an impulse that can't find a way of expression. Then, there's Bud, whose mental images pass through his fingers and out to the world. But even as a master, he knows what it is to lose a bronze in the final stages of development. Let's watch him at work.

Bud starts by kneading and shaping a huge lump of clay into human form—perhaps the face of a famous person. The likeness is striking, right down to a mole on the cheek. Then Bud covers the clay with a white, molasses-like liquid. When combined with a catalyst, it becomes rubber. As the rubber "sets up," the clay presses its image into the inside of the rubber mask. Plaster is used on the outside of the rubber for strength.

After the rubber is removed, the clay image is set aside, its purpose fulfilled. But the clay looks so good that you may say, "Bud, I'll take it as it is."

"No," he replies, "it'll never take the heat . . . it'll never last. One bump and the likeness will be disfigured. One sweltering day and an eyebrow could droop. A freeze could crack it apart. Clay is nothing like durable bronze."

Already an application jumps out at us. Christians often try to shape themselves into Christ's likeness—trying to be servants, trying to practice love and forgiveness. But it's the weak clay of human effort, not the bronze of Christ's nature formed in them. Many of Jesus' followers turned back when the clay of their hearts could not endure the hardness of his sayings (John 6:66).

Bud proceeds to the next step, which is to pour hot wax into the rubber mold. The wax flows into every curve and crevice, recapturing the shape of the original clay. It seems like a backward step to use wax, a substance that's softer and less durable than the clay. But it's a critical step toward the bronze.

Another application emerges for the developing saint. Once God molds you beyond the clay of human effort and self-will, he forms in you a soft willingness. You begin to offer prayers like, "Not my will but thine be done." This is progress, but not yet the bronze of Christ's nature.

Bud discards the rubber mask and forms small, wax sprues on various points of the image. Sprues are nubs that form holes for draining the wax and pouring the bronze. Because the wax will be melted away, the process is called the lost wax method.

Likewise, in your process as a believer, just when you consider yourself advanced, God pokes holes in your life, draining you of the soft wax of partial maturity. This is only a stage in your development, not the end. He is further preparing you for the fullness of Christ's nature.

"Let's go," Bud says. "It's time for the foundry." He grabs the wax image and heads for his pickup truck.

Think about it. There was a moment on high when God said of your church, "It's time for the foundry—time for the firestorm." Nothing happens outside of his purpose and plan.

We arrive at the foundry, where a pungent, burnt smell hangs in the air. A blast furnace, spewing like a hoarse dragon, awaits. Bud dips the wax image into a thick, milky substance, which hardens on the outside of the wax image. But before it does, Bud sprinkles fine sand over it, which clings like a mild irritant to the moist membrane. He repeats the process again and again, adding layer upon layer, each time using coarser sand. The sand and slime solidify into a powerful silicone shell that can endure great heat.

Likewise look at how God prepares you for your firestorm. About the time you're thinking life should be getting better, he sprinkles an irritant over the sticky conflict. You're not yet ready for the full infusion of spiritual bronze, but there's progress. Just a few years ago the slightest criticism sent you tumbling into depression. Not so today; you are certainly beyond clay and wax.

Bud plunges the mold into the furnace. Molecules race faster and faster until they are spinning at a dizzying 2,200 degrees. The wax quickly melts, flowing freely out of the vents made by the sprues.

This is a critical moment. If the wax heats too slowly, it will expand before becoming a liquid and crack the vital silicone shell. Then, it's back to the clay.

So, likewise, just when you think you've arrived at the likeness of Christ, God begins a meltdown in you. He plunges you and your church into the furnace of trial to melt the wax that looked so good on the surface. You feel empty, even abandoned, but the shell of your heart must be hollowed for the true bronze of Christ's likeness. If you respond improperly, then it's back to the clay. He'll start all over again.

Bud tests for leaks by filling the emptied shell with water. All's well. He puts the shell back into the furnace. Timing is everything. Above the husky roar of the furnace, Bud commands, "Now!" The hot shell is removed. The sweaty biceps of a helping craftsman bulge as he tilts the ladle of molten bronze over the shell. A thin metallic stream glistens and flows over the spout, through the vents, and into the shell, filling every human feature: eyelids, lips, nose—even a scar.

"Enough!" The ladle is righted. The craftsman and Bud exchange looks. Time is what they need, but the seconds pass slowly. Should the shell break from heat or weight, it's back to the studio for Bud— back to the clay.

Silence. The wonderful sound of silence, at least so far. Eyes study the bronze-filled mold. One minute passes, then two—hope increases. Eventually ten . . . thirty . . . "I think it's okay. I hope it's a keeper," Bud says, wiping sweat from his brow. As though following a celebration ritual, the craftsman pulls out a large red handkerchief and does likewise.

Bud and the craftsman laugh about some bad times in the past when the shell broke and the liquid bronze coursed across the floor. Talk shifts to Bud's horses up on the mountain and the chilling winds dropping down from the north. The more time that passes the better.

Suddenly, a loud *crack!* shatters the calm. Talk stops. *Crack!* . . . *snap* . . . *crack!*—again and again. But no one is disturbed. This is what Bud has been waiting for. The silicone shell is cooling faster than the bronze. As it shrinks, it breaks and falls off, revealing the mighty bronze within.

Bud whistles while filing off the sprues, touching up small imperfections and applying patina to the bronze—the finishing touch.

Likewise, God allows no shell to cover the marvelous bronze of his Son's nature in his people. It may have the right shape but not the right substance. After the various stages of spiritual growth, the final breaking is often the most bewildering. Why? Because having already passed through so much suffering, you wonder why more painful breaking is necessary, especially since you already bear a great resemblance to Christ. But, without the outer shell broken, people will only see the *likeness* of Christ, not the *person* of Christ in you.

Paul wrote in Ephesians 2:10, "For we are God's workmanship, created in Christ Jesus to do good works." As such, we are not beautiful, soulless bronze statues. No, God is creating living replicas of his Son, forever exhibiting his grace (Eph. 2:7). While creation reveals his glory and handiwork, we reveal his grace, as expressed in his willingness and ability to transform us from sinful clay into the bronze of Jesus Christ (Rom. 8:10; Col. 1:27).

In God's Mold

So, where does this leave you in light of your firestorm? You've fulfilled your responsibility of looking at the various causes of firestorms listed in the previous chapters. You've done all you know to do, and no formulas are working. It's safe to conclude that the Consuming Fire is working in the midst of the firestorm to transform hearts for a greater likeness of Christ.

Perhaps you've already identified where many of your people are in their development. Some never got past the clay stage—shaped like the real, but weak and unreliable. Others have not progressed beyond the rubber mask. Christ is being formed in them, but their exterior is unsightly, unacceptable. Still others stop at the wax stage. They don't want the heat that melts them away, making room for the bronze. Cursing the heat, they escape to another church.

The field narrows as we reach the silicone stage. These people can handle more heat than others, but this is still personal strength, not Christ's. The shell must be broken away from the bronze. If it breaks too soon, God starts all over again. If it breaks at the right time, they emerge as a solid likeness of Christ. One principle is universal:

bronzes are poured when molten. So it is with the deeper formations of Christ in the advancing saint.

Precious few make it to the final stages; many are called, but few are chosen. Stick with the ones who make it. They are the ones who bring God's nature and strength to situations. Encourage them as God files off the sprues, heats and shapes subtle imperfections, polishes and patines them into a glorious display of Christ's nature and likeness. This is God's primary purpose in the life of each believer, so make it yours. If your firestorm produces a stronger Christlikeness in the remnant, then it will be worth the heat.

When you conform to God's purpose, then you will see his hand in your conflict. You can claim the Scripture, "When a man's ways are pleasing to the Lord, he makes even his enemies live at peace with him" (Prov. 16:7). The same God who fires the furnace cools it, too.

Having looked at various causes of firestorms, we will now consider ways to fight firestorms.

PART 3

FIGHTING A FIRESTORM

Church boards are often made up of well-intentioned people who become paralyzed by indecision when conflict strikes. It's a basic law that the longer a board takes to make tough decisions, the harder these decisions become. If leaders wait long enough, decisions will be made for them, with worse consequences than if they had made the tough decisions earlier.

12

FIGHTING FIRE WITH FIRE

ACTIONS THE BOARD CAN TAKE

But it will go well with those who convict the guilty, and rich blessing will come upon them.

Proverbs 24:25

Drive out the mocker, and out goes strife; quarrels and insults are ended.

Proverbs 22:10

Having seen the causes of firestorms, let's turn our attention now to the ways and means God has provided for dealing with them. We'll particularly examine how to handle trouble that could lead to the ruination of the pastor or collapse of the church.

Forest firefighters often start a new line of fire called a backfire to rob the fire of combustible material. Likewise, when your church is enveloped by a firestorm, you may have to deprive it of fuel by building a backfire. Whether your firestorm is caused by behavioral or doctrinal issues, God has revealed how you are to handle it. The first God-given action we'll consider is confrontation and discipline.

A word of caution before we look at this important work of leadership: Most people who appear problematic are not sheep in wolves' clothing; rather, they are sheep in sheep's clothing. They don't mean harm. They just don't know how to handle themselves during times of trouble. So, be slow in your reaction to those who overreact. Don't be guilty of killing sheep for the sake of personal comfort. A sheep may need a serious shearing, but not a throat slashing.

The work of church discipline should fall upon the board more than the pastor. Why? Because the pastor will be tugged at from various camps, yet must attempt to minister to them all. Also, if the attack is against him, it will appear self-serving for him to lead in the confrontation and discipline. The pastor should be part of the process but not the point person. The comments in this chapter, then, are directed to board members. The following is a collection of observations made while the board at Myerstown Grace Brethren Church engaged in a disciplinary process. Hopefully these thoughts will help you prepare for the unexpected and give courage to fulfill God's requirement upon you as spiritual leaders.

Overcoming Personal Hesitation

I've already stressed that when trouble strikes, time isn't on your side, and few things will destroy a church faster than indecision. There are a number of hindrances to hurdle, however, before people with hesitations are free to act.

The first hindrance is failure to distinguish between being a peace*keeper* and a peace*maker.* Peacekeepers tend to be passive, preferring to avoid conflict. That won't solve problems. Avoidance generally leads to anarchy, not peaceful resolution. Generally peacekeepers are not effective leaders amid conflict.

On the other hand, peacemakers tackle conflict head-on, determined to bring peace based upon truth, mutual understanding, and forgiveness. Though this can be initially painful, if it's done with the proper mix of justice, mercy, and grace, it's the only hope for making peace. While peacekeepers try to sweep things under the rug, peacemakers try to sweep issues out the door.

Peacekeepers lead to the second hindrance—indecision. They want to "wait and see," hoping not to make a mistake. But leadership must rely upon bold, clear thinking when time is not a friend. Look at the example of David's brothers when facing Goliath. They may have held prayer meetings, pleading with God to give Goliath a heart attack. Likewise, some want to pray for God to remove a problem, but he is requiring us to face our Goliath eye-to-eye—by *faith!*

Here are some arguments expressed by church leaders paralyzed by indecision.

- These people are not troublemakers, just misguided.
- We will lose the big donor's money. We cannot make it without him.
- Their family has long been a part of the church.
- It's not worth the energy to go through discipline.
- We might get sued.
- What if they respond by causing more trouble?
- Their friends and family might leave the church with them.
- Perhaps there is more to the story than we know.

You must not get stuck on these considerations. If trouble is in your face, you must act!

The third hindrance is board division. Boards divide for various reasons: conflicting perceptions of the problem, insufficient information, loyalties to people who are to be disciplined, pressure from factions in the church, or family complications with people to be disciplined.

The fourth hindrance is ambivalence about the difference between judgment and judgmentalism. Someone may say, "We must not judge lest we be judged." What stalls the board is the lack of understanding about exercising judgment to *evaluate* and being judgmental with the intent to *condemn*. When Jesus said, "Do not judge, or you too will be judged" (Matt. 7:1), he was referring to condemnation. You have no right to condemn people to hell or reward them with heaven. That judgment belongs to God alone. But to judge—that is, evaluate or discern—wrongdoing is both your right and responsibility.

A spiritual person makes sound judgments on all matters, including those relating to interpersonal problems. Paul wrote, "The spiritual man makes judgments about all things" (1 Cor. 2:15). Consider, too, Philippians 1:9–10, "And this I pray, that your love may abound yet more and more in knowledge and in all judgment; that ye may approve things that are excellent" (KJV).

These four obstacles must be hurdled, or your board will be paralyzed. As British statesman Edmund Burke said, "All it takes for evil to prevail is for good men to do nothing."

Statement of Purpose

It will be critical to establish a statement of purpose for both the board and the church. Because church discipline is an emotionally charged experience, it's advisable to have your statement in print. This will help keep your goal straight, even when your emotions get muddied and your motive distorted. Here is a suggested statement.

"We will enact church discipline, not for punishment or retribution, but for the purpose of:

- "*Repentance:* To see the offender turn from wrongful behavior.
- "*Redemption:* To bring the offender into a right relationship with God.
- "*Restitution:* To bring justice where someone suffered wrong or loss.
- "*Restoration:* To reestablish fellowship.

"Our purpose is to be God's instruments as he forms his Son more fully in each heart."

Notice that there is nothing punitive in this statement. Rather, it's a commitment to compassion. Your goal is to encourage conformity to Christ—period! This statement should help you maintain a right spirit when it becomes hard to maintain compassion. This is especially so if the offender is hostile toward your efforts. When fatigue sets in, reasoning blurs, and emotions play funny games, board members will have varied responses:

- False guilt, as though they are bad men for calling people into account for their sins.

- Pity for the culprits, resulting in a desire to drop the matter without proper resolution.
- Anger that could lead to wanting punishment or revenge.
- Hardness of heart, leading to legalistic solutions.

Still, you must confront wrongdoers. The statement of purpose will help you distinguish between emotion and motive. Feelings rise and fall, but motive must be steadfast. Your written statement will help hold that in place.

Personal Preparation

To be right in principle but not in practice is to fail. Spiritual preparation is essential for keeping both principle and practice right. Just as the Scriptures call for self-examination prior to communion (1 Cor. 11:28), so also you must examine your heart before dealing with one taken in a sin (Gal. 6:1). You cannot understand your own heart (Jer. 17:9). While there may be "secret and shameful" things you need to confess and renounce (2 Cor. 4:2), there may be motives hidden beneath your own awareness. These motives can emerge at the most unexpected times, giving Satan an opportunity to destroy you. So ask God to reveal any sins or hidden agendas that may hinder you.

I would encourage you to fast and pray before confrontation. *Being right is not enough.* You must also be blessed and empowered by the Holy Spirit. Such preparation can help you to:

- Maintain a quiet, humble spirit before the Lord amid great strife.
- Foster true dependence upon the Lord.
- Experience the leadership of the Holy Spirit.
- Plead for the repentance of each one facing discipline.

Prepare Your Case Well

Before you call someone to come before the board, be sure your case is well prepared. You should do a better job than even secular courts, since you are not out to fight for a client but to discover the truth. Have all assertions validated and supported by people's testimonials and examples. Never act on hearsay or innuendo. Insist that the accuser faces the accused, unless it's unwise, such as a child having to face a molester.

Gain the offender's viewpoint during the preparation period. But, once your case is prepared, come to the table of confrontation with the issues clearly spelled out and provable.

At times, it may be wise to put the charges in print to avoid emotional misstatement. Then, destroy the file when the matter reaches closure, because love keeps no record of wrongs (1 Cor. 13:5). If the offender has "escaped" to a new church, share the file with this church, since they will inherit the responsibility of disciplining the person. If the case is serious, however, consult a Christian attorney before putting anything in writing, lest the board be held liable for slander.

The Matthew 18 Formula

Now it's time for the confrontation. God has given the general principles in Matthew 18:15–20:

- An offended person is to approach the offender one-on-one to show him his fault. The purpose is to win the brother.
- If the brother will not listen, then one or two other persons are to be taken along to establish every matter by the testimony of two or three witnesses.
- If the offender refuses to listen to the small group, then the matter is to be told to the church. If the offender will not listen to the church, then he is to be put out of the fellowship.

Notice several things about this formula. First, every effort is made to preserve the offender's dignity. You start with the smallest possible circle of people, only increasing it as the offender refuses to repent. Discussions outside of that circle are disrespectful to the offender and degenerative to the process.

Second, the offended person is to confront the offender, not quietly harbor resentment. Otherwise, the offended becomes guilty of sin.

Third, the expectation of closure is established. The person must repent or face consequences—either come to settlement or separation.

Fourth, every step of the process is for redemption, repentance, restitution, and restoration. If it must end with separation, then the offender is responsible for his own fate.

Be forewarned that this formula rarely works without problems. This formula gives the principles to follow, although you may need some adjustments. For instance, if the offender sins against the entire church, you're already beyond the one-to-one level.

Although the offender can throw this formula out of sync, don't be intimidated or let the offender have control. Offenders often try to shift the blame, stating that the board didn't exactly follow the formula. Fulfill the spirit of the text where you cannot precisely fulfill the steps.

Call Evil by Its Name

You can be gentle and still call evil by its name. Most firestorms have an evil core involving very few (one to five) people. I'm using the word "evil" in the technical sense of someone with a destructive agenda who rejects fairness and truth. The mark of this evil is unreasonableness that cannot be diminished. This is not merely a misguided saint.

Mercy, Grace, and Justice

Carry out your work with mercy, grace, and justice. James teaches, "Speak and act as those who are going to be judged by the law that gives freedom, because judgment without mercy will be shown to anyone who has not been merciful. Mercy triumphs over judgment!" (James 2:12–13).

Justice sets the agenda for repentance. Mercy gives the undeserved opportunity to repent. Grace provides undeserved freedom and opportunity after repentance. Mercy, grace, and justice are inseparable in God's nature. Justice preserves the precepts, while mercy and grace preserve the person. Remove any one of the three and you fail the person. Fulfill all three in proper balance and you will best serve the offender.

Be Prepared for Various Responses

Well, here you are at the confrontation. Some of the responses you may encounter are:

- True godly sorrow and repentance (2 Cor. 7:8–11). This is rare.
- Anger that you would invade the offender's perceived rights.
- Blame toward you or another in order to shift responsibility.
- Defensiveness in claiming a right to the offending conduct.
- Efforts to water down the seriousness of what was done.

You have no control over a person's response. You can only control your motive and method. The person is responsible for his or her own response. For instance, Peter was not responsible for the sad end of Ananias and Sapphira—they were destroyed by their own evil.

Have Consequences Prepared

In light of these various responses, it's important to have your plan of action in place. Don't discover at step one that you're unprepared should the accused not repent. Here are some eventualities and ways to be prepared for them.

1. The offender refuses to meet with you. That should not stop you from:

   - Giving the case to another authority who may be able to obligate the person to respond.
   - Dismissing the person from church membership.
   - Disclosing the person's unrepentant conduct to any church where they may seek to attend. This is a responsibility to the church at large, not a punitive measure against the

offender. In a growing number of cities, where pastors are praying together, troublemakers are no longer able to run to various churches without accountability.

2. The offender comes to the meeting to attack and castigate, rather than deal with the issues.

It must be clear that the offender is not in charge of the meeting. You are. If that person feels he has a valid defense, the board must consider it, but don't be deterred from your purpose.

3. The offender cannot refute the statements against him, yet refuses to repent.

Immediately put your plan of clearly stated and fair consequences into motion.

The Ultimate Consequence

The worst consequence to impose upon an unrepentant person is that which Paul instructed regarding the incestuous man in Corinth. "When you are assembled in the name of our Lord Jesus and I am with you in spirit, and the power of our Lord Jesus is present, hand this man over to Satan, so that the sinful nature may be destroyed and his spirit saved on the day of the Lord" (1 Cor. 5:4–5). Let's look at this process one phrase at a time and discover that, even in extreme discipline, the motive is redemptive.

- "When you are assembled" refers to the body of Christ. This important step allows the entire congregation to understand on a deeper level the seriousness of sin (1 Tim. 5:20).
- "In the name of our Lord Jesus" establishes the One who is being offended by the sin. Since it is Christ who is ultimately sinned against, expulsion is for the honor of his name.
- "I am with you in spirit" simply establishes oneness of Paul's agreement.
- "Hand this man over to Satan" is the matter of excluding him from the spiritual protection of the church and exposing him to the realm where Satan can inflict whatever damage God permits. An Old Testament parallel is seen in the life of Saul. "Now

the Spirit of the Lord had departed from Saul, and an evil spirit from the Lord tormented him" (1 Sam. 16:14). It is tragic that Saul did not respond properly to this measure of discipline.

Dr. Jim Logan, author of *Reclaiming Surrendered Ground,* said at a spiritual warfare conference in Gettysburg, Pennsylvania, in 1996 that church discipline is not removing people from the rolls but releasing them to the devil. If they want to live like the devil, Logan said, then the church should give them over to him.

Paul wrote, "What business is it of mine to judge those outside the church? Are you not to judge those inside? God will judge those outside. 'Expel the wicked man from among you'" (1 Cor. 5:12–13; see also Deut. 13:5; 1 Cor. 6:1–4). The two effects of this extreme action are to redeem the sinner and to cleanse Christ's body.

The Divine Court on Earth

While Christians should never take one another to the courts of the land, settling disputes does fall upon your shoulders as a church leader. The church is heaven's divine court on earth, intended to mediate settlements between believers. In 1 Corinthians 6:1–6, Paul writes: "If any of you has a dispute with another, dare he take it before the ungodly for judgment instead of before the saints? Do you not know that the saints will judge the world? And if you are to judge the world, are you not competent to judge trivial cases? Do you not know that we will judge angels? How much more the things of this life! Therefore, if you have disputes about such matters, appoint as judges even men of little account in the church! I say this to shame you. Is it possible that there is nobody among you wise enough to judge a dispute between believers? But instead, one brother goes to law against another—and this is in front of unbelievers!"

Confrontation and discipline (fighting fire with fire) are part of the God-given work of church leadership. Without them, you probably will not stop your firestorm until it has destroyed your church. Let's turn now to the second area—actions the pastor can take.

13

Bold Spiritual Leadership

Actions the Pastor Can Take

> When choosing your course of action, you must first decide what kind of a person you want to be after the conflict. This determines more than anything else whether you win or lose.

Do you remember the noble feelings that surged through your heart as you read Foxe's *The Book of Martyrs*? Or was it the account of the five missionaries slain by the Auca Indians that transported you into a vicarious brush with spiritual greatness? Untested courage may have stirred in your spirit as you read of Martin Luther's bravery at the Diet of Worms and of John Wesley's bold declarations before angry mobs. Perhaps you resolved, "I'll stand with God, come defamation or death!"

That's great, but you thought that in the safety of a quiet seminary campus. Now, you're confronted with a real firestorm that bears your name. Courage melts and your real responses are unexpected: fear, self-pity, anger, bitterness, doubt.

Welcome to real life. Here you kneel beside the real Jesus, facing real spiritual danger. This is your Gethsemane. Here you experience some of the real emotions known to those who suffered in the past—the human reality that historians often fail to capture. You feel abandoned, like any person does who faces human fury. There is no guaranteed happy ending to your situation. Your reward may not come in this lifetime.

More Than Conflict Management

As a spiritual leader, you must be capable of more than conflict management as defined by the secular world, because the dynamics of church conflict are significantly different from secular disputes. For instance, disputes between labor and management are inspired and settled by a motivation of greed—"What do I get out of this?" When each party is satisfied with its gain, a contract is signed and work resumes. It matters not if people like or love each other.

On the other hand, you are bound to a higher standard. Your work is not a matter of getting problematic sheep off your back, but of teaching people who act like wolves how to become or return to being sheep. Nothing is more dishonorable than for a pastor to lapse into wolfish behavior, with fang attacking fang. So, as you choose which option to apply to your situation, be sure that your purpose is to use it for the spiritual benefit of the people and not as a form of self-deliverance. Here are the actions (or combinations thereof) to consider:

Step Out: Set a spiritual example.

Step In: Mediate the conflict.

Step Over: Rise above the conflict.

Step Up: Confront the conflict.

Step Back: Let the conflict burn itself out.

Step Down: Resign from the conflict.

Step Out: Set a Spiritual Example

No one can deny devotion on display. There are times when you are to stay in a firestorm to display the works of God. To illustrate this, I have created the following story out of bits and pieces of some actual events.

The seeds of conflict were sown the night Rev. Fred Murphy met as a candidate with the church board in Rochester, Minnesota. The board explained to Fred that the church was spiritually sluggish and losing people. Some thought Fred's vivacious love for Christ and people would reverse the downward trend. But others, like Jim Blandish, objected, believing that Fred wasn't right for the Rochester culture.

Jim expressed his objections about Fred in terms of market analysis. "This city houses the Mayo Clinic," he began, managing to mention that he worked there in accounting. Cloaking his arrogance with sophistication, Jim continued, "We want to target the upper-class professionals, many of whom hold earned doctorates. They have certain socio-economic tastes and interests."

The implication was clear. Fred didn't fit. Though intelligent, he was scruffy—pleasing but not polished. Tension hung in the meeting like lead, but in the end Fred was called to the church.

The church grew rapidly for three years, but with blue-collar more than upper-management people. This grated on Jim, who served on the high-profile committee of the governor's prayer breakfast. He undermined Fred's credibility at every opportunity. In time, some board members were swayed into believing Fred should be replaced by a more erudite pastor, one who could attract a higher echelon of people. They sowed dissension by criticizing him in well-chosen circles.

Despite the pressure, Fred didn't think he should leave. He fasted and prayed for deliverance and asked for enabling to love his antagonists. But after months of frustration, Fred decided to resign.

It was a cold Monday night when Fred penned his resignation. The conflict had drained his spirit, leaving him feeling old and tired at thirty-six. His bad nerves made even swallowing difficult. The phone rang. Fred hesitantly lifted the receiver. "Hello."

It was Jim, broken and crying.

"Pastor, please come. My daughter was just killed by a drunken driver."

Fred felt tempted to think Jim had received his just desserts, but drove to his home asking God to remove such thoughts. Fred found Jim to be incoherent. He put his arms around Jim and his wife, Betty, letting silence minister. Betty sobbed uncontrollably while Jim stared at the floor. That night Fred said little, just prayed, cared, and then left. Up through the funeral on Thursday, he stayed close, offering them strength.

The following Sunday, Fred opened his resignation letter after the final hymn.

"I want this church returned to peace. It is clear that my presence has become a hindrance—" but stopped when Jim abruptly stood.

"Pastor, no, you must not resign," Jim said. He needed to say no more. Everyone knew of Jim's resistance to Fred, as well as the Blandishes' recent tragedy. People wept. One lone person applauded, then more, until a standing ovation erupted.

Fred stayed. His Georgian background never did free him to don Rochester's Midwestern culture. Nor did the Rochester church ever adopt Fred's casual, Southern ways. But mutual respect grew out of a blend of pain from both sides.

Fred stepped out in an effort to present a Christ-like example in the midst of conflict. On this occasion it worked, but don't assume your story will end this way.

Considerations:

1. There is no guarantee that this approach will produce a happy ending in this lifetime, but God will ultimately protect and exalt this pastor.
2. This is a high risk course and requires enormous physical, emotional, and spiritual strength, since extreme levels of self-death are necessary.

Step In: Mediate the Conflict

You may wonder if the words, "Strike me, I'm a lightning rod" are emblazoned across your forehead. You can be drawn into the middle of conflicts, then be whipped from both sides. To illustrate how this happens, consider the following phone call I received one day.

"Hello, Ron. I have a serious problem on my hands that could destroy our church. I want to bounce it off you for your response."

This man pastored a closely knit church in a small town, the kind in which family conflicts are dragged into the church. In rural settings, resentments can be intense but deeply concealed.

"What's happening, Paul?"

"Well, Ron, one of the key men in my church is being accused by a woman of having an affair with her. Both she and her husband are going after the man, perhaps starting legal action. The man in my church is denying it, although he says they became closer in conversations than they should have."

"Do other people know about the problem?" I asked. The question was somewhat pointless, knowing that tabloid news travels faster than the flu.

"Yes," he replied, "the accusing couple is telling everyone. What I want to know is what action I should or should not take. The couple wants me to meet with them. They say they have proof that there has been involvement."

"Have they given any specific situations?"

"Yes. That's what blew this thing open. The lady has a nighttime job. Her husband went to check on her the other night. Her car was there, but she was not. When he confronted her, she claimed to have been on a sexual exploit with the man from my church. The man from my church says that he was out on a job that night and could not have been with her. I personally questioned the man who hired him and the man corroborated the story. Someone's lying."

I jumped in, "It seems strange to me that the husband and wife are teamed against the accused man. Most people who feel violated are furious with both their mate and the other party."

"I agree. That seems strange to me, too," he replied.

This pastor was being pulled by two families into a conflict for which he could pay a terrible price. If the allegation did not have a clear resolution, then the church and community would take sides. The firestorm that was rolling across the horizon would hit the pastor first. How? Each party would demand that he take its side, destroying him if he did not. The flurry of gossip and side-taking could decimate the church. Here is the potential domino effect of such a situation:

- Two marriages could be destroyed.
- Children could suffer lifelong emotional damage.
- A business may be destroyed.
- A community may get splashed with tabloid talk.
- The church could divide over whose story to believe.
- The pastor could end up too damaged to continue in that ministry.

- The nonbelieving world could be left with a tarnished image of Christ.

Further, chances of ministering in a new church could diminish for the pastor, since no one will be sure if he gave a perfect performance. Thus, he could become an innocent victim.

Considerations:

1. Pastors must decide if it is wise to step in, or if the conflict should be put into the hands of another (counselor, lawyer, consultant, board committee) and act only as a spiritual guide to everyone.
2. Dealing with matters of conflict is the work of the church, but not necessarily the work of the pastor alone.

Step Over: Rise above the Conflict

"If a ruler's anger rises against you, do not leave your post; calmness can lay great errors to rest" (Eccles. 10:4). That was the verse Dr. Ward Felton (not his real name) placed on his desk after members of a committee encouraged him to leave the church. They believed he was denying the power of the Holy Spirit because he wasn't willing to change from a traditional style of worship, didn't make healing the dominant theme of his ministry, and didn't exalt "sign" gifts highly enough.

Ward was gracious in his embrace of the charismatic element in his church, but they were not willing to view themselves as only a part of the body of Christ. They believed their views should sweep through the entire church. Ward couldn't permit that. He met with the members of the group many times, hoping to keep them as a healthy part of the congregation. They tried to "win him with love" to their views, until it was apparent that he wasn't changing his mind. They didn't think he could be their pastor without championing their position.

The group's desire to get rid of Ward and replace him with someone who would give freedom to its agenda sounded innocent at first. "Let's just pray for him," members would say. But there was a superior air in their attitudes. They eroded Ward's credibility by implying that he placed more confidence in his education than in the Holy Spirit.

Pastor Felton chose not to lash out in sermons or enact church discipline. He elected to answer none of the innuendoes made against his spirituality. He took the high road, hoping that by not feeding the fire it would go out. One year later the group departed, stating that Ward was probably not even a born-again believer. The church continued steadfast—even showing growth.

Considerations:

1. Never take this approach because you fear confrontation. That can lead to disaster.
2. This is a good approach if you have an assurance from God that he will handle the problem while you rise above it.

Step Up: Confront the Conflict

When a pastor decides to step up and confront the conflict, he takes many risks. Following is an illustration using real events, with names changed.

Meet Jack Forester—young, soft-spoken, but determined to serve God. He isn't at his new church long before he learns of serious moral problems—past and present—within the congregation. Feeling sure his board members would want him to lead them in confronting the problems, he discusses the need for church discipline. The board responds by forcing Jack out of the church. This is the price tag for touching the "good ole boys' club." The local newspaper catches wind of his mysterious departure and calls the church for an interview. When the board hides behind silence, the following news article appears the next day.

When Expectations Are Not Met, Someone's Got to Go

Priests, reverends, and ministers come and go. They move from church to church, town to town, on a regular basis. Some move to accept greater responsibilities. Others just move on.

Then there's the curious case of Rev. Jack Forester, who has parted ways with the First Baptist Church. Now, normally, a

church and its pastor are only of interest to their own congregation, and the hiring—and firing—of religious personnel does not
make it onto the pages of newspapers. But the departure of Rev.
Forester was brought to our attention by a press release sent to us
by the board of deacons of First Baptist Church. The notice cited
wonderful contributions Rev. Forester made to this community
through his dedicated work and gift for music.

But the seven-sentence press release ends on a sour note by
stating that "because of divergent goals, vision, expectations and
styles of ministry, by mutual agreement, it was decided that Pastor Forester's talents be directed toward Christian service at
another church."

So, it appears Rev. Forester agreed that, for reasons not made
clear, he would leave his flock.

The total irony, of course, is that congregations of Christians
can and do turn on their pastors and run them out of town because
of God-knows-what.

The cartoon accompanying the article shows a pastor standing
in an unemployment office. The headline reads "First Baptist
Church's minister moves on . . . Hmmmm . . . ." The employment
counselor, seated at his desk, asks the pastor, "Other than having
friends in high places, do you have any marketable skills, Rev.
Forester?"

Jack's wife is left to drive an hour each way to work, while he sits
under the care of another church, awaiting a new opportunity. Fortunately, Jack's family is strong enough to handle the abuse that
comes as a result of his choice to "step up."

Considerations:

1. Leadership today is potentially lethal to a career. Taking biblically correct action does not guarantee a biblically correct
   response from the board and/or congregation.
2. The belief that good always wins is valid, but the victory may
   not come in this lifetime.
3. Confrontation can be exhausting. Be sure you are fit in body
   and mind and that your personal relationships are strong,
   because severe pressures will come against you.

Step Back: Let the Conflict Burn Itself Out

Here's how Pastor Bill Oakes (not his real name) stumbled into a no-win position. He went to a church as the fifth pastor in thirteen years—not a good sign. His predecessor was hospitalized, recovering from the ravages of stress. What were routine issues for most churches—style and length of worship time, theological bias, clergy responsibility—regularly caused turmoil in this one. The board's fear of more conflict led to paralysis and stagnation, impeding progress.

On the surface, relationships appeared congenial—everyone displaying Sunday smiles. But under the surface was tension. Power plays were rooted deep in generational soil. However, the people could not confront each other, knowing that they would never recover from such an explosion. So they focused on superficial problems instead, making a whipping post out of the pastor. Herein, they achieved a macabre unity.

Soon they found an issue over which they could make Bill the object of wrath. Being liberal, he offered a Sunday school elective on higher criticism. Surely one would think that a conservative church could handle a liberal pastor in a mature, Christ-like way. Not so. One man gave Bill a threat-filled warning not to have the class, no matter how many people wanted it.

As factions divided over the class, Bill refused to be the sacrificial lamb. He stepped back and forced the two groups to fight it out. Describing the situation, Bill wrote: "The following hour convinced me that the consultant had unmasked the dysfunction in the church by advising me to step back and force them to confront each other. The emotional catharsis was immediate and powerful. Church members cried, shouted, pointed fingers, and stomped their feet. Vile accusations were made.

"With worship minutes away, I called for a vote on whether or not to conduct the class. Three or four members shook their heads no, but many more verbally supported the class. I accepted their decision and agreed to teach it the following week. Those who were using their typical power plays of threatening friendships and removing their memberships (still an indistinct group) did not get their way.

"After worship several members of the church gathered in my office to discuss the ramifications of the decision. One woman became angry over the member who had warned me not to have the class. She asked me who it was. I hesitated to divulge his identity. Little did she know that the member was present in the office and never spoke up—her own husband!"

In the end, the church collapsed, Bill's family suffered serious problems, and Bill underwent medical and psychological care. While Bill's theology is questionable, far more questionable is a conservative church with a systemic problem of destroying pastors.

Considerations:

1. Is the choice to step back an act of obedience to God?
2. Is your health—both mental and physical—good enough to withstand the severe pressures that will come upon it?
3. Are your family members in full agreement and resolved not to let the unfairness and injustice that will come have an adverse effect upon their relationship within the family or with God?
4. Is there a sufficient power base within the church wanting you to stay?
5. Have you sought the unbiased counsel of mature ministers?
6. Do you have a close mentor to openly share with as you pass through this unbearably hard time?

Step Down: Resign from the Conflict

A final approach to settling systemic problems is to resign. Resignation is not a matter of throwing in the towel, unless you wait too long. It can be a cathartic bombshell when done in the right time and spirit.

Such was the case of Pastor Roger Altworth (not his real name), who used this approach just eight months after arriving at his new church. While a candidate, he was never told of the warring factions within the church. A smooth picture was painted, with assurances that the church wanted to grow under his leadership. But he soon found that every idea he presented met resistance. Soon the resistance solidified into attacks. Some accused him of thinking they were not a good congregation. Others suggested he only wanted to use them to build a name for himself. Still others said that he was an ingrate, since he wanted his own home, not a parsonage.

He had been there for barely six months before the swirl around him became hot. He met with each group, trying to understand its grievances, hoping to bring healing. The more he tried, however, the more the groups took their loathing for one another out on him. In this way, they didn't have to confront each other.

He had three children in their early teenage years and a working wife. He decided that it was unfair to put the added stress on them. Further, he was sure that, because the factions were not responding to God's Word, it was useless to hope for repentance and reconciliation. So, on the eighth month he resigned. In his resignation letter he wrote:

> When I accepted the call to be your pastor, I did so in the good faith that what was expressed to me by the board was true—that this is a loving congregation in need of a pastor who would lead you in church growth. But I have discovered that this is not so. There are factions that have existed long before I came, with resentments making progress impossible.
>
> At first I didn't understand why I was met with such intense criticisms every time I presented an idea. Now, I have come to realize that, rather than confronting the sins that you have committed against each other, you prefer to create the illusion that the pastor is your problem.
>
> If I remain any longer, you will believe that you are right. You'll spend all your time trying to resist me, while I spend all my time trying to convince you. That would be futile.
>
> Rather than waiting for such hardening of heart and covering up of issues, I am removing myself from the picture by resigning. You will be left to yourselves, forced to determine whether you want to deal with the real problems that exist or continue in denial. But denial of cancer never produces the surgery necessary to save a life. Likewise, to remain and let you deny your cancer would be to deny you the chance for life.
>
> I am submitting in writing the issues that must be addressed and settled for such surgery to take place. You can choose to throw

it away or undergo the difficult process of facing your real problems head on. If you don't, then you will eventually die as a congregation. If you do, then you may be ready to let a pastor lead you in spiritual and numerical growth.

With that, he was gone.
Considerations:

1. If you resign too soon, you may not be in the position to give the church an accurate picture of its problem.
2. If you resign too late, then you will be viewed as the problem. Your resignation will not carry a positive impact at that point.
3. There is no room for a caustic approach, only a clear, unimpassioned statement of the facts.

I cannot advise which of the six approaches to use in a firestorm. They are presented for your prayerful consideration. Regardless of your choice, however, remember to guard your heart (Prov. 4:23). Keep in mind the attitude we discussed at the beginning of this chapter, and decide what kind of a person you want to be after the conflict. This determines more than anything else whether you win or lose.

Now let's address the role of church members. What can they do in the face of a firestorm? Because this book is designed primarily to address the needs of church leaders, I would encourage you to find a way to communicate the next chapter to your entire congregation.

14 How Followers Can Lead

Actions the Church Can Take

> Whoever wants to become great among you must be your servant, and whoever wants to be first must be your slave —just as the Son of Man did not come to be served, but to serve.
>
> Matthew 20:26–28

If you're a church member who is not in a leadership position, yet you're reading this book to find resolution for conflict within your church, you're to be greatly commended. I know it's frustrating to watch your church family unravel, especially when you feel powerless to stop it. But God has established ways for you to be effective amid the crisis, perhaps even more so than those in leadership positions. At the least, you can be the kind of person desperately needed in a firestorm.

Power and Position

Leadership is not a position so much as a power. Many people have the position of leadership, but not the power. In contrast, it's often true that those lacking the position of leadership still have the power to lead. I am referring to an inner power of spirit that inspires respect—an unspoken authority to lead people's thoughts and feelings. Others instinctively sense you are someone whose opinion bears a divine stamp of approval.

Robert Greenleaf, a management researcher and consultant, titled a book he wrote *Servant Leadership*. Greenleaf writes:

> In this story we see a band of men on a mythical journey . . . .
> The central figure of the story is Leo, who accompanies the party as the *servant* who does their menial chores, but who also sustains them with his spirit and his song. He is a person of extraordinary presence. All goes well until Leo disappears. Then the group falls into disarray and the journey is abandoned. They cannot make it without the servant Leo. The narrator, one of the party, after some years of wandering finds Leo and is taken into the Order that had sponsored the journey. There he discovers that Leo, whom he had known first as *servant*, was in fact the titular head of the Order, its guiding spirit, a great and noble *leader*.[4]

It's that strength to which I refer. It's not an inborn ability but one given by the Holy Spirit and can be had by anyone. I fully understand that servant leadership is a technical term Greenleaf placed upon a style of leadership, but we have every right to claim the term and concept for the lifestyle of the average believer, because Jesus originated the concept for every disciple.

The Power of the Towel

What is the ultimate thing dividing your church? It is the lack of a servant's heart! And a servant's heart is the divine requirement for gaining the *power* of leadership. If people were resolved to serve one another, no issue could divide the household. On the other hand, the degree to which each person tenaciously holds his or her own opinion as divine is the extent to which your church will be debilitated.

The divisive issue merely provides an opportunity for the god of self to reign. This god's means of expression is opinion. The stronger the god, the more unyielding the opinion, thus the more intense the division. The god of self is not concerned with truth—only with one's *perception* of truth, which leads to the perversion of justice. No church can survive this.

The god of self first took the throne of the human heart in the Garden, when Adam and Eve believed the satanic lie about self-deification (Gen. 3:1–6). Divine greatness is the deepest desire of the god of self. This lies behind arrogant, self-willed domination—all of which keeps conflict alive.

The deception is that if there is surrender to one's position, then agreement and peace will reign. Not so. There is never agreement and peace when the god of self in one person is forced to surrender to the god of self in another.

Jesus addressed the desire for greatness with one word—"serve" (Matt. 20:26–28). Grab a towel, get on your knees, and serve. It's that simple . . . or is it? He meant that you must serve everyone, including your enemies—those who spitefully use you, those hotly opposed to you.

Everything inside of you recoils against that, I know. I respond that way, too. We know Jesus is right, but still it sounds unrealistic. After all, your enemy will only get his way, and you will lose. You'll appear weak and indecisive, giving victory to the wrong people. Further, the people have become downright obnoxious, unfair, and demanding. You just don't feel like serving them.

So you're tempted to rush back to the familiar way of handling problems—stand up to them, speak your mind, and try to get them to back down. While there is a time to stand firm in truth, it must be done in love, on your knees with a towel, or it's no more than the god of self confronting another god of self. Herein, you are as pitifully weak as your finite opponent.

In contrast, the sword has never defeated the towel, since true servants are ultimately empowered by God to lead. Throughout history, warring armies met sword with sword. Many of the strong, who fought so valiantly on the battlefield, lay dead, while servants were welcomed at the king's throne.

The servant with a towel often, like Joseph and Daniel, serves in undesirable places. Both were in foreign countries, serving pagan kings. The key is that they were serving, not striving. As a result, they were given opportunities extending beyond the role of attending to that of advising. Their insights literally guided the course of those kings, those nations and, ultimately, world history. In this way, the position of servant can become the most powerful form of leadership.

Unsung Heroes on Display

Read through the pages of biblical history and you'll find a breathtaking display of people who led as servants. Their stories are tucked between the lines of more famous biographies. Yet, in divine economy, some may hold greater reward than the famed people they served.

I think first of Moses' father-in-law Jethro (Exod. 18:13–27). He released Moses from tending sheep to go to Egypt, which also meant the loss of his daughter Zipporah and his two grandsons. When Moses deemed it wise to send his family home, Jethro undertook Moses' responsibility for them. Then he brought them to the desert to visit Moses without the slightest complaint about the inconvenience. Thus the father-in-law, who bore the servant's heart, was in a position to advise Moses about judging Israel. This single piece of advice may have saved Moses' life and ensured his leadership from the Nile to the edge of the Promised Land.

Turning the pages of history forward, there is Abigail, the beautiful woman whose servant's heart won her the right to guide David to the throne without needless bloodshed on his hands (1 Samuel 25). This resulted in her becoming David's wife. While her further effect upon David slipped from the history books into obscurity, one wonders how many other righteous decisions she influenced David to make.

In contrast, we know little of Bathsheba, other than the fact that she was beautiful (2 Sam. 11:2), unfaithful (2 Sam. 11:4), demanding of David (1 Kings 1), and in need of abundant grace—since only grace would establish her as a foremother of Jesus Christ. It is her husband Uriah who emerged in this situation as the servant who led the way of righteousness, showing moral superiority to King David himself. Uriah refused to have sexual union with his wife while Israel was in a time of war (2 Sam. 11:8–13). I have no doubt that after Uriah's martyrdom by David's command, his righteousness preached to David's soul. As a result, who can know how many historical events Uriah influenced from the grave.

Let's turn past many historical chapters and land on the pages ascribed to Priscilla, Aquila, and Apollos (Acts 18:24–28). There we find Apollos, highly educated and brilliant, being helped by a lay couple in the church. How easily they could have been threatened by his stature. They could have become critical of him for not knowing the way beyond the baptism of John. Instead, clothed in humility, they invited Apollos to their home to teach him the more perfect way. How could two people, who were less educated than Apollos, have the right to instruct him? It resulted from their servant spirits.

Servants are welcomed in any place. Servants who motivate others to succeed while resisting the urge to project themselves onto the silver screen are in great demand.

Preparation for Servant Leadership

Robert Greenleaf's book *Servant Leadership* carries this interesting subtitle: "A Journey Into the Nature of Legitimate Power and Greatness." Look at those well-chosen words: legitimate power and greatness. Only those whose towels demonstrate their servant's heart have legitimate power. All other power is temporary and ultimately proves to be weakness. A servant's heart is a belief . . . a disposition . . . a mind-set—in essence, obedience to God.

How did the people in the stories we have looked at become servant leaders? It is something that runs far deeper than their personalities. The person who has the authority to say the right thing at the right moment and in a proper spirit did not start his preparation the night before. As I once heard someone say, "Character is the product of a lifetime and not an instant gift."

The Bible doesn't give us the biographies of Jethro, Abigail, Uriah, Priscilla, and Aquila. Eternity undoubtedly will reveal that these people had undergone more rigid preparation than the public figures they empowered. Such people often show greater signs of wisdom, strength, and morality than their leaders.

They do not gain their positions through self-effort or desire but through divinely bestowed authority—which is the only legitimate authority. When God bestows the *position* (the right of authority) and the *practice* (the ability to exercise authority), nothing can stop the sea from opening, the giant from falling, the walls from collapsing, the armies from dispersing, or the mountains from moving into the sea.

This kind of legitimate authority can be neither withheld nor bestowed by man—nor can it be resisted. It literally moves heaven against hell, drives the church victoriously through the gates of hell, and lifts people out of hopeless situations. Anyone can qualify for it: the pastor, board members, or *you*. All you need is to give yourself over to the long, hard process required—death to self so that Christ, the great towel bearer, can be formed in you.

This is the only way in which you can truly serve the crisis in your church. Consider the life and impact of the One who demonstrated that greatness is found only when a person is on one's knees with a towel. In the time of Christ, there were serious political corruption, social unfairness, moral degradation, and pharisaical religion. Yet, he was not found shouting protest slogans, parading before the emperor's palace, calling for militant action, or trying to splinter Judaism. He spoke truth in love to the secular and sacred arenas, then got on his knees with a towel.

What was the result? This One who had no position had *power*— both the right of authority and the right to exercise it with results. He commanded demons, equipped disciples, defeated sin and death, and turned the course of eternal history. This is the One who said, "Follow me!"

Broken Boldness

What is it that must be formed within you in order to be clothed with this legitimate authority and power? Broken boldness: broken of all self-rule and bold in the Holy Spirit. But how is that achieved?

The answer is first seen in the life of Christ. He was highly exalted by God as a result of his willingness to obey his Father all the way to the cross. Consider Philippians 2:8–11: "And being found in appearance as a man, he humbled himself and became obedient to death— even death on a cross! Therefore God exalted him to the highest place and gave him the name that is above every name, that at the name of Jesus every knee should bow, in heaven and on earth and under the earth, and every tongue confess that Jesus Christ is Lord, to the glory of God the Father."

In my study at home hangs a plaque that states, "No Cross, No Crown." Jesus Christ was made fit for his reign in authority by what he suffered. Hebrews 5:8 reads, "Although he was a son, he learned obedience from what he suffered and, once made perfect, he became the source of eternal salvation for all who obey him."

No one welcomes suffering, yet all treasure its fruit. As it prepared Jesus for his work as the Savior and his eternal reign, so it has a vital role in your life. Part of that is to equip you in broken boldness. It is only out of broken boldness that you can have any effective service—the kind that has lasting value.

Let Moses illustrate what is meant by broken boldness. When God called Moses at the burning bush (Exodus 3), he revealed a keen awareness of his incapability to fulfill the task of taking Israel out of Egypt. Was this humility? Yes. But humility is nothing more than a clear-eyed assessment and acceptance of reality.

Perhaps if God had called Moses while he was an important man in Egypt, he would have complimented God for calling the right man. After all, he was educated, strong, and in the good graces of the authorities. When God called him forty years later, all of that was gone. With the illusions of power and importance removed, Moses, in verse 11, presents to God the picture of reality: "Who am I, that I should go to Pharaoh and bring the Israelites out of Egypt?" That's brokenness. God replies, "I will be with you" (verse 12). That's the basis for Moses' boldness.

In verse 13 Moses responds a second time in brokenness, "Suppose I go to the Israelites . . . and they ask me, 'What is his name?' Then what shall I tell them?" In verse 14 God gives him the basis for divine boldness with these words, "I AM WHO I AM. This is what you are to say to the Israelites: 'I AM has sent me to you.'"

Again Moses demonstrates the depth to which he is broken of improper self-confidence when he says, "What if they do not believe me or listen to me and say, 'The LORD did not appear to you'?" (Exod. 4:1). God demonstrates the boldness of authority he was bestowing upon Moses by the rod that turned into a serpent then back into a rod.

Moses is not suffering from a poor self-image when he pursues God a fourth time with one more reason why he feels he is not the right person for the task. He says, "O Lord, I have never been eloquent, neither in the past nor since you have spoken to your servant. I am slow of speech and tongue" (Exod. 4:10). God draws him into the only place of valid boldness, and that is the strength of the Lord, when he replies in the next two verses, "Who gave man his mouth? Who makes him deaf or mute? Who gives him sight or makes him blind? Is it not I, the LORD? Now go; I will help you speak and will teach you what to say."

Moses is presenting reality to God, a reality he may have arrogantly denied forty years earlier. God did not call Moses because he was capable. It was because Moses was broken (accepted reality) that God could entrust him with divine authority to do the impossible.

And so it is with you who want to be used by God to lead your church out of a firestorm. You may be feeling insecure, still uncomfortable to think that God may be addressing you through the burning bush of this chapter, so let me help put you at ease. Boldness is not arrogance. It is moving with surety, not in yourself, but in God. For instance, no one can stand before God in arrogance, but we are invited to come in confidence (Heb. 10:19). This boldness is not based upon something within you but, instead, upon the work Christ did in your behalf.

To this day, Moses is recognized in Israel as the greatest leader of all time. That is because he never outgrew his brokenness, which in turn fitted him for divine boldness and authority.

So, back to you. Your church is in desperate straits, and you want to be used in working out a solution. What has been presented in this chapter is by far the most effective way you can accomplish something—become great by getting on your knees with a towel. Thereby, God may grant to you the opportunity to strengthen and guide the leaders of your church. Like Leo in Greenleaf's story, you gain the authority to empower by truly being a servant. That's leadership.

Now, let's see how to defeat Satan in your firestorm.

15 STOPPING THE HOT WIND FROM HELL

Confession and repentance: no one will ever come up with a better formula for dealing with the devil.

I hope your convictions about a real devil battling against the church were confirmed as you read chapter 10, "Fire from the Abyss." Admittedly, dealing with Satan is secondary to the problems you face, because human responsibility is always the primary consideration. Still, you'll face additional setbacks if you treat the power of Satan as merely the dark side of human nature.

Satan is rarely responsible for the issues that create conflict, although he does occasionally plot schemes. He is better viewed in most firestorms as a hot wind blowing upon the fires started by people, thereby spreading the damage as far as possible. Stopping Satan is like removing the wind from a firestorm. You're still left with the debris of human issues but will suffer far less destruction.

The good news is that Satan can be stopped. He is not a free agent assaulting the church at will. But there are conditions you must fulfill. First you must realize that Satan cannot be expelled while people are in agreement with him—either willfully or ignorantly. Let's consider that in the following true story.

Pastor Vince Warrington (not his real name) is a brilliant, godly minister who had a troublemaker expelled from the church on solid, biblical grounds. In return, she resolved to destroy him. Every week she held signs as she stood along the busy highway that passed by his church. She twisted statements from his sermons and included derogatory remarks. She was so determined in her evil rage that on one occasion, when Vince was a guest speaker at a church in England, she led a small following of people across the ocean in order to sit in the front pew to harass him.

Her campaign flowed undiminished from days into years. One Sunday, when Vince was feeling exasperated and imprisoned, he inadvertently aided Satan's opportunity to fan the fire in her heart. As she sat in her car near the church, he leaned in the window and said, "I rebuke you, Satan, in the name of the Lord Jesus Christ." He hoped to expel the evil force and set her free. But, since she was not seeking deliverance from Satan, it backfired. Because she was in agreement with the evil, Satan did not have to surrender his grip. As a result, she increased her mockery of Vince.

When a person is in agreement with Satan (whether consciously or not), you may be able to drive Satan away but only temporarily. Their agreement acts as a revolving door, allowing Satan to reenter at will. Sinful attitudes form handles on the soul for Satan to grasp.

Handles on the Soul

Remember, firestorms are generally started by people, then fanned by a hot wind from hell. Misbehavior puts conflict into motion, on which Satan hitchhikes to bring greater damage than people intend. James 3:6 shows the union between people and Satan: "The tongue also is a fire, a world of evil among the parts of the body. It corrupts the whole person, sets the whole course of his life on fire, *and is itself set on fire by hell*" (emphasis added).

In this passage we clearly see the way in which sin is enhanced by Satan himself. It is important to note that this teaching is given to believers. Indeed, Christians can come under Satan's power by allowing sinful attitudes in their hearts.

The collaboration of Satan with people is best explained by Puritan minister John Flavel (1628–1691). This highly educated and deeply spiritual pastor from Devon, England, was greatly esteemed by Jonathan Edwards and George Whitefield. Whitefield ranked him with John Bunyan and Matthew Henry. Out of this seedbed of intelligence and piety he wrote:

"But now we have an enemy within that holds intelligence with Satan without; and this would prove a devil to us, if there were no other devil to tempt us, James 1:14,15. It is a fountain of temptation in itself, Matthew 15:19; and the chief instrument by which Satan doth all his tempting work, 2 Peter 1:4.

"Our several passions and affections are the handles of his temptations. Every thing, saith Epictetus, hath duo labas, two handles to take it by. *Our affections are the handles of our souls. These inbred lusts go over to the enemy in the day of battle, and fight against the soul,* 1 Peter 2:11" (emphasis added).[5]

Simply put, whenever a Christian sins in the flesh, handles form on the soul for Satan to grasp. When people become embroiled in angry conflict, Satan lays hold of those handles to bring fire from the abyss into the crisis. Reason dissolves as intense emotion exceeds the issues at hand.

Perhaps this idea of handles on the soul was referenced by Jesus when he said, "I will not speak with you much longer, for the prince of this world is coming. He has no hold on me" (John 14:30). There was obviously no inner agreement between Jesus and Satan; no fleshly handles for Satan to grasp. This rendered Satan powerless to encourage evil in Jesus. Obviously, then, the fastest way to break Satan's power in anyone's life is to knock the handles off the soul. We'll see how to do that in a moment.

First, however, you must identify the handles found on souls. Look at the list of sins revealed in Galatians 5:19–21: sexual immorality, impurity, debauchery, idolatry (including self-love), witchcraft, hatred, discord, jealousy, fits of rage, selfish ambition, dissensions, factions, envy, drunkenness, orgies.

Somewhere in this ugly list you'll find the evil motivations that provide handles for the devil. People's reasons for causing conflict may differ, but motivations remain the same. A firestorm begins in the heart, then gets fanned across a congregation by Satan. The tough but essential job is getting people to recognize the areas in which they are giving Satan opportunity.

Revealing the Handles

I know of only two effective ways to build such recognition. One is to preach God's Word while asking the Holy Spirit to convict people of their sins. When this fails, the next step is direct confrontation of individuals. There is no clearer illustration of how to handle this than the account of Peter confronting Ananias and Sapphira (Acts 5:1–11). Let's analyze the story.

The first critical observation is that Peter was correct in his assessment of the couple's sin. It's all too easy to assume that someone who intensely disagrees with you is either dead wrong at best, or demon possessed at worst. Be sure that the person is clearly sinning before God and not merely engaging in valid disagreement. What's the difference? Valid disagreement is negotiable. People resolve issues, even at personal loss, for the sake of Christ. But those who have given themselves over to an evil-based disagreement hold forth rigid ultimatums. Saving face is more important than God's glory. It is critical that you fast and pray until God reveals motives.

The church is the dwelling place of God the Holy Spirit on earth. As you fast and pray, the God who revealed the mystery of Nebuchadnezzar's dream to Daniel is also able to reveal the hidden motivation of your firestorm.

The next thing to note is that the evil which Peter revealed may not appear too bad in human terms. Ananias and Sapphira simply wanted to puff their spiritual image—to appear more holy than they were—by claiming to give all the money made on their property's sale. So it wasn't an issue of stealing, but one of lying. They gave only a portion, claiming they gave it all. That doesn't seem too bad to the natural mind, does it? Yet, it was an agreement in attitude and action with Satan, who is known to be a liar from the beginning (John 8:44). Peter saw the connection and said, "How is it that Satan has so filled your heart that you have lied to the Holy Spirit and have kept for yourself some of the money?" (Acts 5:3). Likewise, you must treat sin, even the seemingly small sin, as a surrender to Satan.

Peter exposed the union that formed between Ananias, Sapphira, and Satan. You will also be forced on occasion to expose this in some people in your church. Such bonding between Satan and people is a fact of life. It can happen to you or me, as well as your congregants. When people are driven by sinful interests, Satan quickly grasps the handles on their souls. As a spiritual leader, you must confront them as did Peter: "How is it that Satan has so filled your heart?"

Peter's statement shows surprise. It could be paraphrased this way: "How is it possible that you, a believer who has received God's gift of grace and the indwelling Holy Spirit, have allowed Satan to fill your heart with his malignant desires?"

Above all, you must follow Peter's example and guard against compromise. He saw that the issue wasn't the money but the lie. Peter did not let the lie slide by while reasoning that at least the church had gotten some of the money. Every compromise with sin for present gain leads to greater loss. I think, for instance, of the pastor who was wrongfully undermined by a man who had given the land upon which the church was built. A previous pastor had not checked the man's motives, thus setting the stage for the demise of pastors to follow. Working to destroy the present pastor, the man pounded his fist on a table declaring, "I am an elder, and I gave this land to the church. Therefore, I have more authority." He might have been a dead man if Peter had been there. It's less painful to stand against sinful motives now than to face the consequences of compromise later.

Also notice that it was not Peter who brought death upon the couple. He simply exposed the evil intention. God brought the death. It's most important for you to handle the great power of the Holy Spirit with deep humility and not with boastful threats. You're a minister of grace. Leave the painful judgments to God. It's vital to see, however, that it is your place to confront with truth. If real motives are not addressed, you will leave people vulnerable to satanic control, which opens your church to hopeless destruction.

Breaking Off Handles from the Soul

The fastest, most powerful way to stop Satan from destroying your church is to knock the handles off the soul. This is primarily done through confession and repentance of sin (1 John 1:9).

But, you wonder, how can you make it work? How can you get people to recognize their sin, confess it, and repent of it? How can you dare to suggest they are in agreement with Satan and not get clobbered? You can't. But the Holy Spirit can. He is the Spirit of Truth (John 14:17). It is his work to reveal truth to you. It is your job to lovingly confront with truth. Then it falls back to the Holy Spirit to faithfully convict the transgressor.

Ah . . . confrontation, that's the stopper. You hear all kinds of fears in your heart—voices telling you that you are a sinner, too, so who are you to confront another? Well, the difference is this: You are, one hopes, repentant and walking obediently in God's mercy and grace. On the other hand, the person you must confront is living in disobedience and must be confronted with truth. Agreement with Satan invites the serpent to sink deadly fangs into one's soul. It is for the sake of the erring one that you reveal sinful motives.

Once sin is exposed, fling your most powerful, double-barreled weapon at Satan—confession and repentance! Do not underestimate its force. It wins God's heart and breaks Satan's grip. Nothing else will. You cannot command Satan to permanently release someone who has handles on the soul. On the other hand, Satan cannot hold onto a person once the handles are removed. No one will ever come up with a better formula for dealing with the devil. This is the deepest level of separation between man's heart and Satan's will.

Look at the forthrightness with which the apostles employed confrontation, confession, and repentance in the case of Simon the sorcerer. He wanted to purchase the power that would give the Holy Spirit to people by the laying on of hands. Peter firmly rebuked him with these words, "May your money perish with you, because you thought you could buy the gift of God with money! You have no part or share in this ministry, because your heart is not right before God. Repent of this wickedness and pray to the Lord. Perhaps he will forgive you for having such a thought in your heart. For I see that you are full of bitterness and captive to sin" (Acts 8:20–23).

Envision you and your board speaking that way to troublemakers in the church. Like Simon, they may appear to want something good. What could sound more spiritual than wanting to impart the Holy Spirit? The apostles weren't duped; they saw the sinful motivation. Can you imagine the handles Satan could have grasped for tearing the church to shreds through Simon? Instead, they told him there was only one way out of this mess—repent!

Consider the impact of Daniel's confession and repentance for the sins of Israel. This is particularly important because he had not committed the sins. Israel was several decades into her Babylonian captivity. Daniel read in the book of Jeremiah that God would set Israel free in seventy years. In Daniel chapter 9, he tells of his deep fasting, confession, and repentance before God. He did this knowing full well that the answer could not come for decades, yet it was his intercession that broke God's people free from bondage.

By now you may have already seen that the key to dealing with Satan is to *deal with God*. God sets all the terms, not Satan. God breaks the handles of sin off the soul when sin is confronted and confessed. He does this by forgiveness based upon Jesus Christ's blood sacrifice for sin. Herein, he cleanses. This is how Satan's power is broken—not by us, but by God.

This is the experience of Becky Coronell (not her real name), who is an active member of an evangelical church. She had been through a traumatic divorce. Now remarried, she is raising one child from her former marriage and one fathered by Stuart, her present husband. Life is neatly packaged and seemingly secure.

While Becky sits at work, her phone rings. It's Stuart. He tells her that he won't be home tonight. "Where's he going? Does he have unexpected business?" she wonders. He explains that he is moving in with another woman, whom he believes he loves. He assures her it's not her fault, then hangs up. Becky fumbles to put the phone on the receiver. She breathes but feels no life. This is totally unexpected—completely out of character for her husband of twelve years to act this way. She searches her memory for clues to what went wrong. Surely she'd recall a word or action that should have tipped her off to Stuart's unhappiness.

Her church recently studied spiritual warfare. Becky talks to her pastor to see if he thinks this could be a satanic attack. He affirms that it could be. He says, "I hope it is, since a satanic attack can be stopped easier than mere human disobedience."

With thunderbolt force, Becky throws herself into prayer against Satan and on behalf of her husband. She repents of every sin she can think of. She calls prayer chains and fearlessly asks the entire church to pray. She feels abandoned, yet fights on in every spiritual way she knows to save her marriage.

Telephone conversations with Stuart reveal a man torn by sorrow for hurting her and the children but fully determined not to return home. Three months pass like an eternity in hell. Becky begins to look gaunt. Death is preferable to this pain.

One day the pastor calls her at work.

"Becky, I've been thinking about something. I know that you want to try every proper avenue to save your marriage. If this is a satanic assault, it will be essential to find out why Satan has been able to override the spiritual authority of your home."

"Pastor, I've done what you said. I've searched my heart and confessed every sin I can recall. I think I've confessed some sins I never even thought of doing. What else can I do?"

"Well, Becky, I'm hesitant to mention this, lest it sound self-serving. But knowing your marriage is on the line, I'm going to tell you one area that may have given Satan such opportunity."

"Oh, please do."

"You know that your husband's family has been critical of me without cause. Your brother-in-law has said some harmful things that have damaged my ministry."

"Oh, I know, Pastor. I've been in situations where they have torn you down in terrible ways."

"Now, Becky, you and your family are in need of divine authority to deal with Stuart. It may be that God's authority will not come until they repent of their behavior. I do not have hurt feelings, so they do not need to apologize to me, but I do think they need to deal with God in this matter."

Becky takes the message to her husband's family members. They acknowledge their wrongful attitudes and actions. They have a time of prayerful confession. It is not long before Stuart shows signs of wanting to repent and return to Becky. This story has an ending fitting of God's glory: Today, Stuart and Becky are happily reunited, raising their family and serving effectively in their church.

This story underscores the fact that God has promised to give his limitless power to those who confess, repent, and seek him with all their hearts. Stuart's family broke the handles of sin that gave Satan advantage against them, and God worked their deliverance. Not every situation may end as Becky's, but every person who turns to God wholeheartedly will see him work a grand deliverance from Satan. While this story is about a family, it works the same for church conflict as well.

Areas of Confession and Repentance

It is important to examine every possible area to determine if you have broken off all the handles. Some handles may be fastened to areas long forgotten. A lucid passage that deals with how the past affects the present is Daniel 9. Following are areas to consider.

Is there some ancestral sin that needs to be confessed?

1. If the church has a history of injuring pastors, it may need to offer a proper apology, even reparation to the injured parties.
2. Check to see if anything was done by improper means, such as finding water through a diviner.
3. The church at present may need to repent for a schism that took place years earlier. Even if most of the people are not present in the church today, it still could give Satan handles for harassing the church.
4. Look for a root of bitterness (Heb. 12:15). Such a root in a small group can defile the entire church.

Is there an area where people are not honoring authority and relating to each other in the fruit of the Spirit? Paul wrote to Titus, "Remind the people to be subject to rulers and authorities, to be obedient, to be ready to do whatever is good, to slander no one, to be peaceable and considerate, and to show true humility toward all men" (Titus 3:1–2).

As stated earlier, any problem can be settled provided there is a right spirit. Conversely, no problem can be settled if the spirit is wrong. Do not try to settle issues when spirits are not right, otherwise you'll risk handing the situation over to Satan. On one occasion Dr. Henry Brandt, an author, counselor, and consulting psychologist, was asked to mediate a problem confronting the board of a Christian organization. The people began expressing their divisions with their jaws set in anger. Brandt stopped the meeting and told the people to go home, confess their attitudinal sins, and repent. He said, "When your spirits are right, we will settle the problem." They did as he said and were spared a great calamity.

God does nothing outside of the fruit of the Spirit. If the fruit of the Spirit is sufficient for every problem God deals with, it is all you need. It is futile, even dangerous, to attempt God's work in any other manner. The reverse of the fruit of the Spirit are the works of the flesh. Just as God empowers the fruit of the Spirit, so Satan empowers the works of the flesh.

Is there someone within the church who needs to be disciplined for a sin? It may not seem to be a church issue, but if people are dishonoring the Lord in moral or ethical practices in their personal lives, they could cause trouble in the church. Achan is a prime example. Israel attacked the formidable walls of Jericho and won a great victory, then lost at tiny Ai. Why? Because one man had sinned against the Lord.

You may be disappointed that I didn't offer some clever thing you can say to drive the devil away. Yes, I do believe in the proper exercise of our authority in Christ. At Myerstown Grace Brethren Church, I employed everything I knew about resisting Satan. One Saturday night, when Satan's resolve to destroy the church seemed exceedingly close, I walked through the pews, the choir loft, and every possible nook and cranny, letting Satan know that I was there to hold that turf in Jesus' name, and that he had to surrender the church to Christ.

I have chosen not to go into more detail here about spiritual warfare, however, for two reasons. First, superb books already are available on that topic (see *Spiritual Warfare* in "Recommended Resources"). Second, the principles in this chapter reach to the deepest levels of breaking Satan's grip and involve bringing people to the point of taking responsibility before God for their improper attitudes and actions. Deal first with God and man, then deal with the devil. Often you will not have to deal directly with Satan once the handles have been broken. He must surrender.

It's time to turn our attention to one of the strongest provisions God has made for you to use when facing conflict—the firestorm consultant.

16

FIRESTORM CONSULTANTS

> Neither the pastor nor the church board can act as their own management consultants.
>
> Dr. Ed Peirce, conflict management consultant

No one is more concerned about you and your church than God. After all, it's his Son's bride that is being mugged, and you are part of that bride. God has provided you with many ways to fight firestorms, some of which we have already discussed. Now we come to a vital and wonderful one—the firestorm consultant.

We sometimes view consultants as people who should get a real job and stop charging big fees to tell people what they already know. That may be true in isolated cases, but industry has learned that less money is spent for a greater dollar return by hiring consultants than by slugging it out alone. It's time for the church to use people who have developed ministerial and leadership skills uniquely designed for churches in conflict.

Here's the best news. The magnificent team God is raising up is far more than a management team trying out some new sociopsychology on your church. These are godly people, many of them ministers who went through great conflict and are alive to tell about it. They learned from many sources: books on conflict, seminars, personal experience and, most important, the Holy Spirit. Just as God has equipped you for your ministry, so he has given some consultants unique sensitivities and insights that are just what your situation may require.

Time and again you've heard people say of physical pain, "It'll pass." When they finally go to a doctor, they hear the sad words, "If only you had come sooner." Frankly, it's all too common for church leadership to wait until the problem is too far gone before inviting outside help. As indicated in part 1, the sooner you get help the better. Preventative help is always preferable to restorative help.

I'll tell you right up front what I hope to accomplish in the next few pages. I hope to dash on the rocks the idea that only a wimp needs help, while tough people forge ahead alone. The most gallant mountain climbers take guides. The greatest leaders surround themselves with the best counsel. Gold-medal athletes never outdistance the need of a coach. The most successful enterprises have a circle of consultants. So why is it, then, that ministers tend to act as though they are the consummate whole of the body of Christ, needing no other gift to supplement theirs? That's vanity leading to futility. I hope that by the end of this chapter your hand is already on the phone to call a new friend into your life—a firestorm consultant.

The Body Fitly Framed

God has ordained that his Son's body should gain strength through the interdependence of its parts. But it's common to enjoy serving from a position of strength while despising weakness. Within leaders there is powerful resistance to the thought of needing someone to do something they cannot do themselves. The resistance stems from a number of common insecurities of leaders:

- Fear that they may appear imperfect.
- Feeling that their leadership will be threatened.
- Terror over being out of control.
- Doubt over not having all the answers.

The great tragedy is that by submitting to these insecurities, you will limit the help God would send to you and your congregation. If your concern is for the well-being of God's people, and you're willing to go to any measure to see them come into the strength of unity (Eph. 4:1–16), then there is a limitless supply of divine assistance at your disposal. Admittedly, it can seem threatening to trust your ministry to another for a period of time, but that's a divine requirement. The body must be fitly framed together.

Why is interdependence so important to God? Because it was Satan who fallaciously promised in the Garden that Adam and Eve could be as God—independent, self-sufficient, self-determining— and get away with it. That lie rejects the rule of God, especially if it comes through another person.

So, like many in the past, you may be trying to go it alone. Consequently, you're finding yourself isolated in despair, wondering why God isn't sending help. He is—the church conflict consultant.

Ephesians 4:11–13 is clear that the interdependence of the body is vital to God's plan for the church: "It was he who gave some to be apostles, some to be prophets, some to be evangelists, and some to be pastors and teachers, to prepare God's people for works of service, so that the body of Christ may be built up until we all reach unity in the faith and in the knowledge of the Son of God and become mature, attaining to the whole measure of the fullness of Christ." Here we see a team of equals who have received supernatural gifts from Christ for the purpose of strengthening and equipping God's people.

Of this you can be sure, a qualified firestorm consultant would never enter your situation to erode your credibility. Quite the contrary, this person's work is to do all that is possible to strengthen the unity of the body, which includes the security of your place in the fellowship.

Fear not those congregants who may be enamored of the consultant. Some tried that immature behavior with Paul and Apollos. Rather than competing, Paul honored their individual roles. The believers were told not to be so worldly. "What, after all, is Apollos? And what is Paul? Only servants, through whom you came to believe—as the Lord has assigned to each his task" (1 Cor. 3:5).

The Myth of Leadership

There is a myth that hinders church leaders from seeking help, and it's found in the word "leader." The myth is that leaders are obligated to be out in front, providing answers that no one else can find. Here's a truth rarely understood: No one is ever called by God to be a leader, only a follower. And the better that one follows, the better one leads.

Let me illustrate this truth in the light of men who changed the course of world events—even changed the face of eternity. Moses led as a follower. He followed the great I Am out of Egypt, through the desert, and to the Promised Land. Jesus also led as a follower. He said, "Follow me," while clearly stating he was following the will of his father—calling it his bread (John 4:34). Our idea of leadership is so opposite to his that we're uncomfortable thinking of him in this light. Yes, there is a place in leadership for Christ the righteous king, but not before Christ the submitted Son. Jesus led in "followership" by doing the will of God. Paul, too, led as a follower. He invited people to follow him as he was following Christ (1 Thess. 1:6).

The myth that a leader is an answer man, always courageously out in front, creates an impossible burden that God neither intends nor supports. God never called anyone to lead, but to follow—him. Your work is to invite people to follow as *you* follow.

If you cannot humbly submit to the God-given gift of another person, then it's evident you're not a follower. This will erode and disqualify your authority as a leader. Why? Because an unsubmissive attitude says, "I like people needing *my* strength, but I don't like needing someone else's strength." This is arrogance, not leadership.

The key to leadership in the spiritual realm, then, is good "followership." Humility that follows to the cross always experiences the resurrection power of God (James 4:5–6). And there is no truer test of your growth in this area than the degree to which you work in interdependence with the entire body of Christ.

Dr. Ed Peirce, a conflict management consultant, makes the statement, "A pastor cannot be his own management consultant." Indeed, a pastor may be able to help two people through a dispute in his congregation. Or, if properly trained, he may be able to assist another pastor and church. But rarely can a pastor lead his own church out of major conflict for reasons discussed at length in the opening chapters.

Let's look at some practical things you'll want to know—even ask—of your consultant.

Whom to Look For

Your consultant *must* be more than an industrially trained conflict management expert. There are fine principles to be learned from such people, but the church is unique. It has:

- Certain theological understandings (such as the gospel).
- A particular view of the nature of man (the old and new natures).
- A spiritual foundation for brotherhood (a love focused on Christ).
- Biblical motivational interests (such as the glory of God).
- Satanic pressures unlike anything known to the world.

No one is qualified to deal with church problems other than one who is born of God's Spirit (John 3), deeply advanced in the Scriptures (both in knowledge and personal maturity), and well-trained in assisting groups in crisis. This person may be provided by a denomination or a Christian consultant service.

When searching for a consultant, it is wise to find one who is theologically compatible with your church. The conflict has your church in a state of suspicion and fear. A consultant who cannot give heartfelt assurance that he is "one of you" in the cardinal doctrines of the faith will add to the insecurity.

What to Expect of a Consultant

1. *The consultant must maintain neutrality.* A true consultant will not come into the situation to fight for one side. He maintains a neutral position to carefully reunite people in spirit and in truth—if that proves to be possible. People will want him to validate their positions in the conflict. The fact that he has no vested interest, other than to bring people to honor God with resolution, puts him in a strong position to transcend that pressure and bring the necessary help.

2. *He must work toward a pre-set time of termination.* This helps insure

   - that he develops no vested interest in securing a long-term position,
   - that he makes judgments and decisions geared for the church's benefit, and
   - that people do not transfer loyalty improperly to him.

3. *He will provide the church with clearly defined steps and procedures.* There should be no mystery in what he is doing. Everyone involved will know the *why* and *what* of his work. This does not mean that he will divulge privileged information shared by parties. It does mean, however, that all will know why he is meeting with people and what he hopes to accomplish. This will help assuage mounting fears among the people involved.

4. *The consultant must maintain strict confidentiality.* He will not report his private conversations, just as a pastor would not disclose counseling information. Further, he will not speak of the situation to others. He is hired for a given time to assist with a problem that is highly personal to a church. His professional ethic forbids him from sharing his views or stories in other settings.

5. *The consultant will stay in a hotel of his choosing—and definitely not a home.* No one should know where he is staying. Arrangements, therefore, must be made by his office and not the church. The purpose is to keep him in structured situations. He must avoid those who would attempt to arrange unofficial, private meetings.

6. *The leadership of the church will receive a typed report of the consultant's findings, along with his recommendations for resolution.*

7. *The consultant must agree to remove himself from the situation if he finds his judgment has become impaired by personal bias or emotional involvement.*

8. *His order of priorities should be:*

   - To lead the church toward spiritual maturity through the conflict.

- To guide the church in necessary bold action that is redemptive in spirit.
- To empower the local leaders to continue the process of healing after he is gone.

9. *Under no circumstance should he usurp the pastor's leadership.* He works to undergird all church leadership. Again, if wisdom suggests that the pastor depart from the church, the consultant should have nothing to do with filling the position, lest he appears to have a vested interest in the pastor's choice to leave.

Establish Parameters

Decide what kind of authority is necessary to entrust to your consultant. Following are roles he may assume.

Passive Mediator: He does no more than sit down with parties in conflict (individually and collectively) to attempt to bring about a settlement.

Passive Advisor: The consultant moderates over decision-making but can enforce no decisions. In other words, he is hired to give you advice but not make decisions. This may include organizational as well as interpersonal advice (i.e., how to handle a certain person, or advising that someone be terminated from a job). This is preferable, provided the parties are not at an impasse. If emotions are too intense, you will be wise to entrust your consultant with the added authority of the next role.

Binding Arbitrator: The consultant is empowered by mutual agreement to make certain decisions that each party agrees to honor. This may be the only way to save the church.

This is not an action to fear. Consultants are not on location to condone, condemn, or coerce, but to help the entire church return to a state of relational health. That may demand strong decision-making regarding:

- Whether the pastor should stay or resign (this is rarely done).
- Whether to dismiss certain staff members (this is rarely done).
- Whether a paradigm shift is necessary.

- Whether to engage in church discipline.
- Whether the conflict can be resolved.
- Whether to close the church.

These are some of the many areas where it may be difficult, even damaging, for the people involved to be decisive. For instance, if a staff member who needs to be dismissed has family members in the church, it is better to have that dismissal occur at the hands of someone neutral who leaves town when the crisis has passed.

Decide the parameters in advance and put them into print, then be faithful to the binding agreement.

No Quick Fix

Do not expect your consultant to bring a sudden solution to your conflict. Rarely do people respond this way, and rarely does God work this way. Firestorms generally result from a long-term buildup of conflict and tension. Human emotions will wonderfully adjust to healing, but not quickly, especially if the feelings are deep and intense.

A consultant cannot give a deadline for when the calamity will stop. He generally can start the recovery process, but it may be years before the fruit of his labors shows forth.

What You Should Pay

Consulting ministries will have widely varied rate structures, making it impossible to give an established fee. Reputable consultants will provide that information upon request. The rate will strongly depend upon the complexity of the problem, the time it will take to begin resolution, and the number of people on the consultant's backup team.

The consultant's fee should be viewed as an investment for two reasons. First, the consultant may spare the church from enormous financial loss. For instance, a church that has an income of one hundred thousand dollars per year will save at least one million dollars over the coming ten years by avoiding disaster. Second, the consultant will work numerous hours beyond what is visible, preparing recommendations and directives. In a real sense, you are hiring a co-minister for a short time. You will get more intensity and quality out of his concentrated effort than if he were on staff for a long time.

A church consultant is more than a professional negotiator using human skills to bring parties together. While he must know and employ every proper skill, he first and foremost must be a man under the guidance of the Holy Spirit. He comes to the church for no purpose other than to help define and establish God's will in the midst of a serious conflict.

Well, are you ready to call a consultant? I hope so. The sooner you do, the better his chances will be of bringing you good assistance. The right consultant will help you to

- avoid a firestorm,
- stop and reverse a firestorm,
- stay true to the gospel,
- fulfill the purpose and task God has entrusted to him, and
- help spare you the loss of fortunes.

Perhaps you have gotten your hands on this book after a firestorm has passed, and now you're thinking, "I wish I had known this back then." Obviously, you cannot put time in reverse, but you can sift through the ashes to find the structures upon which to rebuild. So, let's look at what to do after the storm has passed.

PART 4

OUT OF THE ASHES

The firestorm has passed.
The barrenness of the soul is as haunting as a burnt forest.
Brittle grass crunches as smoke puffs from beneath feet crossing
the burnt landscape.
Trees stand disrobed and blackened, and
life-ending vapor rises from the mute statues that once fanned the
world below.
A distant bird calls, though none can save.
Green foliage is now changed to a mountain of ash.
The landscape is draped in death.
The charred remains of the church summon a grave challenge.
It will demand true mastery of spiritual leadership to bring life out
of the ashes.

17
Assessing the Damage

> It is critical that the church makes an honest assessment of the damage done. God will not bless the church that tries to bring a harvest out of poisoned ground.

There are those who pound their chests and bravely declare, "Conflict is good." I disagree. Either they have never been bloodied by conflict, or they have spent too many weekends at self-motivation seminars becoming adept at denying reality. Indeed, you may find good in overcoming conflict, but conflict itself is not good; it is not a product of the peaceable work of the Holy Spirit. In every church conflict a high price is paid by many: the cause of Christ in a lost world, the pastor, the pastor's spouse and children, the leadership, the congregation. Each must be considered and assessed.

Christ and the Lost World

Christ uses many avenues to reach the nonbeliever, such as his revelations through the written Word and natural creation. The church is also a form of divine revelation in that we are called as ambassadors of Christ and ministers of reconciliation. We make direct appeals on behalf of heaven (2 Corinthians 5). The Scriptures and creation never fail in their revelatory purpose. But when a firestorm engulfs the church, one of heaven's finest revelations goes up in smoke—its witness and appeal to the world destroyed.

Christ's revelation through the church is close to people's personal experience. While people can be confused by the debate between creationism and evolution, they always recognize a true act of love. They may not understand some of what they read in the Bible, but they can clearly see the awesomeness of forgiveness, kindness, and selflessness. Ultimately, *people* impress people more than anything else in life. So when the church is embroiled in conflict, the world loses the revelation of Christ that flows through the believers' lives.

What is the revelation of Christ through the church to be like? Jesus said, "By this all men will know that you are my disciples, if you love one another" (John 13:35). So does that mean merely that believers are nice to each other? No, much more. It means that their commitment to one another is so great that they will die for each other. Jesus said, "My command is this: Love each other as I have loved you. Greater love has no one than this, that he lay down his life for his friends. You are my friends if you do what I command" (John 15:12–14).

A firestorm is the antithesis of what Jesus commanded. It is a violation of Christ's heart and a defamation of his reputation. And when this occurs, the world is without a gospel.

Let Israel serve to illustrate the seriousness of failing the divine command. Israel is God's chosen people. That means responsibility, not privilege. By failing her responsibility, she failed the world. It happened on a specific day. No, it was not when she rejected her Savior and Messiah; that was the day she failed herself. The day Israel failed the world was when she asked for a king (1 Samuel 8). From that day to this, the world has had no example of a theocracy (a nation willingly under God's rule). Had Israel been true to God, the world would have had an undeniable exhibit of God's hand of care upon his people.

The church is not called to be a nation under God, as was Israel, but she is called to be a people under God. Our representation of Christ through loving obedience is the only salt and light the world has. Thus, few things are so dishonorable to Christ or disgraceful before the world as a church in conflict. It's a clear statement that, while Christ may sacrificially love us, we will not love one another. Once again the world is without a witness of the working of God in people's lives.

For several millennia, Israel has paid a terrible price for her disobedience to God. Do you think the church, which enjoys the "better things" of the new covenant will escape the price of disobedience? No, Paul strongly warns in 2 Corinthians 5:10, "For we must all appear before the judgment seat of Christ, that each one may receive what is due him for the things done while in the body, whether good or bad."

Think about the impact religion has had upon the cause of Christ. Israel denies him. Pagans reshape him. False religions bypass him. Warring Christians misrepresent him. All the while, God's glory is marred, God's people are traumatized, and a lost world watches . . . and loses.

Following a conflict, it is wise, then, to assess the damage done to Christ's name. This is the time to make difficult decisions. Here are factors to look at when deciding whether to disband or forge ahead.

1. Is the church able to exist financially, or will the budget be an endless burden, stripping the remnant of needed vitality?
2. Is the church in a high population area where there are many new prospects to be evangelized who knew nothing of the firestorm, or is the church in a low population area where the stigma will make it hard to rebuild?
3. Is the church so damaged that you are not able to attract a pastor capable of helping you rebuild? To hire a maintenance pastor will only prolong your plight.
4. What motivates those who want to continue on with the church? Is it a clear commission from God? Is it nostalgia? Is it a prideful determination not to give up? This is important to determine, because the motivation will affect the long-term success or failure of the church.

The Violated Pastor

In the natural world, sheep never attack shepherds. But in the church, they do. Pastors are in a precarious position as they strive to turn people away from danger. They can never be sure whether their efforts will be appreciated or devoured. Pastors who become overly transparent generally will find that they have been sharpening the knives of their enemies.

There is invisible bleeding. That's the only way to describe a pastor when the church is in conflict. Wounds are inflicted from every direction. He experiences the pain from

- attackers who care not for his spiritual well-being or value as a person,
- people who love him, but are powerless to help,
- having his efforts condemned as inadequate,
- having his professional credibility brought into question,
- his wife, who bears his agony worse than he, and
- his children, who wonder if the faith of their father is worth their loyalty.

It's like a divorce. At one time you laughed, cried, prayed, and worked together. The people of the church welcomed you into their lives. You left your world of self-interest to give your life to their joys and sorrows, hopes and dreams. Now, people guard their words around you. Your place at the table of fellowship is in question. Your office becomes a prison.

You are left defenseless. You cannot defend yourself without appearing self-protective, as one with something to hide. The more you try to explain yourself, the more your words are twisted.

Dignity is denied. You're an open book for people to read or misread at will. People feel free to wound you, then gather around to stare at your wounds, laugh, and feel justified in their conduct.

Your world is crumbling and few, if any, stand with you. It is easy for unscathed bystanders to say you need to "take it like a man," but this isn't a movie in which actors are shot, then get up and go home. This is the real world, in which men are destroyed, never to rise again. Pastors carry scars on their souls that affect them for the rest of their lives.

The strongest of biblical characters staggered under pressure from evil people. Jeremiah questioned why God allowed the wicked to prosper (Jer. 12:1–4). In anger Moses broke the tablets inscribed with the ten commandments (Exodus 32). David often asked God to harm his enemies (Psalm 3:7). The apostle Paul spoke sternly of those who gave him trouble (2 Tim. 4:10, 14–15). These men staggered because, apart from divine intervention, people do destroy people.

It is critical that the church makes an honest assessment of the damage done to the pastor. The issue is not whether the pastor was right or wrong but the church's treatment of the pastor. It is vital to make amends for any improper treatment, even making restitution where necessary, or the seeds of self-destruction will reside in the church. God will not bless the church that tries to bring a harvest out of poisoned ground.

The Pastor's Disgraced Wife

Since the great majority of pastors are men, this section is designed to represent the many women who have suffered as a result of the cruelty poured out upon their husbands. The pastor's wife is directly affected each time her husband is struck. She suffers beyond measure, since both her family and primary ministry are being unfairly torn. Her love for the people faces rejection. Her need for social acceptance is denied.

Take June Baldwin, wife of Rev. Henry Baldwin, for instance (a true story with a change of names). He is young, energetic, and brilliant, a strong leader who doesn't need a lot of affirmation to feel secure. But June is quite the opposite. Her need of strong affirmation is not obvious, however, because of her beauty and poise. She has learned to hide her painful fears behind a bold facade.

June is like a fragile doll ready to break at the slightest bump. She doesn't know why, but she lives with a hidden terror that someday someone will unmask and destroy her. She also fears what this could do to her husband's ministry.

Then it happens—the nightmare becomes reality. A man has asked June not to speak with his wife about a certain situation in the church. He wants to do that himself. As they stand in the church aisle following the morning service, the man's wife asks June about the problem. A woman standing nearby overhears June say that she isn't free to talk about the matter. The bystander suddenly grabs June, shakes her and shouts, "Tell her what she wants to know!" People are stunned into silence, but no one thinks to rescue June.

June's inner strength pours out like water on the ground. Her sense of well-being is crumbling, collapsing. No thought can reestablish her sense of security. When the raging woman stops, June walks away unable to feel her legs beneath her.

Henry cannot know the damage occurring within his wife, since she herself does not understand her problem. It will be sometime later that repressed memories of childhood abuse surface, revealing the cause of her deep-seated insecurities and fears. The screaming woman thinks she is attacking a poised, self-confident woman. She has no idea that she is devastating a frightened little girl within the woman, who has no strength for defense.

The story becomes more complicated. Henry decides to take his wife away for a rest. He says to the church board, "I will expect you men to handle this problematic woman before I get back, or I will resign from the church." The board, afraid to deal with the situation, writes to the pastor, telling him he is to terminate his ministry.

Now June's inner world is destroyed. She still doesn't know that her inability to handle the angry woman is the result of childhood abuse. All she knows is that she felt her insides disintegrating during the encounter. The transfixed people who stood by watching only added to her humiliation. Henry was not able to perceive the depth of help she needed. The church board openly declared that the angry woman would be protected and the pastor and his wife expended. June feels shamed before her children and experiences a crippling sense of guilt that screams out her full responsibility for Henry's pastoral demise.

The very place where she should have found unconditional love and acceptance—the church—is the place where she was ambushed in guerrilla warfare.

There is a postscript to this church's story. The secretary of the church suffered such verbal and emotional abuse from the board for defending the pastor and his wife during this period that she sued the board and was awarded fifty thousand dollars. In the six years that followed, the church devoured three pastors. Today the church no longer exists. A destructive woman is on the loose, potentially endangering another church, because of the incompetence of the church leaders.

All of this is small comfort to June, who remains in therapy, and Henry, who may never reenter the pastorate. Above all, it is an utter disgrace to God's reputation.

June doesn't represent every pastor's wife, since she had deep, unresolved hurt in her past, but every pastor's wife suffers deeply all the same. So consider:

- How did the firestorm affect the pastor's wife?
- What needs to be done to minister kindness and help to her personally?
- Has her position ever been heard, or is she treated as a nonentity?

The Pastor's Betrayed Children

A church firestorm can cause reactions in the pastor's children, ranging from hating the church to attempting suicide. That may sound overly dramatic, but it's not. Young people do not have enough depth of experience to know that terrible circumstances can be out-lived—that God always has a dawn for those who endure the night. There is no tomorrow for a young person—only today, and if today falls apart, life is over.

Thus, I believe God will hold church members accountable for the impact they make upon "preacher's kids" through their treatment of the pastor and his wife. When a church ruthlessly brings about a pastor's departure, the children suffer deep insecurity compounded by embarrassment and, worse still, shame. They want to know if they'll have a home, or even be able to afford sneakers for school. After all, being humiliated before friends can "end" their world.

The parents of such young people helplessly watch as their children draw negative conclusions about church and even life itself. They cannot know, or control, the choices of their children. The stories they taught them about how good always wins appear untrue. Individuals they saw as extended family members turn out to be vitriolic and untrustworthy. Indeed, many pastors and their families are paying an enormous price while a lost world watches.

Here is a true story. A hard-driving, successful businessman approaches me after a service where I have just spoken on discipleship. "If I did what you said today, I'd be out of business tomorrow," he says in an aggressive, belligerent manner. We end up having many discussions over the following days. In each discussion, he agrees that one must obey Christ at all cost, but he insists that this is unrealistic in today's world.

He invites me to his place of business. He has become somewhat legendary as an entrepreneur. People seem to fear him, as well as respect him. He keeps coming at me as though I, too, should fear him.

In time, his exterior cracks, and I am privileged to see into his heart. Deep inside, he is not a tyrannical man but a hurt and angry one. The story is painful to hear. His father was a minister who was greatly abused by a church. He had resolved that there would be a payback. He determined to become wealthy and powerful, then when the church (any church) approached him for help, he would let it hang.

Fortunately, he repented, but many pastor's children do not. They go through life with either ambivalent or antagonistic views of the church. Often they forget what made them this way; however, they rarely come to serve Christ fully, since it was his church that harmed their father.

We sing the song "Jesus Loves the Little Children." Does your church? That will be seen in the care given to ensure that conflict doesn't negatively affect the pastor's children.

- Repeatedly assure the children that they are safe and that the church will be sure the family doesn't fall into harm.
- As a church, pay for professional crisis counseling for the children.
- Protect them from embarrassing public exposure. Remember that they have to go to school and hear their peers discuss their parents' plight, and young people can be cruel in what they say.

The Wounded Congregation

The price paid by the congregation involved in a firestorm is high.

- The fallout can leave those remaining with severe debt that will bind their hands for years to come. They built in faith during the good days, planning on an expanding future, but now they face brutal financial bondage.

- Terrible strain is put on friendships as people are called upon to take sides.
- Families experience dangerous tensions as they disagree on issues.
- The congregation must endure social embarrassment. It bears the stigma throughout the religious and secular communities as the church that underwent a major fight.
- The remnant grieves and feels guilt for not doing more to avoid or stop the firestorm.
- Children often reject the belief system of the church as payback to the culprit.
- There is a great letdown in initiative after a firestorm. This feeling of defeat is deepened every time the people look around to find friends and family members who are no longer present, or when they realize that the issues which tore them apart were never settled.
- There is the slow realization that recovery will be years in the making, if it ever comes. The likelihood that it will not is strong. Who wants to put money and effort into a church so badly damaged that it's like putting putty onto walls that need to be completely rebuilt?
- If the board and church failed to properly handle the firestorm, then serious consequences could flow for three to four generations (Exod. 20:5). While God is full of grace, he will not honor a violation of authority. Peter wrote, "The Lord knows how to rescue godly men from trials and to hold the unrighteous for the day of judgment, while continuing their punishment. This is especially true of those who follow the corrupt desire of the sinful nature and despise authority" (2 Peter 2:9–10).

Because all authority originates with God, to despise authority is to despise God. Ruthless people who despise authority and cause firestorms must be dealt with by the church. If not, then chastening will fall upon the leadership for failing to protect the church. Many churches have "Ichabod" figuratively written over their doorways because of unresolved violations of authority in the past. I firmly believe that there are families under bondage because of unrepentant ancestors who were destructive to pastors and churches.

In nature, firestorms scar the landscape for a season, but then new life emerges from the ashes. Not always so with church firestorms. The price is high and often permanent. On occasion, individuals and congregations do emerge in better condition, but not without much support through good theology and good people.

We have assessed the damage a firestorm can inflict on the church. Now let's look at how the church needs to care for the person who is often at the center of the conflict—the pastor.

18 The Church's Responsibility to the Pastor

As Israel was judged for her treatment of the prophets, so the church is held responsible for the treatment of her pastors.

Discerning and ministering to your pastor's real need is critical during both productive times and a firestorm. It's especially vital if the pastor who endured the firestorm remains to help you rebuild.

The Pastor's Real Need

The real need of your pastor is to find people who can help him in the lifelong process of becoming an effective pastor. Don't assume that seminaries create pastors. They don't because they can't. Seminaries can only provide the tools for becoming a pastor. The church, more than any human factor, will determine the shaping of a pastor. Here's how it works: Christ gives the pastoral gift (Eph. 4:11), the Holy Spirit enhances and empowers for service (Acts 1:8; 4:29; John 14:25–26), and the pastor develops and exercises the gift (1 Tim. 4:14). But the church will either nurture or dismantle that gift.

How can you help your pastor develop? I'll answer that with two stories—one from my own life and the other from the Bible.

A Tribute to Mentors

Roll back your calendar to the mid-sixties. While studying at Washington Bible College, I was the student pastor of a church in Alexandria, Virginia. I was full of ideals and zeal and ready to knock down every Goliath with one stone.

Life seemed simple and obvious. I naively assumed that the congregation would rejoice if I preached truth and applied its righteousness. It wasn't long, however, before "Goliath" showed up. One Sunday I announced that I wanted a friend from the West Indies to sing at the church. Deacon John approached me after the service: "Ahhh, Pastah . . . well, uh . . . uh . . . wouldn't a person from Jamaica be black?"

"Sure would," I answered, impressed by his global awareness.

"Well," he continued, looking at the floor, "we . . . ah . . . we don't allow no black people in this church."

Civil rights demonstrations were under way just across the Potomac River in the nation's capital. I never expected, however, to find myself embroiled in this debate of hatred in my own church. I looked stunned, which boosted John's confidence. He stuck a fat, unlit cigar in his mouth and continued, "If a black person evah enters this church, Pastah, we'll throw 'im out." He said "Pastah" in a contemptible tone, while twisting the cigar in his lips as a power prop. Beside him stood Jim, his cohort, wearing a sickly grin.

My confusion turned to anger as I responded, "The day you remove any black from this church you'd better plan to throw me out with him."

"We will," harmonized the determined duet.

I had no choice but to seek their removal from the deaconate, as well as from teaching Sunday school. I felt certain that everyone would stand with the truth, only to find many afraid to state their convictions. Eventually the situation came to the floor at a congregational meeting.

I presented a biblical case against John and Jim. They scowled and whispered loudly to each other. When I finished, they rose in unison, threatening to crawl over the pew and attack me. "Do you want him first or do I get him?" asked Jim.

Jim, was a thin, cowardly man who hid in the shadow of John's bullish personality. He seemed relieved when John countered, "No, let me get 'im."

The moderator, who was a secret service agent serving as a bodyguard to President Lyndon B. Johnson, stood, pointed his finger and said, "Sit down or I'll break both of your arms." That sounded spiritual enough for me. They sat down, giving me a we'll-get-you-later stare.

The whole nation seemed to be howling under a full moon, and I seemed to have two of the most wolfish individuals in my congregation. They were losing, however, which made them all the more dangerous. They warned me of what may happen to me, suggesting they had "friends." Phone calls came in the middle of the night with no words spoken, just threat-filled breathing. This couldn't be taken lightly, because civil right's workers had been maimed and killed and a president assassinated.

This was the firestorm I faced . . . and the perfect setting from which a remarkable man emerged. Mr. Charles Sterling, known as Pop Sterling, silently watched me fight this righteous cause, often with unrighteous attitudes. His silence didn't condone the evil I was facing. Rather, he was preserving his soul for the work that would make the most lasting impact—to mentor his pastor.

I was at that stage in life when you sense your immaturity but don't know what to do about it. I was easy game for destructive people. Pop Sterling's quiet disposition, however, suggested there was something more important than the raging firestorm. In time I saw it. It's found in Proverbs 4:23, "Above all else, guard your heart, for it is the wellspring of life." While two men were bent upon destroying me, Pop Sterling was bent upon developing me. Before I could govern a crisis, I had to learn to rule my heart. He taught that truth by example more than words.

Pop often placed his hand on my shoulder and, with composed authority, would say, "I'm praying for you. Let's trust the Lord through this. God will make a way." He gently suggested spiritual things for me to think about, being careful not to be condescending. While I held the position of pastor, he held the position of power. He was what every minister needs—a mature person committed to maturing a pastor. Technical training doesn't grow saints. People like Pop

Sterling help to do that. Every successful minister I know has a string of Pop Sterlings in their past, enabling their minds and souls to endure impossible situations.

The evidence of the mentor's maturity is his or her ability to grow from the relationship with the person they are seeking to develop. The immature person behaves as though the person being helped can make no contribution in return, but a true mentor is growing, too. The growth that takes place is mutual. This is Christ's body fitly joined together with supporting ligaments (Eph. 2:22; 4:1–16).

The Example of Priscilla and Aquila

The Bible tells the story of two Pop Sterlings, Priscilla and Aquila, who affected the lives of the venerable apostle Paul and the brilliant elocutionist Apollos. Priscilla and Aquila were tent makers by trade but enablers of leaders by commitment. The Corinthian Christians, acting out of spiritual immaturity, tried to divide Paul and Apollos with a wedge of public opinion. On the other hand, Priscilla and Aquila had a ministry to each one.

The Impact on Paul

As the curtain rises on our story, Paul is in a prison cell in Rome, nearing his life's end. There he is, the great apostle, awaiting the executioner's blade as a wrongfully condemned felon. Paul picks up a quill to pour out his heart to the church. Rather than reflecting a disgruntled old man, Paul's writing reveals a fiery faith: "For I am already being poured out like a drink offering, and the time has come for my departure. I have fought the good fight, I have finished the race, I have kept the faith. Now there is in store for me the crown of righteousness, which the Lord, the righteous Judge, will award to me on that day—and not only to me, but also to all who have longed for his appearing" (2 Tim. 4:6–8).

There is no sign of resentment or self-pity for the misunderstandings, rejections, beatings, imprisonments, and betrayals. Paul's mind is focused on godly thoughts and even expresses his desire to study the Old Testament (2 Tim. 4:13). His heart is ablaze with love for God's Word. Weathered wisdom causes him to instruct Timothy to endure hardship (2 Tim. 4:5), the lot of all who would be spiritual leaders. He painfully remembers those who failed and harmed him. He talks about Demas, who failed him for the love of this world. He warns Timothy to be on guard against Alexander the coppersmith, writing, "Alexander the metalworker did me a great deal of harm. The Lord will repay him for what he has done" (2 Tim. 4:14).

The church, likewise, will be remembered for its treatment of those who have committed themselves to Christ's service. It is not a small issue to be known as one who deserts or disturbs spiritual leaders. Many individuals who have serious family disturbances may find their trouble rooted in the way they once abused a pastor. Consider again Peter's words, "The Lord knows how to rescue godly men from trials and to hold the unrighteous for the day of judgment, while continuing their punishment. This is especially true of those who follow the corrupt desire of the sinful nature and despise authority" (2 Peter 2:9–10).

While Paul gives an honest assessment of people who have wronged him, he turns to the sweet memories of those who blessed and enhanced his work. His special love for two of them can be felt flowing from the parchment: "Greet Priscilla and Aquila" (2 Tim. 4:19).

This greeting is loaded with affection. First, it is highly unusual for Priscilla's name to be before her husband's in first-century culture. Paul showed this honor to her in four out of the six biblical references. Also, in some translations he calls her Prisca, a shortened and more personal form of Priscilla, giving further evidence of heartfelt appreciation. To speak so affectionately of her also shows the mutual trust and love between Paul and Aquila. So, as Paul faced death at the hand of the deranged Nero, he is deeply warmed by the memories of Priscilla and Aquila.

We first meet this couple in the book of Acts in connection with Paul's journey. Whenever Paul entered a new city, he walked through the marketplace seeking opportunities to share Jesus. He would also look for opportunities to make tents to support his ministry.

In Corinth he sees this couple making tents. They are in the market area near the famed Bema seat. The area is corrupted with prostitutes from the temple, who also service men who come to the harbor from other countries. Aquila is a Jew, though his Latin name means "eagle." His wife, Priscilla, bears a Roman name that means "little old lady." When they providentially meet Paul, the chemistry between them proves dramatic. Paul works with them in their shop and stays in their home. He probably leads them both to a saving knowledge of Jesus Christ. We also know that Paul remains in their city for an unprecedented year and six months (Acts 18:11).

But now Paul is old, with failing eyes, housed in a prison cell. It's been sixteen years since he met Priscilla and Aquila. He writes, "They risked their lives for me" (Rom. 16:4), hereby revealing to Timothy their rich character in caring for spiritual leaders.

We don't know what danger Paul faced. But in a life-threatening situation, Priscilla and Aquila considered Paul's life more important than their own. That's certainly different from the actions of Peter, who denied Christ on the night he was betrayed and judged.

Does Paul have flaws? Yes, he openly speaks of them. Could they take his failures into account and decide to "look out for their own hides"? Yes. Could they think Paul must have done something to deserve his troubles? Yes. Do they do any of these things? No.

Likewise, a church must minister to its minister for Christ's sake and not because the pastor maintained a good approval rating on the public opinion poll. Even if a pastor must be removed from a church, it is essential for Christians to stand with him, insisting that removal be done in a God-honoring way. The work of the church must always be redemptive in every aspect, especially in its treatment of pastors. Only when churches care for their pastors can they bring security to the sheep. And only then will the church encourage the best of its pastor's potential, since no one ever works well in fear and insecurity.

The Impact on Apollos

Priscilla and Aquila's story takes a dramatic turn when they meet Apollos after accompanying Paul to Ephesus during Paul's return trip to his home church in Antioch. "A certain Jew named Apollos, an Alexandrian by birth, an eloquent man, came to Ephesus; and he was mighty in the Scriptures. This man had been instructed in the way of the Lord; and being fervent in spirit, he was speaking and teaching accurately the things concerning Jesus, being acquainted only with the baptism of John; and he began to speak out boldly in the synagogue" (Acts 18:24–26 NASB).

The word "fervent" means "boiling over, bubbling" and is a picturesque expression of Apollos's zeal and spiritual enthusiasm. Availing himself of the opportunity afforded him as a visiting rabbi, Apollos powerfully declares his message to his Jewish audience. The phrase "to speak out boldly" translates "to speak freely, openly, fearlessly."

When Priscilla and Aquila hear this dynamic speaker, they are impressed by his love for God, knowledge of the Old Testament Scriptures, and oratorical skills. They don't say to each other, "We sat under the great apostle Paul for eighteen months, and Apollos is no Paul." Rather, their attitude is that there is unbelievable potential in that man to be developed for Christ's sake.

But Apollos's message is defective. He only understands part of the message. It would be easy for Priscilla and Aquila to be critical of him, especially in the light of Paul being their former pastor. They could "poison the well" for Apollos and kill his credibility. Think of the damage they could cause by saying to their friends, "We don't like him. He might be brilliant, but his theology and doctrine are terrible. We've sat under Paul, and Apollos doesn't compare."

The Bible warns against pridefully resisting rather than reinforcing God's servants. "If anyone destroys God's temple, God will destroy him" (1 Cor. 3:17).

"If anyone teaches false doctrines and does not agree to the sound instruction of our Lord Jesus Christ and to godly teaching, he is conceited and understands nothing. He has an unhealthy interest in controversies and quarrels about words that result in envy, strife, malicious talk, evil suspicions and constant friction between men of corrupt mind, who have been robbed of the truth and who think that godliness is a means to financial gain" (1 Tim. 6:3–5).

Priscilla and Aquila were taught better than that, both by Paul and the Holy Spirit. Paul had modeled Christ-likeness in word and deed. They knew he had rebuked the Corinthian believers for their carnal behavior in choosing sides between Apollos and himself (1 Cor. 1:10–17). Their rich character is demonstrated by their love and loyalty to men who seek to serve God—even when God's servants have weak and lacking areas in their lives.

Look at the kind, gentle approach the couple uses: "When Priscilla and Aquila heard him, they invited him to their home and explained to him the way of God more adequately" (Acts 18:26).

Why would the brilliant Apollos listen to two tent makers? First, they had something to say, and second, they said it with the right spirit. A right spirit bears greater authority than argument. So they lovingly, humbly, patiently, and courteously approached him in the hospitality of their home. I am sure they didn't begin by asking, "Have you ever heard the apostle Paul? Man, what a teacher! Did you know that he was caught up into the heavens?"

Rather, it was probably after a good meal that they openly discussed the life and ministry of Jesus Christ—how it fulfilled the words of the prophets: his sacrificial and substitutionary death, his victorious resurrection, his glorious ascension into heaven, the necessity of personal faith in him and his finished work, and the coming of the Holy Spirit at Pentecost.

Yes, Apollos had an imperfect, inadequate, and incomplete message. But instead of undermining him, Priscilla and Aquila undergirded him by more adequately explaining the "way of God." As a result of their delicate and discerning ministry, Apollos became more effective in his ministry. Although the Corinthians were wrong in choosing favorites between Paul and Apollos, it's a high tribute to Priscilla and Aquila's work that they placed Apollos on a level with Peter and Paul.

The church will never develop good pastors until people like Pop Sterling, Priscilla, and Aquila are found in our churches. People far less than these are in our churches destroying potential firebrands of the gospel. If you are a lay person, what about you? Will you commit yourself to building pastors? Will you open your heart and home to these imperfect people? Will you gently help, instruct, and protect them? Because of you, they can experience a wider, more powerful ministry for Jesus Christ. And you'll share in their reward.

But many pastors do not have mentors in their lives. That is not good for a pastor in a healthy church but is especially damaging when church conflict is under way. These pastors get badly burned in firestorms and need Christians' care to help them recover.

19

CARE FOR BADLY BURNED PASTORS

> Whether pastors stay or leave, the primary goal is to preserve them as people and enable them to more effectively minister in the future. You must not think in terms of how to get rid of a problem but how to help a life. That's love.

Having discussed how to serve your pastor's real need, let's look at what your church must provide for every pastor, whether arriving, leaving, or still in residence. I am setting forth a plan I hope will find its way into every church budget and practice.

Pastors must receive professional help. I am not referring to the general help found at conferences and seminars. I'm referring to the personal kind, like that provided by the personal coach of a world-class athlete. Pastors need highly personalized help at three points in their ministries: when leaving a church (under good or bad circumstances), while serving a church, and prior to entering a new church.

No person can succeed in any area of life without adequate support—God has so designed life. Pastors cannot be nonstop work machines simply because they are serving God. Moses would never have survived without his father-in-law's advice, which led to helpful judges. If Moses needed to be "coached" to lead Israel, so pastors need to be coached to lead the church.

Here is a three-part plan to provide the pastor professional assistance. First, budget money for an incoming pastor to invest thirty days at a professional retreat center for pastors and Christian workers to evaluate the past and establish direction for the future. Second, every three to five years, send your present pastor to such a place for refocus. And, third, send every departing pastor to such a place for debriefing and preparation for his next place of service. In following this plan, you will help insure that your new pastor will arrive at his best, your present pastor will remain at his best, and your departing pastor will leave at his best.

You may see the value in doing this for an incoming or existing pastor, but why a departing one? Because you have a responsibility to the body of Christ. The ministry your departing pastor is entering is directly linked by God to yours. It will be ideal when most churches have this plan in place and you only have to pay for one coming to you. Until then, do it for your departing pastor as an investment in your brothers and sisters in Christ.

This plan is essential to the health of the church. Why? Because your church will not grow beyond the spiritual and personal strength of your pastor. Individuals in the church may, but the church as a whole will not. Just as the Bible says that out of the mouth flow the thoughts and intents of the heart, so it can be said that out of the church flows the spiritual condition of the pastor.

Here is a little-known fact. Christian ministry is one of the rare areas of life that has few benchmarks for success. And the ones that exist are terribly blurred and even shift. In other fields, there are clear, unmovable benchmarks. The businessman has a financial bottom line. The carpenter builds a certain number of houses. The artist paints so many pictures. Such professions even have shows or exhibitions to gauge the value of one's accomplishments.

But pastors live with ambiguity about their performances. For instance, a couple in whom months of counseling have been invested decide to divorce, or the elder who has received years of training moves to another city, and sermons that have taken countless hours to prepare barely remain in people's memory to Sunday's end. Add to this the endless flow of counseling overload, political pressures within the staff and church, personal family difficulties, and a host of other complications, and it's easy to see why pastors burn out. And very few people have the training and discernment to understand the unique needs that rise out of their world of nebulous benchmarks.

Pastors are generally tough, resilient people who find it hard to face and accept their own needs. They function out of personal initiative, faith, and prayer. When they do not periodically gain professional help, the church pays the price. They become blinded by the light of self-evaluation and cannot see their own needs. Behind every badly burned pastor will be found a long, slow burn that took place before they became engulfed in the final flame.

Tuscarora Resource Center

To help your pastors maximize their abilities, thereby giving their best to your church, turn to a place like the Tuscarora Resource Center, located in the foothills of the Pocono Mountains along the Delaware River in northeast Pennsylvania. There are a few such places across the continent (and many more needed), so we'll model the plan with this one.

Remember when your church had just hired a new pastor? You could hardly wait for the first Sunday to hear him declare your church as the fulfillment of God's will—a virtual dream come true. But behind the glowing smile could have been a deeply pain-filled, trouble-gouged soul. Further, your new pastor would have had no time or opportunity to receive help in smoothing those rugged grooves into wisdom.

Unlike flesh wounds, heart wounds don't heal on their own. While God has built restorative powers into the body that perform without our awareness, the heart and mind demand conscious care to heal. And that is best done with a professionally trained person to assist the process.

That was the vision driving a businessman named Radar Senum and his wife, Norma, to establish a place where pastors could revitalize their lives and refocus their ministries. Feeling adamant that pastors should have a beautiful place for personal enabling, much like that provided for the business world, Radar and Norma bought a German manor house and property with several ponds and swans. They built twelve efficiencies, two duplexes, and two cottages near the manor house. Only a mile and a half away was the three-hundred unit Tuscarora Bible Conference that could also be utilized.

The Senums' next step was to acquire a competent staff. They developed a team of men and women with at least one year of theological training and significant ministry experience, along with graduate and mental health degrees. This combination was important because the staff needed to understand the unique problems faced by pastors and missionaries and possess the expertise to help them. Jim Cheshire was one of the team members chosen. He had faced burnout as a pastor, worked through his recovery, and prepared professionally to assist others.

Restoration

Jim knows that he is only an instrument and God is the Counselor, so he strives to not come between a person and God. High on the agenda is time to be quiet and alone before God. The breathtaking beauty of the Poconos provides a grand, open-air cathedral, while the enchanting campus of the TRC provides relaxed warmth. Here a person who may be drained of vitality can spend time letting God do what only God can do. And there are many things God will only do when one gets alone and quiet before him.

While people must draw their inner strength from God alone, it is also within God's plan that people draw from one another. It is not infrequent that one will gain a divine perspective only through the assistance of another person. TRC counselors are trained to listen for the symptoms of burnout or other problems. They may take their cues from hearing pastors mention such symptoms as listlessness, lack of motivation, sleeplessness, tentativeness, loss of creativity, withdrawal from people, detachment, cynicism, and anger. They know that failing to get at the heart of these symptoms can lead to serious physical problems, as well as the destruction of ministries and homes. Their purpose is to help God's servants restore strength for service.

Frankly, every person in ministry periodically needs to sort through the complexities to understand his or her inner motivations and responses. These areas are often worked out by talking with a loved one or a friend, as in iron sharpening iron (Prov. 27:17). Leaders who would reach greatness, however, must find someone trained like Jim who can fulfill Proverbs 20:5: "The purposes of a man's heart are deep waters, but a man of understanding draws them out."

What is Jim working to draw out of the heart? Those wrong perceptions and distortions that inevitably come from living too close to a situation. His purpose is to restore a healthy view of God, a proper understanding of oneself, a debriefing of responses to various people, and an unbiased assessment of decisions to be faced.

Let me illustrate one of many areas in which this help is essential. A pastor may discover that while one difficult person is upsetting, another is not. What makes the difference? It's not the difficult people, rather an undeveloped area within the leader. One difficult person may push an emotional hot button inside by reminding the pastor of a person who inflicted great pain upon him in the past. The other difficult person may provoke no such memory, thus the leader is less threatened and more tolerant of the second. Add countless other encounters and frustrations that build like barnacles on the soul, and you'll understand the need for a professional to chip them away.

Refocus

Jim has gone on to develop other programs that are geared to help Christian leaders make in-flight adjustments. One program is called Reentry and is geared to help missionaries prepare for either a return to the States or to the field. Much debriefing is needed at the beginning and end of every Christian endeavor, to say nothing of the help needed while in the process.

At TRC, special seminars have been prepared for Christian leaders, ranging from pastors to missionaries. One may find himself sipping hot cider, coffee, or tea at a small-group gathering in the manor house to gain and share information on one of the following topics:

- Conflict resolution
- Assertiveness versus humility
- Anger: internalized or expressed
- Forgiveness
- Loss and grief

- Identity in Christ
- Depression
- Burnout
- Self-care

Downtime

Jim knows that Christian workers must have planned downtime if they are to be fit for the long haul of ministry. Your church must realize that, too. This isn't family vacation time; that's another matter altogether. Just as every pilot must have downtime before another flight, so Christian workers need downtime designed to enable them for further service. Downtime includes:

- *Quiet time for meditation and contemplation.* We live in a day of information overload flooding into our minds from every direction. It's essential to pull back from it all to give God sole access to the heart and mind.
- *Rest for physical restoration.* We know from Scripture that a willing spirit does not automatically guarantee physical strength. The body must be properly serviced, or there will be serious consequences.
- *Recreation (best spelled re-creation).* Within a stone's throw of TRC is access to canoeing, hiking, and ball fields. One may also walk down the hill to the Tuscarora Bible Conference to take in a concert or favorite speaker. Within an easy drive are New York City, Philadelphia, Gettysburg, Hershey Amusement Park, and Pennsylvania Dutch Country, which includes the famous Sight and Sound theater where live productions with biblical themes are performed.

Places like TRC are not a luxury but a necessity for pastors to be enabled to perform at their best. Pastors can only rightly set the compass of the present by keeping an eye on a distant star. The TRC and others are designed to help Christian leaders do just that.

A Perspective on Responsibility

Churches have the right to expect good performance from their pastors. But that leads to the responsibility of providing the assistance pastors need to keep their performance levels high. That can only come by churches being willing to fund such help. Remember that your budget must include the pastor's cost of living for the month, plus the cost of attending a thirty-day restoration and refocus retreat at a place like TRC.

Before you conclude that this plan is too grandiose, let me illustrate its value another way. If you were hiring someone to head a billion-dollar-a-year corporation that yielded nothing more than temporal value, you would consider a thirty-day preparation time as money and time well invested. How dare we consider anything less for the people whom we call to lead the church in matters of eternal consequence? A thirty-day period is not always possible and, at times, a week or weekend may have to be the alternative. But between pastorates, especially, and every three to five years within a pastorate, a thirty-day period is essential. At every point that this is neglected, the church will suffer loss. On the other hand, your pastor's gain will directly result in your church's gain. Your church will pay one way or the other—either by equipping and enabling your pastor to be a bright beacon, or allowing him to merely exist on a low energy charge, resulting in a dim signal to the world.

If you are a pastor, you cannot wait on the church to provide for your needs. Whether churches awaken to this retreat concept or not is beyond your control. Therefore, you must take immediate action to keep your own life in peak condition, as we shall see next.

20   Self-Help for Badly Burned Pastors

Guarding Your Heart

> Above all else, guard your heart, for it is the wellspring of life.
>
> Proverbs 4:23

We've been talking about what the church should do for a badly burned pastor. But that doesn't often happen. Generally you'll find compassion only in a few, and they are unable to extend much help beyond friendship. If you are a pastor in that situation, you probably feel reduced to a piece of tabloid news.

Your vacillating emotions may cause you to feel out of control, swinging from solitude to warlike fury in the flash of a second. Fear not, you're not going out of your mind. These are normal eruptions when the soul is overpowered by unfairness, injustice, and disappointment. Add to that list the twin fiends of betrayal and rejection.

But as life disintegrates, there is one bastion over which you have ultimate control—your heart. When all is said and done, no one can determine the condition of your heart except you. God has put you in charge of it. Proverbs 4:23 states, "Above all else, guard your heart, for it is the wellspring of life." God has provided all the tools you need, but the work is yours. Jesus made that clear in the parable of the four soils (Luke 8). It is the person, not God, whom Jesus said determines the condition of the heart. God has placed a circle around your heart, forbidding any to enter without your permission. You are the guard, then, of all that comes or goes.

In wanting to show you how to do this, I searched for the story of one who succeeded in guarding the heart. It wasn't easy to find this person for two reasons. First, many pastors have failed to guard their hearts, thereby being reduced to John Greenleaf Whittier's dismal observation, "Of all sad words of tongue or pen, the saddest are these: 'It might have been!'" They never gained what could have been. Their bitterness robbed them of wisdom. The second reason is quite different. Many who succeeded in guarding their hearts preferred to quietly bury the past, never sharing their stories because recall stirred undesirable emotions.

Fortunately, I stumbled across Rev. Dan Caldwell, whose story is time-tested and true. He was willing to tell me his whole story based on the hope that it will awaken courage and offer help to you who are in the middle of great conflict. The names and places have been changed so that his years of taming and befriending his enemies won't be disrupted.

Return to 1972. Forty-four-year-old Dan and his wife, Martha, arrive at Silver Spring Independent Bible Church in Berks County, Pennsylvania. The church of seventy-five people sits amid a rural population of five thousand. Dan is a smashing success, increasing the attendance from 75 to 250 during the next six years—a remarkable feat, because the youth tend to leave the area. Dan says his formula is preaching the simple gospel in a humble way.

The church formed out of a split from First Presbyterian Church, with painful memories lingering in both camps. But when a church is growing, it's easy to forget that the seeds of destruction planted by the founding fathers will, in time, bring forth a destructive harvest. Success also blurs one's assessment of an oncoming problem. So it was with First Presbyterian leading up to the firestorm that resulted in the founding of Silver Spring Independent Bible Church.

While the church is strewn with destructive seeds, there is another area of trouble that none can see, not even Dan, and that is the condition of his heart. Although he believes he is preaching the gospel in a humble way, he is driven by prideful competitiveness with his brother, who is also a pastor. Dan is deeply concerned with the size of attendances and offerings, two visible criteria of "success."

With the stage set for trouble, enter the antagonist, Larry Broadson. Larry has just finished his studies for the ministry. He feels ready to pastor and decides there is no better place to start than riding on the crest of Dan's success. Larry plants the thought in his parents' minds of how wonderful it would be for him to pastor the family church. But first, Dan must go.

Ed Broadson, Larry's dad, isn't an evil man, but he fails to test the source of the "inspired" thought. That's hard to do when it comes from a son. Oh yes, and did I mention that Ed was one of the key figures in the earlier split of the church?

Ed leads a home Bible study class for the purpose of helping to disciple people in light of the church's growth. His wife, Bertha, is also teaching Evilyn Christiansen's book, *What Happens When Women Pray,* to a ladies' group. You see it coming don't you? Once again, two sacred platforms will be used to launch an attack to destroy a pastor.

Meanwhile, Dan attends a conference led by Ray Stedman at Pensacola Bible Church. The theme of the conference is based on 2 Corinthians 5, where Paul shows that our sufficiency, both for reconciliation and service, comes from Christ and not ourselves.

Dan finds liberation from his prideful, competitive spirit toward his brother. He also discovers that anger had strongly motivated him—and he surrenders to love. He no longer does things for God but allows God to do things through him. He is a new man with a new message. He can hardly wait to teach these liberating truths to his church, illustrating them from his own life. He boldly declares his insufficiency apart from Christ. This sword of truth keeps cutting deeper into Dan's heart, resulting in greater liberation from the bondage of self. But Larry sees his opportunity to swing this sword of truth at Dan's head. This truth becomes the crux of his plot.

Larry rushes to his dad's Bible studies expressing how insufficient Dan is to be the pastor and that according to his own words! Furthermore, Bertha asks the ladies to pray about the sad failure their pastor is admitting to be. Did they miss the point of Dan's teaching? Obviously. Is this the first time truth has been twisted to meet a private agenda? A trillion tragic times no!

"Pastor, they are crucifying you at those Bible studies," warns Fred Bainer, who has stopped attending because of what he sees happening. Dan is hurt but decides to put his new belief to the test, a test that will last longer and go deeper than he expects. But divine truth is generally branded into the heart by heat, pressure, and time.

Dan thinks God's sufficient help is on its way when the board, headed by Warner Linquist, says it will stand with him. "These people have driven previous pastors away, and we're not going to let it happen again," they say. Warner is the most vocal, insisting, "This isn't right!"

But accusations continue from the home Bible studies and ladies' prayer group. Then, one Sunday, a special congregational meeting is announced. Dan is shocked, having no knowledge of it. He can't stop it, because the constitution states that any five families can call for such a meeting—a questionable addition to any constitution. Ed takes Dan aside, places a fatherly hand on his shoulder, coughs up a spiritual tone, then proceeds: "Pastor, I don't want you to attend the meeting, but I feel it's only right that you know what we will present to the people."

He shifts his weight to both feet for support and clears his throat again. Deep inside he feels foolish, but it's too late to back out, especially since he has wrongfully pledged his loyalty to his son. He continues:

"Inadequacy is the first charge, Pastor. Ah, we don't feel you are adequate to be the pastor of this church. Well . . . ah . . . you have said so yourself many times from . . . ah . . . you know . . . the pulpit."

His pinched voice reveals his uneasiness as he continues. "Deceitfulness is the second charge. One time you quoted from Dave Roper's book on the New Covenant and didn't give him credit. Ah, well . . . ah, we think that is plagiarism. You know . . . ah, that's deceitful.

"Slothfulness is the third charge. I mean . . . ah, you went to this seminar, and now you're preaching everyone else's ideas and none of your own. That suggests that you don't study and think for yourself."

Dan is numb. Questions scream from his heart: "Where are you, my sufficiency? I need you *now*, yet you seem so far away. There is no truth to these charges. How can you let Ed stand here and do this? I have accepted my insufficiency. If you don't prove sufficient, then I'm sunk." Dan is hurled to those deepest pits spoken of in the Psalms, and his thoughts echo those who have previously known their terrifying, lonely darkness.

Ed walks away, subconsciously aware that he has just made a total fool of himself. But he can't apologize. The Judas kiss is planted. The crucifixion must proceed.

Three months of destructive talk has turned the tide of opinion throughout the congregation. The board, too, has lifted its finger from God's Word, moistened it, and thrust it into the wind of public opinion. England's former Prime Minister Margaret Thatcher said, "Consensus is the negation of leadership." That's not always true, but in this case it is. Even Warner surrenders in fear to public opinion. Despite the outrageousness of the accusations, he prefers to betray Dan rather than risk surfing the growing tide of anti-Dan sentiment.

Still, Dan resolves to fight on. His legs are kicked out from under him, however, when the board tells him to take a leave of absence for a month. He is free to go to the office, counsel people, and do other chores, but not preach. With the love of his heart cut out, Dan resigns.

Shell-shocked and disgraced, he picks up the tools of his former trade and begins building homes for a construction firm. Day after day he goes to work dragging a heavy heart, clotted with confusion. He doesn't doubt God's sufficiency but is staggered at the difficulty of proving it as an outcast in the community he once served.

Signs of clinical depression set in. He feels listless and at times finds it hard to keep his thoughts together. He doesn't want to leave the house, knowing that people look upon him with suspicion and scorn. The very people who once doted upon him now shun him without valid reason.

In the midst of this, there are two saving graces. First, the home Dan is building is a geodesic dome, which demands all of his mental energies and skills. Second, next to his lunch pail sits his radio, which carries the voices of Charles Swindoll, Chuck Smith, J. Vernon McGee, and others bringing biblical truths into his heart and encouraging his faith. The binding chains of bitterness begin to loosen.

And he needs all the support he can get, especially in light of the additional public disgrace imposed upon him by Rev. John Straight, pastor of the small Independent Fundamental Church of America in Silver Spring. John announces to his congregation that no one is to speak to Dan, since he has been put out of his pulpit for sinning without repentance—a strange nontruth coming from John's imagination.

Some of his people carry out the ungracious dictum. Dan goes to the local grocery store, where one of the IFCA members works. "Hi," says Dan, with cheerful hope that he still belongs to the human race. The man turns away without saying a word. Another man from the IFCA works as a carpenter with Dan. He won't speak to Dan, other than to say things like, "Hold that chalk line tight," or, "We need more lumber over here."

Months drag like years as the shunning continues. But Dan is amazed at the increasing strength he feels, despite being robbed of nourishment from fellow Christians.

Dan musters up the resolve to confront John Straight, who will not meet with Dan in his office, but instead escorts him to the front pew of the church. Dan tells his story. John remains inflexible. He insists that Dan has committed sin, although he can't specify what it was. Therefore, John continues, Dan needs to confess it to the congregation and place himself under the board for discipline. He doesn't explain how Dan can place himself under a board that has kicked him out. Further, John believes Dan should not pastor again until he confesses and repents.

Dan shakes with anger. How can a fellow pastor be so ignorant and so lacking in compassion? But he resolves to trust God's sufficiency even in the face of John's misjudgment. Dan muses over how unfair Earth and heaven are toward him. Earth unfairly abandons him, and heaven unfairly accepts him. One brings grief, the other grace.

The next day he returns to work, fighting the one great fear that daily wraps its fingers around his heart—the fear of never pastoring again. Despite his spiritual resolve, he can't be sure of God's mind. And God sends him no discernible assurances.

He reminds himself that where there's no cross, there's no crown; if there's no death, there's no resurrection. He clings to Matthew 28, where Jesus told his disciples that all authority was given to him in heaven and on earth. "If that's true," thinks Dan, "then nothing can come into my life without passing by God's throne. It's allowed by him for my good. So I must learn . . . I must submit . . . I must prove God." Each day he clutches a hammer in his hand and truth in his heart.

Nearly a year passes before Bill Wisehorn, a school principal who attended Dan's former church, asks him if he'd teach the Scriptures to his family in his home. "No," Dan replies, "I'm committed to do nothing in Silver Spring that would compete with the church."

"Well," Bill responds, "what if we hold it in my school? That's twelve miles away in Winebrook."

Winebrook is a new, growing community. Dan and his wife had prayed God would send someone to start a church there. "Give me thirty seconds to pray about it," Dan replies, then says yes with a Grand Canyon smile.

Bill rounds up twelve men to meet with Dan. The idea of starting a church in Winebrook is born. Forty people show up on the first Sunday. God's sufficiency to sustain Dan over the past year is about to empower him in a new ministry.

But Dan is convicted to do something that goes against all that is natural to human nature. He feels that if he is to pastor a church, teaching others how to overcome anger and bitterness, he must take the lead. He has to do all within his power to bring peace between himself and his enemies. If not, he knows that as a founding father, he will sow the seeds of future destruction in the new church. Dan has experienced God's sufficiency as a rejected outcast. Now he must experience it as a peacemaker.

Dan begins by asking to return to the Silver Spring Independent Bible Church pulpit to apologize for his wrong attitudes and actions, as well as preach one final sermon—a request flatly denied. Dan doesn't quit. He pursues his desire from different angles until he is invited.

The Sunday morning arrives. Dan stands to speak, hoping not to miss one vital point. "I'm here today to extend to you my deepest apology for my behavior in the trouble that fell upon us."

But aren't the charges made against Dan false? Yes. Shouldn't people be apologizing to him? Yes. But that isn't Dan's concern. He has learned that he can't govern anyone's behavior except his own. Leaving his accusers to the Lord's judgment, he is here to take responsibility for his own behavior. He doesn't recount the past, just takes responsibility for his part.

"I want to apologize for holding some hard feelings. I also want to apologize for not resigning sooner. I had no business staying here to fight for what I perceived as right at the expense of the church." One third of the people had scattered to other churches, one third attended no church, and one third remained. While one could still argue that this was the church's fault, Dan remains committed to clear his own soul, no matter what anyone else would do.

"Further, I want to apologize for speaking too much about the problem. I talked to people in an effort to sort out what was happening, but that only complicated it. I tried to talk out my bitterness, but it only hardened. It took me too long to learn that talk doesn't always bring solutions."

The service ends at twelve fifteen. The new pastor (who is not Ed Broadson's son) says, "I'm going to ask Rev. Caldwell to stand in the front of the church. If anyone has anything you'd like to say to him, you can come forward and do so." The service closes. So many people stand in line to talk with Dan that he isn't able to leave until one thirty.

Ed is the last one in line. The hand that laid on Dan's shoulder while the charges were presented now drapes over Dan's neck. Ed buries his face on Dan's shoulder and weeps. Struggling to speak he says, "I'm so sorry for my part in all that's happened. I could have stopped it at any time, but I didn't. I'm so sorry. Will you forgive me?"

"Of course I forgive you, Ed. Will you forgive me for the hard feelings and judgmental spirit I've carried toward you?"

"Yes, of course."

Two men rise to godly manhood. Dan doesn't know if this will end his bitterness, but at least it's a start. He is determined not to enter future ministry with such a weight on his soul.

Dan doesn't stop there. He decides to go to every individual who had offended him and try to make peace. This doesn't necessarily mean he'll become a coffee-drinking buddy again, just a man at peace with them, with himself, and with God. The most difficult one proves to be Warner Linquist, the man who had vowed to stand with him. Dan drives to the Park and Ride, where Warner carpools into Harrisburg.

Dan sits in his car near Warner's truck. Everything in him cries out not to do it; after all, Warner is clearly a turncoat and should apologize to him. Further, what if Warner reacts badly? Every fear is confirmed when Warner arrives, exits a car, and ignores Dan as he walks to his truck.

"Warner, I need to talk with you." Warner, fixing his eyes on nothing, marches past Dan like a mute statue. Dan goes home feeling like a fool.

The next day, the scene repeats itself, only this time the statue speaks: "I don't want to talk to you." Dan returns home explaining to God that it is time to let the man alone, that enough is enough, but he has no peace at the thought of giving up.

Day three is identical to day two, except that Warner says more emphatically, "I *don't* want to talk to you! We have *nothing* to talk about!" With two Gestapo-like clicks of the heel, he's gone.

Day four is slightly different. Warner speaks while walking past Dan, "I don't have time now. I have to take someone else home."

Undaunted, Dan shows up on day five, but Warner is nowhere to be found.

On the following Monday, Dan is back with irritating persistence. Finally Warner breaks, saying, "Well, it looks like I'm not going to get rid of you."

Dan replies, "That's right. I need to talk to you." So, they set up a meeting for Thursday night.

When they meet, Dan tells Warner of the damaging things he has learned that Warner is saying about him, thereby harming his reputation as far away as Harrisburg. He reminds Warner that he had promised to stand firm with Dan to stop this kind of pastor bashing. Then, he launches into his reason for being there. "I'm not recounting these things to accuse you or to hope for an apology, but to tell you that my reaction toward you has been one of bitterness. I really want your forgiveness. I can't pastor this new church, telling other people how to settle disputes with love and forgiveness, if I do not take the lead. Will you extend forgiveness and friendship to me?"

Warner says yes, but fails the test of spiritual maturity by letting Dan bear all the responsibility. However, that is not Dan's concern. Dan has extricated himself. He is resolved to learn God's sufficiency on every level of life.

Do Dan's efforts pay off? Fortunately we can evaluate it now, nearly twenty years later. Dan is pushing seventy and still pastoring the church in Winebrook, which averages nearly three hundred in attendance. Dan is a free man, even an honored man, in the very community that once unjustly shamed him. He has proven Proverbs 16:7, "When a man's ways are pleasing to the LORD, he makes even his enemies live at peace with him." Above all, Dan is experiencing the mental, emotional, spiritual, and physical well-being that comes from obeying God and proving his sufficiency. He's fulfilling David's words, "Find rest [completion, well-being], O my soul, in God alone" (Ps. 62:5).

The essence, then, of guarding your heart is to fulfill life according to God's Word. God alone resolves life according to his faithful character and power. While none can duplicate Dan's story, because every situation is different, the divine principles are the same. Jesus wasn't being poetic, but rather prophetic, when he said, "Blessed are the peacemakers" (Matt. 5:9).

To handle his conflict in a biblical manner, Dan had to go against his own nature. But in so doing, he saved his heart, which resulted in personal health and success in his relationships. He also opened the door to a highly productive and fulfilling ministry.

Although you cannot stop people's attacks, you are the one who determines the good or bad impact they will make upon you. God has established you as the caretaker of your heart. As you handle your conflict God's way, he will keep you in all your ways—that's his promise.

21   SELF-HELP FOR BADLY BURNED PASTORS

REBUILDING

Success is the product of growth through conflict.

Dan resolved to follow neither the natural instincts of his heart nor the methodology of the world. Instead, he sought to honor God through his ordeal. God in turn honored him, making him triumphant over his adversaries. Your story can be every bit as victorious because the divine promises that Dan proved apply to you as well—God will demonstrate his sufficiency. With Dan's story as a backdrop, let's look more deeply into the various areas demanding your attention in order for you to rise up from your calamity to be mightily used by God.

Rebuilding Spiritually

Times of devastation are rare opportunities for you to start at ground zero with God—returning to the simple faith of a child. Don't let degrees or advanced knowledge become a stumbling block. God requires childlike faith on all levels of the Christian experience.

Perhaps the simplest, yet most profound, restoration is found in the psalmist's words, "Be still before the Lord and wait patiently for him; do not fret when men succeed in their ways, when they carry out their wicked schemes" (Ps. 37:7). "Be still, and know that I am God; I will be exalted among the nations, I will be exalted in the earth" (Ps. 46:10).

In the Hebrew, "be still" carries the picture of an army marching in full battle array, fevered with readiness to fight. The command is to stop marching, lay down all weapons, and be at ease. The assurance behind the command is that there is a greater one than you who will be glorified by proving his sufficiency as your defender and deliverer.

This truth became deeply personal to me when, toward the end of my second year at Myerstown Grace Brethren Church, I found myself exhausted. Along with the late nights and high tension of assisting this troubled church, I was maintaining a daily television program and traveling to evangelistic meetings. I got to the point where my body let me know that I could go anywhere I desired, but it wasn't going to take me. Both my board and the MGBC board agreed to give me a month off to travel to Israel for studying, fasting, prayer, and rest.

When I arrived at the Saint Gabriel Hotel in Nazareth, which would be my sanctuary, I sat down and said out loud, "Here I am, God. Where are you?" That wasn't doubt or despair, just the emotional emptiness that accompanies fatigue. I began to read the Scriptures, gulping them like a man at a water hole in the desert. One day I read the Scriptures for fourteen hours, slowly feeling their refreshing power.

On day seventeen of my stay, I happened to read Psalm 46:10, and something completely unexpected happened. I felt that inner motor that tends to race twenty-four hours a day shut down—literally. For three days I enjoyed such peace that I felt it too crude to request anything of God. I knew that he desired to answer all prayer; therefore, there was no need to inform him of my need. This was a time for worship and praise.

That encounter with "being still" not only fully reinvigorated me, it became one of the most cherished memories of my life. I know that God restores the heart, the mind, the body. I experienced that in its full, wonderful force. I know he can restore you, but you must take the time to get alone with God and be still.

Do not argue that you have too many responsibilities. I did, too. It's amazing how God undertakes for us while we are seeking him on his terms. From the time I took that trip until the end of my stay at MGBC, we experienced an extraordinary infusion of peace in the congregation, such as had not been known for years. I urge you strongly, before you spend thousands of dollars for minimal help, to get alone with God and *be still.*

In this stillness there is a faithful waiting upon the Lord. Herein strength is renewed. Isaiah writes, "But those who hope in the LORD will renew their strength. They will soar on wings like eagles; they will run and not grow weary, they will walk and not be faint" (Isa. 40:31). The word "faith" is like a mighty stream branching out and feeding the tributaries of hope, trust, obedience, faithfulness, fear, waiting, seeking. Each of these words represents a nuance of faith. Thus, the verse could be read with each tributary flowing into the message:

- *Hope:* The soul's anchor (Heb. 6:19); the substance of the unseen (Heb. 11:1).
- *Trust:* Childlike simplicity and reliance (Matt. 11:25; 18:3; Job 13:15).
- *Obedience:* The conduct resulting from confidence in God (James 2:14–26; Heb. 11:4, 7–8, 25, 29–30).
- *Faithfulness:* The steadfast character of faith (Eph. 4:12–16).
- *Fear:* The awe-filled worship and respect of faith (Ps. 111:10; Eccles. 12:13).
- *Waiting:* The conviction that God brings his purposes to pass (2 Peter 2:9).
- *Seeking:* The longing of faith (Ps. 63:1).

Think not, however, that being still and waiting on the Lord denotes doing nothing. Faith is not passive. You are told to *walk* and *run* while resting. But as you rest in the Lord, new energy fills your heart, even invigorates tired muscles. You are energized by resting in divine strength.

The renewal comes from the rest found in the stillness of faith. But what is this rest? Is it mere relief? No, much more. It is *completion.* For instance, when God rested on the seventh day, it was not a matter of regaining lost strength but of looking upon the completed works of his hands. All was in a state of wholeness.

Likewise, the rest that God will bring to you, even amid devastation, will be an inner completion—a wholeness. Well-being comes to your body, mind, and soul. I strongly encourage you to give the highest priority to being still, believing, and finding God's rest in your rebuilding process during and after a bad conflict.

Rebuilding Emotionally

Conflict is a great distorter of emotions. Part of your recovery will be to get your emotions back into alignment with your faith. Most inner breakdown comes not from a crisis of theology but of emotional energy. During the early stages of the conflict, your emotions were manageable, but sustained conflict can send your emotions into surges that seem to be beyond your control. You can talk yourself to sleep, for instance, only to be awakened in the middle of the night with a rage in your heart that produces cold sweat.

Emotions can be like children, running in a circuitous frenzy—demanding, crying, pouting, forgiving, then not forgiving. This is not the time to make serious decisions. Find a trusted friend with whom to safely share these emotions. This friend must have the right to say what you *need* to hear, not just what you want to hear. Use this friend as a benchmark of sanity, helping you to sort out emotions that can distort reason and result in poor decisions. The Bible teaches, "Wounds from a friend can be trusted, but an enemy multiplies kisses" (Prov. 27:6).

Along with finding the right friend, do some things that are emotionally simple and provide physical exercise, such as walking or playing golf. Emotions have amazing restorative power, provided they are given relief from constant pressure. Also, exercise is vital to good health during times of great stress, helping to keep down blood pressure, among other benefits.

Emotions that are not properly serviced will attempt to force you to serve them rather than Christ. You will say and do things based on how you feel, rather than on what is right. Careful management of your emotions, then, is vital to your recovery. I strongly recommend spending a lot of time in the Word and prayer and being with friends in pleasant situations. Your emotions will be manageable again, but it will take time and care.

Rebuilding Physically

Don't underestimate the importance of caring for your body. The body suffers terribly when conflict is in the soul. Many people in physical care fields may be willing to donate their services if they know they are helping to restore you to ministry. Try to put together a team of people to enable you to endure your calamity. Doctors will help you know your level of endurance. Chiropractors will help keep nerves free to function. Physical therapists will aid in vital neuromuscular reeducation. Massage professionals treating the body with deep tissue massages can cleanse the body of toxins and increase blood flow for rebuilding. Nutritionists will help determine your body's needs.

The care of your body is a ministry unto the Lord. You don't own your body. You're a caretaker of God's property. "You were bought at a price. Therefore honor God with your body" (1 Cor. 6:20). "Therefore, I urge you, brothers, in view of God's mercy, to offer your bodies as living sacrifices, holy and pleasing to God—this is your spiritual act of worship" (Rom. 12:1).

On the practical side, it is necessary to maintain a healthy walking or running program, unless you are able to do more strenuous exercise. One minister, who was passing through a severe trial, was under such pressure that he could not engage in heavy workouts, so he found great relief in taking walks on a nearby golf course. While he did this he prayed. In so doing, he was rebuilding both the physical and the spiritual.

Rebuilding Professionally

Success is the product of growth through conflict. How can you accomplish that? Reflect upon chapter 7, "TRIM: The Pastor's Four Pillars of Strength." Dissect the chapter, then take your discoveries about yourself to the professional who can best help you prepare for your future. This is not necessarily a highly paid person asking you to force round pegs into square holes. I would encourage you to start with another minister, one who has weathered some storms. Herein you may find the ultimate professional. Often the deepest mystery is unlocked by a rightly spoken word. And the Holy Spirit knows how to reveal the right word through the right person.

You must also give thought to future opportunities. Surround yourself with leadership, making them aware of the entire situation—they will not recommend you if their vision is colored by incorrect information. However, you will find leadership highly tolerant of mistakes you've made, providing you take ownership of your missteps and give evidence of trying to correct them.

Above all, don't wait on someone to take care of your recovery. God will fulfill his promises, but you must do your part. With providence, there is always a tomorrow. Let nothing stand in your way of getting ready for it.

Let's turn from you, as the pastor, to the broader picture—care for the church after a firestorm.

22

CARE FOR BADLY BURNED CHURCHES

> The congregation must discover sound, theological reasons God allowed the firestorm to erupt and what value can be brought out of the conflict.

Whether you are called to a badly burned church or remain as a pastor or member of one, it will be essential to analyze the state of mind produced by the conflict. Only then can you determine how to assist the church's recovery.

Understanding Group Mind-Set

You have heard of mob psychology. It's true, there is such a thing. When caught up in a group frenzy, people will engage in behavior they would lack courage for alone. Anger reaches a critical mass, and an explosion of destructive behavior results. Your firestorm produced that critical mass and left your church in emotional and spiritual shambles. Now that it has passed, new critical mass attitudes are forming. They must be understood and addressed, or a new firestorm could break out, leveling what remains.

Most people will not understand what is troubling them. The leadership must help them define and resolve the inner responses to the calamity that shook their church. There is a subconscious search for a leader—one to guide the church out of the nightmare. This leader must help people deal with collective confusion, fear, insecurity, disappointment, anger, guilt, discouragement, despair, and paralysis.

Collective Confusion

The congregation will be overrun with opinions about the cause of the firestorm. Each person will have a fragment of the truth, but few will possess the whole story. Also, even if the whole story is known, a positive solution isn't guaranteed.

It is critical to put a stop to speculation, since this only prolongs and deepens the problem and offers nothing for resolution. While it is natural for people to want to analyze and pinpoint the cause, the wiser person leaves such work to the right authorities. Otherwise the issues keep smoldering, even breaking out into new firestorms.

Proverbs 26:20 states, "Without wood a fire goes out; without gossip a quarrel dies down." Of course, people do not view themselves as gossips and quarrelsome, and they may not be. But the congregation must realize there is a time when further discussion will only fuel the crisis and add to the confusion.

Collective Fear

It may not be verbalized, but an underlying concern has developed over where God was during the crisis. Why didn't he stop it? Why didn't he answer the many agonizing and sincere prayers? Can we really rely upon him for the recovery? How will this crisis affect our children's attitude toward the faith? Can we survive financially? Will we ever regain respect in our community?

Unanswered questions create fear that will make the congregation overly cautious, even resistant to recovery efforts. The church leaders must not ignore the reality of these concerns. It will take one to two years of steady success for the fear to subside. Boldly address the questions and fears head-on with sound biblical explanations. For example, the pastor may want to present messages on topics such as the following:

- God's unshakable sovereignty and power to fulfill his purposes
- Divine purposes for suffering
- How to respond to the sifting of Satan
- How unanswerable questions can develop faith
- The power of persistent prayer

To preach as though no problem exists, or to keep speculating about the crisis will only deepen the fear. It is the Word of God preached in the power of the Holy Spirit that will dispel the timorous spirit and restore confidence.

Collective Insecurity

Collective fear is coupled with a collective loss of confidence. While most people will not openly admit to a loss of confidence in God, it is there nevertheless. It will express itself through undue questioning of the leadership. The leaders already appear to have failed since this terrible problem has swept through their midst. The congregation will care little about the long, hard hours the leaders are investing to stop the crisis and remedy the problem. Instead, quick-fix solutions will be demanded. This is a typical expectation set forth by those who have lost confidence.

It will be necessary for the church leaders to implement an open door policy. If information is withheld—such as disciplinary action being taken against someone—the reason for silence must be explained. When decisions are made that affect the congregation, details must be given. It must be made clear that no information vital to the life of the body will be withheld.

If people are going to get upset, be sure they are upset over the facts and not a rumor. If the leadership is to take flak, let it be over the truth and not for some made-up reason. When the congregation sees that the board is acting on responsible, well-considered decisions, confidence gradually will be restored.

Do not respond in panic, however, every time a member challenges a decision or action. If the decision or action is based upon biblical reasons and carried out in humble obedience to God, it generally will prevail and quiet the disturbance. "If a ruler's anger rises against you, do not leave your post; calmness can lay great errors to rest" (Eccles. 10:4).

Collective Disappointment

The pastor may have behaved in a way that betrays the truths he preached. Those who believed he was their greatest example of godliness will be overwhelmed with disappointment. Other leaders in the church may have proved to be unfit for the firestorm. When people know what a leader should be doing and how he should be acting but find him lacking integrity, disappointment will reign.

When issues become more important than people, disappointment ensues. People who had assumed they were valued and appreciated for who they are discover they are derided for not lining up on a certain side of the issues. There is great disappointment when this shallow basis for friendship is revealed.

People also suffer disappointment if they come to realize that their value to the church is no greater than their contribution in money or talent. When the firestorm has burned away the facade of congeniality, congregants may see that they were mere pawns.

Whatever the cause of disappointment, it is a real emotion that must be addressed and resolved. Otherwise, disillusionment can result, and this can cause people to fall from the faith.

Collective Anger

There will be many reasons for anger throughout the congregation.

- *Betrayed* people are angered over being considered as fools.
- *Hurt* people are angered over the pain that was inflicted.
- *Violated* people are angered over the injustice.
- *Quiet* people are angered that they didn't say more.

People must not be made to feel guilty for the anger, because anger is a valid emotion. However, the leadership must direct people in how to handle and resolve their anger, so that they do not sin in it (Eph. 4:26).

If anger is not recognized and addressed, it will manifest in various ways. Tensions lead to disputes among the people, even after the real storm has passed. These disputes may take the form of resistance to decisions or prolonged arguments over insignificant issues. Anger may surface in arguments at home. People will fly off the handle over someone forgetting to feed the dog, when the real problem is unresolved anger over the calamity at the church.

Anger can also take on a more subtle form. People may continue to attend but won't get involved in church programs. Because they feel powerless to conquer the problem, they withdraw as a form of passive protest.

Anger is no small reality to be faced when a church has been assaulted by a firestorm.

Collective Guilt

There will be a sense of guilt in the congregation. Are we bad people? Is God punishing us with this trouble?

Those who caused the storm will not feel this, but the true saints will. They are sensitive to sin. The calamity will raise a question in their minds about themselves. They will feel unworthy of love and respect.

Only genuine love and reassurance over a long period of time will dispel this sense of guilt. It will also be necessary to preach sermons on the false guilt that Satan, the accuser of the saints, imposes upon God's people. Also, state clearly that the guilt falls on the people who set the storm into motion and that it must not be shared by those who sought to honor God through the unity of the church.

Collective Discouragement

When the church is so damaged that special programs for your elderly, young married couples, and children are reduced or obliterated, discouragement cripples the remnant. There is no easy solution, because people who love the church and want to stay also may feel the need to go where their specialized needs can be met.

Strong sermons must be preached on the greatness of God to deliver the church from the impossible. Faith must be reawakened and positively challenged to engage in seeking God for his mighty works. Then, practical steps must be put into place to focus the people's hope on a fresh vision. The congregation will extend a period of grace to the leadership as long as it sees a plan of action being put into place.

Do not berate the church members for their discouragement. Instead, gently encourage them with biblical teaching, along with a plan set in motion by hard work.

While discouragement will exist in the congregation, there is no place for it in the leadership. One of the most effective ways of maintaining a positive attitude in the leadership is to hold retreats. These times should be used for spiritual refreshment, building trust and unity, and sorting out the myriad problematic issues to be faced.

Collective Despair

Discouragement is the doorway to despair. And despair is understandable. People who are plagued with personal problems must now deal with a church crippled by emotional conflict and potential financial collapse.

How can people in despair recover? People can endure any crisis providing they have a big enough reason. Such a reason must be set forth—one that can inspire special faith and sacrifice. The congregation must be taught that historically God allows the worst of calamities to come upon his finest people. To believe and obey God through this crisis can produce great spiritual growth. Never set forth a lesser reason than the glory and purpose of God for dispelling despair.

Collective Paralysis

All of this leads to a fear of making decisions. Conflicts often break out over what corrective measures need to be taken. This leads to a deepening paralysis. People lean toward making no decision rather than risking action that could bring a new disturbance. Herein, the church will lose the vitality needed to rise from the ashes.

Healing through Theology

How can you care for a church with these areas of collective difficulties? Build an adequate theology that brings perspective and answers to many questions. The congregation must discover

- why God allowed the firestorm to erupt,
- why God didn't stop it before it did so much damage,
- why God doesn't seem to punish the troublemakers,
- why love and forgiveness were overpowered by anger and divisiveness,
- why prayer seemed so powerless in the firestorm, and
- what value can be brought out of the conflict.

Incorporating specific doctrine that reaffirms the role of God in the church will be essential to rebuilding.

23

The Intentional Interim Pastor

> The "Intentional Interim" is a specialized ministry which combines an apostolic function with proven consulting experience designed for churches in transition or crisis.
>
> Rev. Steve Richardson, Titus Task Force

What a serious predicament you're in if your church fits the profile of the last chapter. The leadership is either confused or at a stalemate. Worse still, your pastor may have left in the midst of the calamity. You know the church will soon stagnate and atrophy. Your first instinct is to say, "We need to find a new pastor, fast!"

It's true that you need a new pastor, but not necessarily the one you hope will stay for years to come. For many reasons, it will probably be in the best interest of the church to find what has come to be called the intentional interim pastor—one who comes for a predetermined amount of time to take the church through the transition from its firestorm to a new future.

There are a number of reasons to have an interim pastor. It will not be easy to find a pastor of high caliber until your church has regained stability. Such pastors are in great demand and are not looking for a struggling church. I know that may not sound spiritual, but that's reality. Also, your church cannot afford to be the testing ground for an untried pastor, especially not in its weakened state. And you need more than a semiretired pastor looking to supplement Social Security, unless he is highly qualified.

Did that last one throw you? Are you wondering why a person with years of experience won't do? Your church needs a person who is wired by God to handle impossible challenges and, much more, has developed special skills to lead the church out of its crisis. It is critical to find the right person, because it will be necessary to give that person extraordinary authority to assure success. That's exactly why the time of stay should be limited. It is not good to give extensive authority to one who has come for the long haul.

Reason to Give Authority

When the Chrysler Corporation was in deep trouble, the board had the wisdom to know it would never be saved by committees and consensus. It had to find a person like Lee Iaccoca and invest him with great power to tap into his entrepreneurial genius. Otherwise, Chrysler would be lost today.

The church that is in deep trouble must do the same. Believers have more to rely on, however, than raw human talent. They have people with apostolic gifts, as well as God-given talent and learned skills, which enable them to raise a church from the ashes of a firestorm.

It is disheartening to see some churches remain in needless defeat for years because of board members who will not exercise the same wisdom as that of the Chrysler board. While Chrysler went on to become a great American success story, many churches remain ineffective.

Value of an Intentional Interim

A church in crisis cannot be led by a person who is thinking of a long-term ministry. The reasons are as follows:

- He must make decisions that may be unpopular. For example, a financially draining or useless program may need to be eliminated, but some people may want to keep it for nostalgic reasons. A long-term pastor will move understandably slower when making unpopular decisions, which may result in irreparable setbacks.

- He may have to engage in church discipline. The healing process may be served best if this person is not long-term.
- A church in crisis needs a change agent. Not every pastor has that kind of temperament and skill. It is best for long-term pastors not to be radical change agents. It is the duty of the change agent to prepare the church for the work of the long-term pastor.

Stated Goals of the Interim

The interim pastor first must discern whether a church should attempt recovery or begin the termination of its ministry. In either case, the interim pastor's assistance is vital. Recovery will require his unique abilities, while termination will demand his unencumbered and unbiased perception.

If it has been established that the church will begin the process of recovery, specific goals will need to be met by the interim.

1. Resolve conflict. To resolve conflict the interim needs neutrality to assess if there can be compromise or if some people need to be dismissed.
2. Restore effective leadership. This means spiritual restoration as well as being sure the right people are in power positions.
3. Refocus vision and ministry (establish a master plan). The firestorm has devastated the church's ability to fulfill its purpose. All attention has been given to the problem. Now, a positive vision must be set forth for recovery to take effect.
4. Revitalize worship and service (teach the church to be the church). It's vital to get the congregation's mind off the problem and set on God and service to one another.
5. Refine the organization for the future. The church may have collapsed under the weight of unnecessary, even dead, committees. Now is the time to be sure every structure is an important undergirding to the future life of the church.
6. Restaff the church effectively. The presence of the interim pastor gives the church time to carefully select the right people for permanent positions, rather than fill jobs hastily and inherit new problems.

When an Interim Pastor Is Needed

Not all churches are candidates for an intentional interim ministry. Factors that indicate it's time for an interim pastor:

1. The previous pastor was fired or left after a stormy conflict between him and the congregation.
2. The congregation experiences significant internal conflict, which may or may not focus on the previous pastor.
3. The pastor has resigned or retired following an unusually long ministry (some experts have indicated seven years or more to be a considerably long ministry).
4. The church has had a series of short-term pastorates (three years or less). This indicates a systemic problem that needs to be uprooted.
5. The congregation is in major transition due to such things as changes in the community or economic conditions, a need to relocate the church building, or rebuilding after a fire. A transition may result from a major change in the focus and emphasis of the congregation's ministry, such as the completion of a church building program, paying off a debt, or setting new goals.
6. An extended interim ministry has proved to be relatively unproductive.
7. The pastor in active service to the congregation has died.
8. There has been serious moral default in leadership.

If more than one of the above conditions exist, the need for an interim pastor becomes more serious. Of course, the decision ultimately rests with the congregation and its leadership, but these conditions may serve as guidelines.

Profile of an Interim Pastor

God builds into people certain temperaments that equip them to serve in various ways. A well-intentioned person can fail in a position for which he is not equipped. The role of intentional interim pastor requires unique traits.

1. *His focus of ministry is on the established church.* This person must be geared to honor the traditions and history of the church. It would be unethical for an interim to attempt to lead a church away from its roots, simply because he doesn't share the same roots.
2. *He has a high-risk personality and is able to:*

   - envision potential in others,
   - confront sin and mediocrity, and
   - challenge the saints for renewed activity in the kingdom.

3. *He has leadership training and gifts as:*

   - A team player: Multiple relationships exist between the interim pastor, the local church and, where applicable, the denominational leadership. These relationships are key in enabling the interim period to be used effectively to build and strengthen the life of the congregation and prepare it for a productive future.
   - A transformational leader: Leith Anderson, in his book *Dying for Change,* aptly describes the nature of a transformational leader as one who is close to the action, gets authority from rank and file as they affirm him, has God-given authority, excels amid adversity, and takes the initiative.[6]
   - A transition specialist: Persons serving in this type of ministry need to possess finely tuned skills for being able to assist a congregation in the transition from grief to reflection, reflection to recovery, and recovery to new beginnings. They also must provide exceptional strategic planning, leadership, development, conflict resolution, and decision-making. Note the difference between transformational and transitional leadership. In his book *The Once and Future Church,* Loren Mead states: "Organizational specialists distinguish between 'transitional' and 'transformational' change. By transitional change they mean the adaptations

and shifts brought on by temporary dislocations and dis-
comforts, moving to a new stability. By transformational
change they mean the shattering of the foundations and
the reconstitution of a new entity."[7]

- A tenacious investigator: Tenacity is needed to pursue
issues that may be unpleasant or even controversial. These
ministers must be willing to be at risk in identifying and
exposing problems that may have been long-buried, and
then offering biblical solutions.
- A temporary shepherd: The interim pastor must care for
the flock during the transition period. On many occasions
it is necessary to call on every member at home to determine the health of the flock. (This also assists the inves-
tigative part of the ministry.) From this, the particular needs
of the local church may come into focus.

Critical Interim Teams

Several teams must be put into place to assist a church in the
speediest possible recovery.

1. *The Interim Pastoral Team.* The intentional interim pastor may
   have a team behind him, especially if he comes to you from
   an organization that specializes in helping troubled churches.
2. *The Leadership Team.* It is essential that the elders work closely
   with the interim pastor. They are the leadership that will insure
   continued success after he departs. The elders must be a working board, not merely a decision-making board. They must
   lead by example, because it will require serious commitment
   by many members to bring the church into a new future.
3. *The Worship Team.* The interim pastor must honor the culture
   and style of worship found in the church served. It is essential, however, that a team of people be assembled to lead a
   vibrant worship service. This will help throw off the heaviness
   that has settled over the congregation during the conflict.
4. *The Pastoral Search Team.* The interim pastor is intentionally
   temporary and must not be considered as a candidate for a

permanent position. A search team must be working throughout the transition period to find the most qualified person to
continue the turnaround.

The Pulpit during the Interim

Here is what the interim pastor should do from the pulpit.

1. *Reinforce interim goals.* A vision must be stated and restated.
   While one leader may have a clear view of where the church
   is headed, that view must be constantly reinforced to the
   congregation.
2. *Allow gifted laity renewed access to the pulpit.* The interim
   period is a golden opportunity for the church to learn to be
   the church. The real work of any pastor is not to perform Christianity for the people, but to equip the people for works of ministry (Eph. 4:12).
3. *Present a clear course of action.* The church must know that the
   authority given to the interim pastor is not a matter of free rein
   but one of freedom to carry out a stated plan. That course of
   action, along with its observable points of evaluation, should
   be presented regularly to the congregation.

I hope you clearly see the value of the intentional interim pastor
and have considered whether this may be the best option for your
church. I also hope you have seen that, indeed, major church conflict
can be overcome . . . *but not without stretching you beyond measure.*

We have looked at the life cycle of a firestorm, its causes, how to
fight it, and how to rebuild after its devastation. Now, let's look at the
ultimate end of your firestorm . . . and your ultimate reward.

24   Coming Forth as Gold

I consider that our present sufferings are not worth comparing with the glory that will be revealed in us.

Romans 8:18

Scene 1: The Trial

How unfair can life get? You returned home from the congregational meeting with your tattered world slapping wildly in a wind of hopelessness, while the other members returned to their neatly packaged lives. They are lying on beds of ease. Yours feels like rock. You never dreamed that a forced resignation would awaken every fear, insecurity, and sense of inadequacy that has dogged you since childhood. Over the years you developed great skills to compensate, thereby leading people to view you as fully self-assured. But the mood of the church was turned against you by a handful of detractors, and people clawed at your soul as though you couldn't bleed.

Now you sit, head pressed into your hands, imprisoned by the impossible. No explanation can vindicate you, since no one will listen. The very people whose lives you sought to build are shredding yours. You're experiencing the aloneness that comes with integrity. You're reminded of the historic heroes of the faith who suffered abuse. But in this empty hour, they seem like lifeless statues incapable of giving comfort.

Your emotions swirl and fight against one another. One moment you want to rise up in vengeance, returning the pain that has been imposed upon you. Then, in the next you feel the urge to extend forgiveness to your worst enemy. Waves of thought and emotions course through you all night long. The intensity is so great you don't know which ones are genuine, so you fight against them, trying not to be driven to something rash, something foolish, something dishonoring. You force yourself not to act at all.

You look at your Bible but feel resentment toward God. Where was he? Why did he let it happen? When will he vindicate you? Your spouse sees this as an occasion to reinforce why you should leave the ministry. Your children are confused by the betrayal—after all, the people who are rejecting you are the very ones you taught them to call "uncle" and "aunt."

Everything in you wants to do something radical: leave the ministry, get drunk, curse God. You hardly recognize yourself. Never did you dream that such thoughts—no, demanding emotions—would have such a grip upon you. You want to get as far away from Christians as possible. You pace late into the night, fighting the fires that break out in your heart.

At long last it's 5:30 in the morning. The sun is slicing across the horizon, opening a new day, but you feel cold. How can there ever be a new day for you? The vileness you wrestled against throughout the night leaves you feeling dirty. Your dry mouth tastes bitter. You feel a bondage of evil wrapped around your soul.

Suddenly, unexplainably, some Scriptures come to your mind. Somehow they seem to be weakening the grip of the hellish vise. The more you say them out loud, the more life you sense reentering your being. The atmosphere of the room lightens, as though an evil cloud is lifting. You feel it happening.

You turn on the light, open your Bible, and underscore the verses. They seem to be soaking up the spilt blood and binding the deep cuts in your soul. Spiritual courage and determination brace you anew. You read, "He who overcomes will inherit all this, and I will be his God and he will be my son" (Rev. 21:7). Hope for divine vindication increases as you choose to leave all vengeance to the perfect Judge. You resolve to honor Paul's admonition, "Do not be overcome by evil, but overcome evil with good" (Rom. 12:21). Knowing part of your struggle has been a battle with Satan, you rush to John's writings: "I write to you, fathers, because you have known him who is from the beginning. I write to you, young men, because you have overcome the evil one" (1 John 2:13).

Then the hand of memory offers you a look into the future through Christ's revelation to John, "To him who overcomes, I will give the right to sit with me on my throne, just as I overcame and sat down with my Father on his throne" (Rev. 3:21). The resolve to win strengthens as you continue, "Then I heard a loud voice in heaven say: 'Now have come the salvation and the power and the kingdom of our God, and the authority of his Christ. For the accuser of our brothers, who accuses them before our God day and night, has been hurled down. They overcame him by the blood of the Lamb and by the word of their testimony; they did not love their lives so much as to shrink from death'" (Rev. 12:10–11).

Emboldened from on high, you authoritatively address Satan out loud. "This is one battle you will lose! I will not betray my Lord and my God!"

You turn to John 16:33 and read, "I have told you these things, so that in me you may have peace. In this world you will have trouble. But take heart! I have overcome the world."

The victory Christ established is dispelling the awful evil of this night, which is the culmination of months of destructive conflict within the church. Peace floods your heart. You sense that a great war is passing, and a victory is being won that could not have been gained by you alone. Something extraordinary has happened during the night. You will never be able to explain it fully to anyone. But you know its immensity—its reality. You lift your Bible toward heaven and declare, "God, I am resolved to prove you as you are revealed in this Book!"

Scene 2: The Triumph

Years later you step on heaven's shore, having served two more churches prior to your death. While you spoke little of your firestorm and the night that nearly took your life, you found yourself repeatedly calling upon the wisdom and insights gained through that time. A profound death occurred deep within your heart—a death to self-rule. Christ was given the right to reign in you in practical ways, governing your thoughts, desires, and decisions. The seeming paradox was hard to adjust to at first: Through death you found life.

Indeed a harvest of eternal fruit grew out of what you allowed to happen to your heart during the firestorm. You became noted for your ability to enter into people's lives, helping them to resolve crises. People often wondered how you had developed the deep, rich faith that helped carry churches through troubled waters. At your funeral, ministers spoke of the uncanny grasp you had of spiritual matters, your confidence in God's Word, and the many lives you affected.

Now, you find yourself amid the church of all ages, bowing before the judgment seat of Christ. One at a time all are being called before the Lord to be rewarded according to what they had done. The dark hour of your life that nearly caused you to turn from your calling seems eternally behind you. You reflect upon Paul's words that carried you through many valleys, "I consider that our present sufferings are not worth comparing with the glory that will be revealed in us" (Rom. 8:18). He was right. This is glory more brilliant than a trillion suns.

And over there, not far from you, is Paul. He just returned from his appearance before the throne, but isn't wearing a crown. Of course, he was given one, but he took it off and laid it at the feet of his Lord. You catch his eye. He senses that you're wondering about the crown. He points to where scars once rimmed his body and whispers, "Remember these? They're my crown."

Suddenly, your name is called. The voice bidding you to approach the throne is far beyond what you imagined John meant when he said, "And his voice was like the sound of rushing waters" (Rev. 1:15). It sounds like a thousand oceans thunderously colliding, yet it is kind, like a gentle brook. It has the personal warmth that Mary felt when she heard him call her name in the garden on the resurrection morn.

You step before his thrown, overwhelmed by the reception. You approach him, understanding more fully why John fell as though dead when encountered by Christ on the Isle of Patmos. But you are sustained by the same fullness of mercy, grace, and love that upheld John during the revelation. There's no unspoken trace of rejection or disappointment coming from the Almighty's heart. Still, it is no small adjustment for you, having crossed the vast divide between the crude world of sin to appear in the presence of absolute purity, truth, and light.

He begins to unfold the story of your life, showing pleasure in the disciplined way you studied, prayed, and tended his sheep. Then comes the page you often wondered about—that dark night when you nearly surrendered your reward. The firestorm is replayed, with special focus on that night. How will he judge you? You know that you would have failed without the supernatural help that came on the wings of the early dawn. There is deep silence across the heavenly host, since the outcome will determine your eternal reward.

As the night is replayed, your eyes are opened to see the reality you had to accept by faith. You see now what was then unseen. Standing in the corner of your den, snarling slanderous thoughts into your mind was Satan—not just a demon, but Satan himself. Now you understand the dark energy that charged your thoughts. This was your Gethsemane, and there was the enemy of your soul whispering with violent force, trying to discredit God and provoke you to loss. You didn't realize at the time how fully God was fulfilling the promise made through Paul: "But the Lord is faithful, and he will strengthen and protect you from the evil one" (2 Thess. 3:3).

As you relive the dawn that drove the deep chill from your bones, you see an angel of magnificent stature enter the room and address Satan with divine finality, "Enough. Leave at once!" That was the moment the Scriptures burst anew into your heart like the force of the sun dispelling the darkness. Ah, but in addition to the Scriptures you see angels are surrounding you, ministering strength to your human frame.

Overwhelmed with gratitude for having been delivered, you want to fall among the twenty-four elders and angelic hosts, to join them in crying out, "Holy, holy, holy is the Lord God Almighty." Without his intervention, you would have fallen. In your frailty you nearly listened to the satanic whisper above the divine promise.

The moment has come. The decision is made. The Lord looks deeply into your eyes. How has he evaluated you? "Well done," he says, pointing to an imposing crown. "You have overcome. I give you the right to reign with me. Because I found you faithful in a small matter, take charge of ten cities."

You quickly kneel, lest you collapse. Such a reward . . . and you nearly failed. Then you remember his words, "Without me you can do nothing." Indeed, the victory was all his, but you walked through the trial by faith. You did not turn away in bitterness, judging God unfair to allow you such hardship.

The church of all the ages bursts into songs of praise to the One who is the merciful yet mighty Lion of Judah. You raise your crown to salute your Savior and King, then lay it at his feet.

You return to your place in the throng, filled with thanksgiving that the night when you endured such hell proved to be your most glorious triumph in heaven.

To him who is able to keep you from falling and to present you before his glorious presence without fault and with great joy—to the only God our Savior be glory, majesty, power and authority, through Jesus Christ our Lord, before all ages, now and forever-more! Amen.

Jude 24–25

Appendix

A Plan of Action Guide

Well, here you have it—the things I learned while working with the Myerstown Grace Brethren Church and in the subsequent writing of *Firestorm*. My friends at MGBC and I will be deeply rewarded if some things in this book clear away the smoke of confusion and empower you for great achievement in overcoming conflict.

To assist you further, here is a guide to use as a church board to determine the health of your church, along with the action you need to take to prevent, stop, or recover from a firestorm.

Life Cycle of a Firestorm

List as many symptoms as you can for each level of the firestorm's life cycle. For each phase, judge the number of symptoms that exist in your church, along with their intensity, as you determine what action to take.

Phase 1: Sparks

1. Symptoms include:

2. To prevent these "sparks" from igniting a firestorm, we are resolved to engage in the following action:

Phase 2: Sparks Igniting a Firestorm

1. Symptoms include:

2. To prevent the firestorm from becoming more severe, we are resolved to engage in the following action:

Phase 3: Firestorm in Full Fury

1. Symptoms include:

2. To prevent the firestorm from becoming more severe, we are resolved to engage in the following action:

Phase 4: Consuming Winds

1. Symptoms include:

2. To prevent the firestorm from becoming more severe, we are resolved to engage in the following action:

Phase 5: The Final Burn

1. Symptoms include:

2. To prevent the firestorm from doing irreparable harm to the church, we are resolved to engage in the following action:

Phase 6: Rebuilding on Burnt Timbers

1. Symptoms include:

2. To repair the damage done to the church, we are resolved to engage in the following action:

Causes of a Firestorm

The Pastor's and Church Leader's Personal Evaluation

If your church is to have spiritual power, *every* leader in the church should be responsible for determining personal areas of strength and weakness.

1. In view of the four pillars of strength, as outlined by TRIM, I see that my strengths and weaknesses in each area are:
   a. Truth (presenting Christ in concept and communion)
   - Strengths:

   - Weaknesses:

   b. Relationship (presenting Christ in companionship)
  - Strengths:

  - Weaknesses:

   c. Integrity (presenting Christ in character and conduct)
  - Strengths:

  - Weaknesses:

   d. Mission (presenting Christ in conquest)
  - Strengths:

  - Weaknesses:

2. To bring the four pillars of strength into greater balance, I am resolved to:

3. From chapter 8 "Social Pyromaniac Madness," I have discovered some areas in which my family and psycho-social needs still affect me too deeply.
   a. I have a destructive family background that still negatively affects my relationships in the following ways:

b. The unresolved psycho-social needs still negatively affect my relationships in the following ways:

4. With God's help to overcome any unmet needs from my past, I am resolved to make Christ my deepest fulfillment by:

Evaluating General Causes

1. Our church is being affected by each of these factors in the following ways:
   a. Cultural Resistance to Authority:

   b. Rapid Church Growth:

   c. Marketing Jesus:

   d. The Clash of Freedom and Form:

   e. Systemic Problems:

   f. Culture Crashing:

   g. Wounded People Who Wound:

h. Multiple Staff/Hidden Agendas:

i. Empire Building:

j. The Human Heart:

2. We need to take the following action to curtail the impact these factors are making upon the church:

Evaluating the Fire from the Abyss

Here are the evidences we see that Satan is involved in our conflict:

Evaluating the Fire from On High

Here is what we believe God is trying to do with us and our congregation through this conflict:

Fighting a Firestorm

Church Discipline

1. Before we can begin the process of church discipline, the following hesitations must be discussed and overcome:

2. To keep our goal before us, we have made a statement of purpose for church discipline. Our statement can be summarized as:

3. Understanding that discipline is only to be an act of love and redemption, we are going to take the following necessary steps:

4. In the event that "things turn bad" during the disciplinary process, we will put the following plan into motion:

Bold Spiritual Leadership

1. As the pastor involved with a church in conflict, following much prayer and counsel, here is the position I believe I am to take:

2. My reasons for doing so are as follows:

How Followers Can Lead

Knowing that the principles in chapter 14 are essential to the well-being and success of our church, here is how we plan to educate the congregation in these ideas set forth by Jesus:

Stopping the Hot Wind from Hell

Knowing that Christ has made every provision for us to overcome Satan's role in our conflict, here are the "handles" we are going to remove to break his grip on us:

Firestorm Consultants

We believe the time has come to seek the assistance of an unbiased person whom God has equipped to help us work through our conflict.
1. We will investigate the following people from whom to choose a consultant:

2. In the consultant we will vest the authority of the role of:
   Passive Mediator   Passive Advisor   Binding Arbitrator

3. Other action we will take to pursue hiring a consultant:

Out of the Ashes

Assessing the Damage

1. The firestorm has affected all areas of the church. We see its impact in these specific areas in the following ways:
   a. The Pastor:

   b. The Pastor's Wife:

    c. The Pastor's Children:

    d. The Congregation:

  2. Here's the action we will take to remedy the pain brought to
     each area in the body:
     a. The Pastor:

    b. The Pastor's Wife:

    c. The Pastor's Children:

    d. The Congregation:

The Church's Responsibility to the Pastor

  1. The importance of the pastor/mentor relationship was dis-
    cussed in chapter 18. Is your church effectively meeting this
    important need in your pastor's life? As you consider the
    answer, use the chart below to evaluate what percentage of
    your congregation impacts your pastor as did the people the
    apostle Paul referred to:

Personality	Person	Impact
a. Unreliable	Demas	Failed Paul for worldly gain
b. Troublemaker	Alexander	Opposed Paul

c. Mentor   Aquila and Priscilla   Helped Paul,
                                                        matured Apollos

   2. With a desire to love as we have been loved by Christ, and in
an effort to be known as disciples of Christ, we resolve to do
the following to help pastors mature in our church:

Care for Badly Burned Pastors

Our goal is to be sure any pastor who leaves our church is better
equipped to serve future congregations. We commit ourselves to the
following care for any pastor who faced conflict here:

Self-Help for Badly Burned Pastors

Recognizing that I am ultimately responsible before God for the
condition of my life and ministry, I am resolved to do the following
things to:
   1. Rebuild spiritually:

   2. Rebuild emotionally:

   3. Rebuild physically:

   4. Rebuild professionally:

Care for Badly Burned Churches

1. Of the signs described in chapter 22, our church shows the following:

2. Here is how we plan to address and hope to resolve these collective difficulties:

Intentional Interim Pastor

1. We need an interim pastor. These are the items we want to be sure to discuss with the people we consider for the position:

2. Following are the people we have in place (or need to put in place) for each interim team.
   a. Interim Pastoral Team:

   b. Leadership Team:

   c. Worship Team:

   d. Pastoral Search Team:

NOTES

1. *Webster's New World Dictionary,* Third College Edition (New York: Webster's New World Dictionaries, 1991), 702.

2. Erwin Lutzer, *The Serpent of Paradise* (Chicago: Moody, 1996), 119.

3. Herbert Lockyer Sr., *The Psalms: A Devotional Commentary* (Grand Rapids: Kregel, 1993), 355.

4. Robert Greenleaf, *Servant Leadership* (New York: Paulist Press, 1977), 7, emphasis in original.

5. John Flavel, *Banner of Truth,* vol. 6 (Carlisle, Pa.: Banner of Truth, 1968), 62.

6. Leith Anderson, *Dying for Change* (Minneapolis: Bethany, 1998).

7. Loren Mead, *The Once and Future Church* (Washington, D.C.: The Alban Institute, 1993).

Recommended Resources

Most of the following resources affected this book to some measure, although they were not directly quoted. They are all valuable tools in developing strong churches.

Abusive Leadership

Johnson, David, and Jeff VanVonderen. *The Subtle Power of Spiritual Abuse.* Minneapolis: Bethany, 1991.

Avoiding Culture Crashing

Arn, Charles. *How to Start a New Service.* Grand Rapids: Baker, 1997.
Leisch, Barry. *The New Worship.* Grand Rapids: Baker, 1996.

Biblical Assessment of the Human Heart

Susek, Ron. "Discovering the Real You" video series. Gettysburg, Pa.: Susek Evangelistic Association, 1991.

Church Outreach

Miller, C. John. *Outgrowing the Ingrown Church.* Grand Rapids: Zondervan, 1986.

Confronting Destructive Excesses

Hill, Clifford, Peter Fenwick, David Forbes, and David Noakes. *Blessing the Church?* Surrey, B.C., Canada: Eagle, 1995.

The Percentage Principle Found in Every Organization

Kock, Richard. *The 80/20 Principle.* London: Nicholas Brealey Publishing, 1997.

Spiritual Warfare

Anderson, Neil T. *The Bondage Breaker.* Eugene, Ore.: Harvest House, 1990.
———. *Setting Your Church Free.* Ventura, Calif.: Regal Books, 1994.
Bubeck, Mark I. *The Adversary.* Chicago: Moody, 1975.
———. *Overcoming the Adversary.* Chicago: Moody, 1984.

Understanding the Spirit of This Age

Bork, Robert H. *Slouching Towards Gomorrah.* New York: HarperCollins, 1996.
Guinness, Os. *The American Hour.* New York: The Free Press, 1993.
Lindsell, Harold, *The New Paganism.* San Francisco: Harper and Row, 1987.

Worship

Engle, Paul E. *Baker's Worship Handbook.* Grand Rapids: Baker, 1998.

My Debt of Love

Credits scrolling across the screen at the end of a movie could win an Oscar for boredom. But this credit listing is different. These are the people who loved you enough to give of their time and abilities to help prepare *Firestorm*. And do I ever owe them a debt of love! Would you please read this list, then thank God for them, even ask his blessing upon them? They'd consider that a wonderful reward.

Paul Engle, editorial director of Baker Books, first read *Firestorm* because his father, George, led in my ordination to the ministry. Eddy Hall and Rev. Tom Schwanda, both professional writers and editors, saw early drafts of *Firestorm* and rushed to my side to apply their professional craftsmanship to the manuscript. Be assured that I didn't just watch them, I studied them and read all the books they recommended on writing. They taught me that, while writing starts with an inspired idea that demands release, it's the craftsmanship of writing that determines its impact.

Dr. Roy Roberts, a pastor who experienced his own firestorm, assisted with the section about Aquila and Priscilla, plus more. Dr. Roy Johnston and Dr. William Secor Jr., psychologists, offered wonderful counsel to pastors—and that without charge—for the chapter "Social Pyromaniac Madness." Dr. Ed Peirce gave his expertise as a conflict consultant for the chapter "Firestorm Consultants." Rev. Jim Cheshire offered his assistance with the section regarding the Tuscarora Resource Center. Rev. Steve Richardson presented his field of service in the chapter "The Intentional Interim Pastor." All of these men were selfless in wanting their knowledge and experience to assist you.

Mrs. Sherrie Stohler was the secretary who endured the Myerstown Grace Brethren Church firestorm. Having felt the heat firsthand, she resolved to get this book into your hands.

Mrs. Chris Mummert got a stiff neck from proofing the manuscript while vacationing in Hawaii. This was a special effort in light of the enormous task she carries out as the executive secretary of Susek Evangelistic Association.

Mrs. Sharon Mummert exhausted a number of red pens making corrections and shared wise insights for improvements.

Mr. Terry Ortman and his wife, Doris, read each chapter with a critical eye and friendly heart.

Wanting a well-developed book, I had an array of friends respond to the manuscript with their own insights. They are, in no specific order, Dr. Jimmy DiRaddo, Dr. John DeBrine, Mr. Gary Rutherford, Dr. Erwin Lutzer, Rev. Gleason L. Archer, Rev. Chet Joines, Dr. Vander Warner, Rev. Mick Allen, Rev. Mark Moore, Rev. John Kuert, Dr. Keith Skelton, Dr. Jamie Mitchell, Rev. Hayden McClain, Dr. Phil Yntema, Mrs. Orpha King, Mrs. Wilma Buss, Rev. Keith Shearer, Rev. Dan Jackson, Mr. Bryan Crouse, and Rev. Carl Holwerda.

Then, please whisper a special prayer of thanksgiving for the elders of Myerstown Grace Brethren Church, who overcame their firestorm and encouraged the writing of this book: Mr. C. P. Brezeale, Mr. Ed Dechert, Mr. Paul Horst, Rev. Jim Link, Mr. Ray Mahoski, Mr. Joel Moehlmann, Mr. Robert Mountz, Mr. Ken Seyfert, and Mr. Lee Wenger.

I am grateful for the steady support and commitment of my SEA boards: USA—Dr. Ben Atkins, Mr. Jack Fleming, Mr. Clyde Horst, Mr. Bob Mauk, Rev. Bill Mummert, Mr. Bob Uber, and Mr. Warren Wolbert; Canada—Mrs. Edna Buss, Mr. Peter Falk, and Mr. Norman Woltmann.

Remembering my wife, Diane, in these acknowledgments is not just being nice. She has a natural brilliance that glows behind many of the sentences. Further, for three years she put up with hearing, "I'm sorry, I can't go shopping with you tonight. I'm working on *Firestorm*."

Finally, there are all of the pastors and their families who graciously allowed me to share their stories in this book for the sake of the body of Christ.

These are perhaps faceless names to you, but people impassioned for the success of your church and ministry. I owe them all a debt of love that will have to wait until heaven to be paid, because it's too big to handle now. Thank you, everyone!

Ron Susek is an evangelist and Bible teacher. He is the founder of the Susek Evangelistic Association, headquartered in Gettysburg, Pennsylvania. Ron speaks at evangelistic crusades, deeper life seminars, and leadership conferences throughout North America and in poverty-stricken countries, which recently resulted in the granting of an honorary doctorate. He has pastored three churches, including the one that gave birth to *Firestorm,* and is the author of *Seeing Is Not Believing* and *You Can Handle Stress.*

As a result of *Firestorm* breaking into its third printing in only six months and calls for help coming from churches all across North America, the Susek Evangelistic Association has opened a conflict consulting division to assist churches through these difficult times. They are committed to bringing the highest of Christian ethics combined with excellence in professional standards to help churches from every background. For information and a listing of additional resources designed to assist ministers and churches in crisis, contact:

Susek Evangelistic Association
P.O. Box 3007
Gettysburg, PA 17325
Phone: (717) 337-1170
Fax: (717) 337-1833
E-mail: RonSusek@aol.com